Obentoo 1

Teacher Notes

Peter Williams

Sue Xouris

Kyoko Kusumoto

Nelson

an International Thomson Publishing company **I(T)P**®

Melbourne • Albany, NY • Belmont, CA • Bonn • Boston • Cincinnati
Detroit • Johannesburg • London • Madrid • Mexico City • New York
Paris • Singapore • Tokyo • Toronto • Washington

Nelson ITP®
102 Dodds Street
South Melbourne 3205

Email nelsonitp@nelson.com.au
Website http://www.nelsonitp.com

Nelson ITP® ***an International Thomson Publishing company***

First published in 1998
10 9 8 7 6 5 4 3 2 1
05 04 03 02 01 00 99 98

National Library of Australia
Cataloguing-in-Publication data

Williams, Peter (Peter B. C.), 1956-.
Obentoo 1.
ISBN 0 17 009136 8 (Teacher notes).

1. Japanese language - Textbooks for foreign speakers - English. 2. Japanese language - spoken Japanese - Study and teaching (Secondary). 3. Japanese language - Writing - Study and teaching (Secondary). I. Xouris, Sue. II. Kusumoto, Kyoko. III. Title.

495.682421

Designer Judith Summerfeldt
Cover designer Deborah Gilkes
Cover illustrator Donna Cross
Editors Col Cunnington and Catriona McKenzie
Project editor Ingrid De Baets
Publishing editor Sally Happell
Production controller Sandra Abela
Printed in Australia by Australian Print Group

Nelson Australia Pty Limited ACN 004 603 454 (incorporated in Victoria) trading as Nelson ITP.

Contents

Icon legend

S 1–3	Student Book pages 1–3
Cassette 1A	Cassette 1A
W 2/T1	Workbook page 2, Task 1
B 1.1	Blackline master Unit 1, Number 1

Introduction

There are two parts to this introduction. The first, *About Obentoo,* provides general information about the course and its components. The second, *Using Obentoo,* provides practical suggestions for using the material and includes teaching strategies, ideas for presentation of new material, exercises, activities, ideas for planning lessons, suggested extension work, links with the *Yoroshiku National Curriculum Guidelines* and a section about assessment. The suggestions in *Using Obentoo* are provided as a guide only and will need to be adapted to suit your preferred teaching style and the needs of your students.

About *Obentoo*

Setting

Obentoo is set in *Nakayama Gakuen,* a fictitious school in Japan. The school is attended by Japanese students and a number of international students who together make up the *Obentoo* students portrayed in the course materials.

Language

While *Obentoo* has a 'real' setting, the main language elements in Stage 1 are presented in their polite or *desu-masu* forms. In electing to use this pathway, the authors consider *desu-masu* to be the most appropriate forms for learners outside Japan who are likely to have limited contact with native speakers of their own age. There was also concern about the organisational and pedagogical implications of basing the course around informal forms, which would inevitably require introduction of *desu-masu* forms in addition to the introduction of kana and kanji.

Obentoo students and teachers

The *Obentoo* students and teachers who appear in Stage 1 are:

- Emma Jennings from Australia
- Takako Moriyama – Japanese student and Emma's host sister
- Ben Summers, also from Australia – Ben has been living in Japan for some time. He likes to give advice about learning Japanese and narrates his own section in the Student Book called *Benkyoo no Ben* (Brainy Ben), which introduces Japanese script. His nickname is based on the Japanese system of giving children names which have good meaning according to the kanji used to read the name. So *Benkyoo no Ben* refers to the use of the kanji 勉 meaning 'to be diligent' or 'studious'; therefore 'Brainy Ben'.
- Kate Henderson from New Zealand
- Yuki Matsuda – Japanese student and Kate's host sister
- Carla Toledo from the United States
- Chieko Ishida – Japanese student and Carla's host sister
- Tony Cruise from Canada
- Shingo Hayashi – Japanese student and Tony's host brother
- Harjono Sudarga from Indonesia
- Yuusuke Satoo – Japanese student and Harjono's host brother
- Sanae Katoo – a Japanese student
- Kenichi Fukuda – a Japanese student
- Nakamura Sensei – the homeroom teacher
- Suzuki Sensei – the Physical Education teacher.

While the experiences of the international students (as they learn Japanese) provide the context for much of the material in the course, they are not intended to dominate classroom activity and discussion. Where students want to question 'advice' given by the *Obentoo* students, they should be encouraged to do so, particularly if the students' own ideas work more effectively and/or improve their attitude or performance. Students are reminded during the course that, if an idea works, it's a good idea!

Let's meet the *Obentoo* students (⊖ viii)

This page is designed as a reference page to set the scene and identify the students introduced in *Obentoo.*

- It can be used as a reading task for students.
- You could read out one of the captions and students must then match this information with the appropriate *Obentoo* student. (Flashcard images of the *Obentoo* students can also be used.)
- You could photocopy the page, cut up the pictures and captions (leaving out the English) and have groups of students match each caption with its correct picture in a limited time.

Linking *Obentoo* with the *Moshi Moshi National Curriculum Guidelines for Japanese*

Stage 1 of *Obentoo* is designed to cater for a junior secondary school beginners' program (approximately 100 to 200 hours) and is arranged into 12 units. The units are developed around the themes of the suggested units of work in *Moshi Moshi* of the *Yoroshiku National Curriculum Guidelines for Japanese* and cover language introduced in Modules 1, 2, 3 and part of Module 4.

Obentoo is designed to support the *National Curriculum Guidelines* by providing ways for students to achieve the goals and objectives in *Moshi Moshi,* and to prepare them for the suggested activities in the *Moshi Moshi* materials. Suggestions about which *Moshi Moshi* activities are appropriate to each unit in *Obentoo* are given on the last page of each unit's notes in this book.

In planning a teaching program based around *Obentoo* and *Moshi Moshi,* it may be useful to bear in mind that, because *Obentoo* has been designed as a 'course' (and therefore devotes much attention to the presentation of new language, consolidation material and extension work), it has not been possible to cover the entire range of language exponents and vocabulary presented in *Moshi Moshi* – a curriculum 'framework'. Most *Moshi Moshi* activities will therefore require some supplementary language, particularly during the first few units of *Obentoo.*

Obentoo components

Student Book

As the name suggests, *Obentoo* is a package of interrelated language sections developed around the theme of the Japanese *bentoo* (lunch box). These sections are intended to give the course an easy-to-use structure, and at the same time build in the important connections between language, culture, learning and general knowledge.

The Student Book contains 12 language units and, at the back of the book, detailed grammar notes (*Setsumei*) and vocabulary lists (Japanese–English and English–Japanese) covering all units. Each language unit follows the same structure and consists of nine sections:

- *Itadakimasu* – introduces the new language through a manga-style cartoon strip. Dialogue is recorded on tape.
- *Donna aji?* – develops the new language through listening and conversational exercises.
- *Benkyoo no Ben* – addresses the use of script.
- *Gohan to okazu* – provides the grammar and vocabulary reference, supported by examples.
- *Teeburu manaa* – presents cultural and socio-cultural background and stimulus material for follow-up activities.
- *Ohashi* – focuses on essential learning-how-to-learn skills.
- *Oshooyu* – provides colloquial expressions and related vocabulary.
- *Okashi* – presents songs.
- *Gochisoosama* – summarises key learning outcomes.

Students are also provided with a quick overview of these elements on p. vii in their Student Book.

Workbook

The Workbook provides the essential hands-on material designed to practise and extend language introduced in the Student Book. It contains a variety of enjoyable and stimulating exercises and activities to support each unit in the Student Book. In general, material in the Workbook helps students use the language they have learnt, rather than simply translating it from one form to another.

Material in the Workbook covers four main categories:

1 Listening

- Students listen to short, lifelike situations and extract simple details, for example by writing brief notes, answering questions in English, selecting pictures from a number of alternatives or completing a table.
- Through the listening tasks, students practise the learning-how-to-learn skills discussed in *Ohashi* (in the Student Book), for example listening and picking up familiar material, listening and guessing, listening and not being distracted by unfamiliar material, and listening for gist.

2 Oral interaction

- Students perform simple tasks, with a partner or in a small group, in response to stimulus pictures or written texts. Tasks emphasise the new language in each unit; however, there is recycling of language from previous units.
- Students talk about themselves and/or other people in response to questions in Japanese, short written texts, or situations presented in English.
- Students are encouraged to speak in more imaginative ways, for example by saying a few words or sentences in response to a stimulus picture or situation.

3 Script recognition and reading

- A variety of word puzzles and games involve identifying or extracting characters and words introduced in each unit.
- Students practise their understanding of key vocabulary through a variety of matching and sorting tasks, for example matching words to pictures, extracting words from sentences, piecing together broken sentences, and unjumbling sentences.
- Students extract information from a variety of text types such as short letters, charts, menus, captions, labels and advertisements.

4 Writing

- Students practise writing single characters by tracing and copying model characters in the *Kakikata* section at the start of each Workbook unit.
- As a next step, students write the missing characters in a word or sentence following a picture cue, for example.

- Students practise writing words by selecting the correct word from a number of alternatives and rewriting it, completing a sentence according to a question or pictorial cue, selecting a word to label a matching picture and writing words to complete simple sentences.
- Students practise writing sentences by producing short responses to simple questions, short spoken and written texts, situations in English and pictorial cues.

Teacher Resource File

The Teacher Resource File comprises three main sections:

1 *Teacher Notes*

These contain, in order:

- a general introduction to the course and its components *(About Obentoo)*
- general suggestions for using the materials *(Using Obentoo)*
- general information on assessment and reporting of students' progress *(Assessment)*
- a reference list of classroom instructions
- unit-by-unit notes comprising:
  - concise unit overviews
  - suggestions in the form of games, role-plays, pairwork tasks, research ideas, class discussion topics, and so on, for leading into each section of the Student Book and consolidating learning outcomes. You will notice that there are many more tasks suggested than you will be able to cover in a given unit of work. Many of these are five-minute tasks which you can slot into your lesson plan if needed or use to consolidate a point if students are having difficulties. We suggest selecting from the large number of tasks to vary your approach as you teach the unit to multiple classes or as you teach the unit in subsequent years.
  - references to relevant tasks contained in the Workbook
  - notes on particular teaching points
  - cultural notes and tasks
  - suggestions for linking units to the *Moshi Moshi* materials
  - suggested structures and vocabulary for extension
  - references to blackline master extension tasks
  - scripts of the audio recordings
  - teaching register proforma
- solutions for tasks in the Workbook

2 *Blackline masters (BLMs)*

These contain the following:

- illustrated vocabulary flashcards and word flashcards for each unit
- supplementary material (speaking activities, script practice, cultural activities, game boards, ...) and solutions. Speaking activities contain pairwork tasks (from Unit 3 onwards) and role-plays.
- extra stroke order practice
- assessment materials for each unit covering listening, oral interaction, reading and writing skills, and solutions

3 *Overhead transparencies (OHTs)*

These contain the manga-style cartoons from each unit (without text) for presenting and consolidating the new language in each unit.

Audio cassettes

A set of six audio cassettes containing the *Itadakimasu, Donna aji?, Benkyoo no Ben* and *Oshooyu* sections of the Student Book, listening material from the Workbook and the listening tests. Cassettes 1 (Side A) and 6 (Side B) also contain the *Obentoo* song. You can find the lyrics at the back of these Teacher Notes on p. 132.

Using *Obentoo*

Before presenting some general suggestions for using the different sections in *Obentoo,* here are a few pointers on introducing script. We stress that the techniques below are a guide only and will need to be adapted to suit your own teaching style and the situation in your classes.

> Emphasise the excitement in learning another language (with a new script). Beware of giving the message that Japanese is difficult. It can easily kill students' enthusiasm.

In *Obentoo* we opted to gradually introduce hiragana, katakana and a small number of useful kanji from the outset, and have avoided the use of *roomaji*. Using *Obentoo,* it is not necessary to suspend oral-based teaching while students learn to read hiragana and katakana.

The following is a step-by-step guide to introducing script using *Obentoo.*

1. Allow students to flip through the text just to *look* at the script, focusing on the shapes of characters (are they simple or complicated? do they all look the same?), the use of numbers or the use of 「。」, and so on.
2. Students listen to pages 4 and 5 on tape. As they listen they should point to the words and characters indicated. After listening once, you may like to continue the discussion of patterns in the script, the use of hiragana, katakana and kanji, shapes of characters, and so on. Then listen again to the conversation on the tape.
3. Give students the opportunity to recognise examples of hiragana, katakana and kanji throughout the text, or in magazines and other authentic material. Once students are familiar with the shapes of hiragana, katakana and kanji, it is easy to teach examples of each of the scripts as they need them.
4. Certain key characters are introduced in each unit

so that students are able to work with script from the outset without having to learn every single character. These key characters have been carefully selected. In early units they are the first characters of a limited number of key words. For example:

お　おはようございます
こ　こんにちは
さ　さようなら

Where two or more words begin with the same character, the second character of one of the words is introduced so that the words can be distinguished. For example:

ゆ　ゆうすけ
き　ゆき

お　おはようございます
な　おなまえは

> The individual characters should be introduced in the order presented in the *Benkyoo no Ben* section in each Student Book unit. They have been selected so that students can recognise key words in each unit.

5 Students should first listen to the explanation in the *Benkyoo no Ben* section on the tape whilst following the relevant pages in the Student Book. You may like to help students to remember the characters using *Hiragana in 48 Minutes* or a similar mnemonics system.

6 You should then use the *Obentoo* word flashcards to practise students' recognition of the key words. See if students can recognise the first character in the word or expression. Then ask them whether they can remember a word they have learnt in this unit which begins with that sound. Students should also be asked to reflect on the length of the word, or any other sounds in the word they might know in order to work out what the word or expression is. For example:

おはようございます　(long word)
おなまえは　(students also know な and ま)

> The most important thing about introducing script by this method is that students are familiar with the key words (aurally and orally) **before** they are required to read them. They will have heard them in *Itadakimasu* and practised saying them in *Donna aji?* You should use the vocabulary flashcard images provided in the Teacher Resource File to reinforce these key words.

7 Once students can recognise the character on its own and the character within words or expressions, they should do the *Kakikata* section in the Workbook. This section focuses on writing individual characters with correct proportion and stroke order.

> In summary: students listen, speak, recognise a limited number of single characters, recognise words starting with or containing these key characters, and finally learn to write the key characters.

Students will have learnt to read and write all of the hiragana and some katakana by the end of Unit 6 and all of the katakana by the end of Unit 12. Twenty-one kanji are introduced for recognition and writing throughout the text:

Unit 2　日本
Unit 3　一、二、三、四、五、六、七、八、九、十
Unit 4　人（じん）
Unit 5　一人、二人、三人、四人、五人、...
Unit 7　日、月、火、水、木、金、土、休

For teachers who prefer not to teach katakana at this stage, *furigana* are placed above each word written in katakana. For those students who have studied Japanese at primary level and who already know some hiragana, the first six *Benkyoo no Ben* sections can be used for revision and students' knowledge can be extended using the extra script tasks in the BLMs.

いただきます

Itadakimasu has two main purposes:

- to present the key language
- to help students work the new language out for themselves (by guessing and noticing)

> It is recommended that drilling is left until *Donna aji?* The emphasis in *Itadakimasu* is on listening and understanding. (Avoid just reading and translating the manga.)

Suggestions for using *Itadakimasu*

1 Warm-up

Set the scene of the cartoon by showing the OHT. Ask students what they think it is about. Write their ideas on the board.

2 Listen and discuss

- Talk about *listening and guessing* as a means of understanding. Discuss guessing overall gist and guessing specific details. Discuss what makes a good guess.
- Using the OHT, give a taste of the story by playing a short excerpt from the recording. Ask students to guess what the people said. Replay the section until students are comfortable with it.

Students may become quite vocal after hearing recorded natural speech for the first time, but this is not necessarily an indication that the task is impossible! To increase the students' confidence, simply replay the 'taster' section three or four more times, asking students to identify the words they picked up after each replay.

- After listening to the whole story, ask students to tell you what it was about in their own words. You could then replay the whole story (without stopping) and see if students can follow it.

The OHT can be used until students have worked out the gist of the story and the key language. Text overlays are provided as BLMs separating the OHTs in the Teacher Resource File. In later units, when students are familiar with some of the script, you may choose to use the overlays to present the text before students refer to their books.

- After listening, refer students to the cartoon in the Student Book and discuss cultural points which emerged, for example bowing, people's clothing, and so on.
- Answer the questions at the end of the story.

3 Follow-up

- Do some practice tasks using the new language, then revisit the manga. For example:
  - Listen to sections of the recording and find the matching panels in the cartoon story.
  - Act out the whole manga.
  - Ask students to act out each section, modifying or adding to the story where they can.
  - Copy the OHTs. Number each frame randomly, enlarge and cut up. The students form groups and are given one set each. The winning group is the first one to assemble the frames in the right order.
  - Make flashcards out of the manga to practise key expressions.
- Recapitulate the process of listening and guessing. You could ask students how they could pick out clues more easily.

- Avoid listening to the cartoon story *cold*. Students should spend time exploring the OHT (looking for clues) and talking about their ideas before looking at their books.
- During the listen-and-guess phase, focus students' attention on the main details, not every word.
- The first time a sentence is played, students might only pick up one small detail. This is quite acceptable and should be praised.
- Encourage and praise guessing and avoid giving the message that you are only interested in the right answer.
- During the listen-and-guess phase, ask the students if you are playing them too much (or too little) at a time. Encourage students beyond their comfortable limits from time to time.
- Don't worry about script during the first encounter with the cartoon and discourage students from taking written notes. At this stage, work should be limited to listening and guessing.
- Students should repeat new words as they are picked out from the story.
- Avoid explaining something before students have had time to work it out for themselves. Replaying a sentence, giving a clue or asking students to verbalise their hunches will encourage students to develop their own resources and their confidence.
- No listen-and-repeat reading of *Itadakimasu* is provided on the tape; however, teachers can pause the tape for students to repeat if desired.
- If students are keen to learn some of the hiragana and katakana characters in the story, you could move on quickly to the *Benkyoo no Ben* sections. If in doubt, ask your students if they are ready to learn how to read Japanese.

どんなあじ？

Donna aji? is organised around the two (or three) key language functions emanating from *Itadakimasu*. It is designed to help students make the transition from listening and understanding to speaking. Each set of dialogues appears twice on the tape. As the icons on the Student Book pages indicate, students are expected first to look at the pictures, listen and repeat after the speaker, and then second to listen, look at the text and repeat.

Using Donna aji?

1 Warm-up

- In Unit 1, revise the expression *Donna aji?* (What flavour?).
- Ask students what the pictures might be about and what language they remember from *Itadakimasu* which fits the pictures.
- Use flashcards of the essential vocabulary to help students internalise the key language before they start.

2 Listening and repeating

- You may like to play the dialogues right through first and ask students what they were about.
- Then play one dialogue at a time while students repeat. Encourage active listening by getting students to perform a simple action for each key word, for example rubbing their 'tired' eyes for おはようございます. If students need more time to repeat, press the pause button.

3 Listening, looking at the sentences and repeating

- Students should listen to the sentences and follow the text with their finger as they repeat. In later units they will be able to *guess–read* the key words by recognising the first character or the first couple of characters. Encourage them to point to words as they 'read' as this will help consolidate the key characters they have learnt in previous units.

> You may like to come back and do this task again **after** doing the *Benkyoo no Ben* pages or experiment with introducing the characters in *Benkyoo no Ben* before doing the 'listen, read and repeat' section of *Donna aji?* (This is advisable for Unit 1.)

- After all the dialogues have been repeated, ask for volunteers to take the parts of the speakers and perform the dialogues themselves.

4 Speaking with a partner

- Ask students what other words they have learnt which could be used with the dialogues.
- Ask for volunteers to demonstrate the patterns in the boxes. Students can then practise these with their partners.
- Explain how the dialogue pattern at the bottom of the page is used. Refer to *Gohan to okazu* for other useful vocabulary.

5 Follow-up

Set up a ふくしゅうをしましょう *(Let's revise)* segment: at the end of the lesson, students take turns to provide a quick recap of what was learnt.

べんきょうのベン

Benkyoo no Ben:

- introduces and explains how to use the hiragana and katakana charts
- presents in each unit a set of hiragana and/or katakana (and a small number of kanji in some units) which will enable students to recognise the key words contained in *Itadakimasu, Donna aji?* and *Gohan to okazu*
- introduces the conventions for combining and changing sounds
- revises characters introduced in previous units.

On the *Benkyoo no Ben* page the new characters introduced in each unit are boxed in yellow, the characters introduced in previous units are printed in solid black and the characters yet to be introduced are a legible grey shade.

You may like to use your own mnemonics for teaching the hiragana and katakana characters or let the students make up their own.

The characters presented in *Benkyoo no Ben* provide the framework for the reading and writing practice tasks in the Workbook. You may wish to present extra characters in some units.

Using Benkyoo no Ben

1 Warm-up

If you use mnemonics, you may wish to revise any mnemonics the students have already learnt.

2 Playing and discussing the narration

- Play the tape and follow Ben's instructions. When you hear a 'ding', press the pause button to give students time to complete the task.
- In Unit 1, help students work out the pattern for combining the consonants and vowels.
- If you use mnemonics, decide on any new mnemonics required to reinforce the new characters.
- After students have found words which start with (or contain) each new character, use the word flashcards in the Teacher Resource File to practise word recognition.
- Do the *Find the odd sound* quiz.

3 Follow-up

- Make large hiragana and katakana charts. Fill in the characters as they are introduced in each unit.
- If students are coping easily with the number of characters presented, you could try introducing extra characters, for example the equivalent katakana character for each hiragana introduced, and vice versa.

4 Kakikata

This can be found in the Workbook at the start of each unit and is used to introduce students to writing. Students should trace the shaded characters, taking particular note of the stroke order, then continue writing characters to the end of the row. It is advisable for students to use pencil for this task so that it can be easily corrected if necessary. At the very end of each row the printed as well as the handwritten version of the character is presented. Point this out and discuss the differences with students.

The tasks immediately following the *Kakikata* focus on script practice without any particular reference to the functions introduced in the unit. It is recommended that these tasks be done as follow-up to the *Benkyoo no Ben* page.

ごはんとおかず

Gohan to okazu:

- focuses on form and structure of new language introduced in *Itadakimasu* and *Donna aji?* (*Donna aji?* focuses on function.)
- provides a summary of all structures and new vocabulary. Refer students to the more detailed grammatical explanations in the *Setsumei* section towards the end of the Student Book if more explanations are needed.

> It is recommended that information about grammar is provided on a need-to-know basis. Some students may find the information in *Gohan to okazu* adequate and not need the information in the *Setsumei* section.

Using *Gohan to okazu*
The following suggestions may be helpful:
- In Unit 1, talk about how *gohan* (rice) and *okazu* (side dishes) are the foundations of an *obentoo.*
- Indicate that this section can be used to look up English translations of the key words and sentences.
- Explain how the tables relate to *Donna aji?*
- Show students how to refer to the *Setsumei* (pp. 198–211 in the Student Book) for more detailed explanations as they are required.
- Discuss the language patterns used, showing how other words can be substituted into the given sentences.
- Note the *Need some extra words or expressions? Ask your teacher!* prompts in the Student Book and consider other vocabulary which students might find useful in this section. Suggestions are given on each unit overview page in these notes.
- Ask students how many characters and words they can recognise.

テーブルマナー

Teeburu manaa has a number of broad purposes:
- to introduce cultural information related to the language of each unit and, in some units, to address topics of broad cultural relevance
- to serve as a springboard for classroom discussion, displays and collections, project work, library research and cultural excursions
- to provide general knowledge about Japan, its people and their lifestyle
- to offer a balanced focus on cultural differences and similarities
- to provide a forum for balanced discussions about Japanese culture in the context of what students pick up from friends, parents and the media.

Using *Teeburu manaa*
Read and discuss the information on the *Teeburu manaa* pages and use it as the basis for further class discussion on the topic. A follow-up activity for each *Teeburu manaa* section is provided as a BLM in the Teacher Resource File. There are also suggestions for culture-based activities in the unit-by-unit notes.

おはし

Ohashi has been designed to:
- focus on the tools or skills associated with learning a new language
- address underlying issues and attitudes which are likely to have a bearing on students' success or confidence
- serve as a stimulus for discussing and evaluating the students' own learning-how-to-learn experiences
- encourage students to modify the learning techniques they use and make up new ones as required.

Using *Ohashi*
While specific suggestions for using the *Ohashi* section are given in the unit-by-unit notes, the following general suggestions may be helpful:
- Encourage students to talk about when they do not feel confident. Talk about your own uncertainties when using another language.
- Encourage guessing. *Listen and guess* is a key facet of using this course which will require careful nurturing in some (less confident) classes.

> You may like to finish a lesson (or group of lessons) by asking students how they are finding learning Japanese, and which aspects they find easy or difficult and/or satisfying or frustrating. Ask students to suggest remedies where appropriate.

- Encourage students to evaluate the advice given by the *Obentoo* students in the light of their own experiences learning Japanese.

おしょうゆ

Oshooyu highlights a number of expressions and useful extension language typically introduced in *Itadakimasu* (and not covered in *Donna aji?* or *Gohan to okazu*). These expressions may be useful when working through the *Practise with a partner* sections in *Donna aji?*, during role-plays and for other oral interaction tasks in the Workbook and BLMs.

Using *Oshooyu*
Ask students to find the expressions in context in other sections of the unit. Discuss their meaning and use as a class or in small groups. Ask students to invent other situations where the expressions could be used. Refer to the unit-by-unit notes for further suggestions.

おかし

The *Okashi* section provides a change of pace and an alternative way of reinforcing new language. It consists of a song or rap (in the Student Book) and a board/card game or craft activity (described in these Teacher Notes).

Using Okashi
The *Okashi* section can be done at any time within the unit. You may choose to teach the song after introducing the new vocabulary and structures if

students are having trouble remembering them. Refer to the unit-by-unit notes for further suggestions.

ごちそうさま

Gochisoosama has several purposes:

- to summarise the intended learning outcomes of each unit (note the mixture of skill, attitude and understanding outcomes)
- to provide students with a checklist for measuring their progress at the end of each unit
- to provide revision checklists, for example for end-of-unit and end-of-semester assessment
- to give broad indications of the scope or depth of particular outcomes, for example *I can read and write at least seven sentences which describe what pets eat.* (Unit 6)

Using *Gochisoosama*

While specific suggestions for using *Gochisoosama* are provided in the unit-by-unit notes, the following general suggestions may be helpful:

- You could place a large photocopy of the unit outcomes on a pin-up board and tick each item as it is introduced, using a different colour when it is completed.
- Modify the learning outcomes to better reflect the situation in each class and/or your school policy; for example, the suggested target number of expressions or vocabulary for each outcome could be modified. The wording of some outcomes could be changed.
- Visit *Gochisoosama* regularly so that students can see their progress rather than leaving it as a final end-of-unit task.
- The list of outcomes could be used to profile students' achievements at parent–teacher meetings and when student reports are written.
- Ask students to write a few sentences assessing their progress with each outcome. These will serve as a valuable reference to place against your own judgements when students' reports are written.

Assessment

The purposes of assessment

On page 35 of the *National Curriculum Guidelines for Japanese (Moshi Moshi)* the purposes of assessment are described as follows:

- *to provide an additional purpose for learning*
- *to find out what learners can do and how well they can perform, rather than simply reporting a numerical score*
- *to understand learners better*
- *to judge the effectiveness of a sequence of lessons*
- *to give learners an understanding of the part they play in their own learning*
- *to inform relevant people about learners' progress.*

In recognising these principles, assessment in *Obentoo* is intended to serve two main purposes: summative and formative.

Summative assessment using *Obentoo*

In general, summative assessment is viewed as end-of-unit or end-of-semester assessment, where the aim is to determine what level students have reached and how effective the teaching program has been. In this form of assessment, it is useful to consider how well students have integrated what has been taught, and how well they are able to use their Japanese for active and purposeful communication. For students to demonstrate their integrative skills, assessment activities should require students to use language from several units and reflect a balance of modes of language use (listening, oral interaction, reading and writing) which have been practised in class.

Here are some general examples of summative assessment tasks using the *Obentoo* materials:

- *conversation* – students answer questions, for example in an interview, covering the units which have been taught. Include questions covering extension material which has been taught.
- *role-play* – students perform short role-plays, for example using the suggested activities in *Putting it all together* in the unit-by-unit notes.
- *prepared talk* – students deliver a short talk on a topic taught in class.
- *listening for information* – students listen to a short spoken text and record information in a chart or fill in gaps, and so on. While students will hear Japanese, it is quite appropriate for them to note details of what they hear in English.
- *reading for information* – students read a short text and extract information from it. Again, while the text is in Japanese, it is quite appropriate for students to note details in English.
- *written expression* – students write a short letter introducing themselves to a friend in Japan. The letter could be in the form of a reply to a letter from their friend and could include supporting illustrations with labels in Japanese.

In grading and reporting students' progress, teachers may wish to consider the criteria for judging performance used in the sample listening and speaking activity and reading and writing activity on pages 44 and 45 of *Moshi Moshi*. In general, the criteria for judging assessment will vary from one assessment task to the next. Teachers may wish to discuss the criteria with students before the assessment and encourage students to suggest how they could best prepare for the assessment. Post-assessment discussion can also serve to show students how they can improve in the future.

Formative assessment using *Obentoo*

In general, formative assessment tasks are designed to provide feedback on students' progress in particular aspects of the course. Vocabulary tests, character-writing quizzes and spot-tests are examples of formative assessment. Many of the tasks in the Workbook can be used as formative assessment. Here are some other general examples of formative assessment tasks using the *Obentoo* materials:

- *Gochisoosama* checklists – students tick their progress with objectives described in *Gochisoosama*, including perhaps a self-rating. For example:
  - ☆ I can do this but I need to refer to my book or ask for help.
  - ☆☆ I can do this without help but I still make mistakes.
  - ☆☆☆ I can do this easily.
- *short tests* – students complete short listening and/or reading tasks based on particular language objectives and vocabulary.
- *oral work folio* – students provide examples of several pieces of oral work they have completed, for example short talks they have recorded on cassette at home or recorded role-plays, and give an assessment of their performance.
- *written work folio* – students provide examples of several pieces of written work they have completed and give an assessment of their performance in each task.
- *self-assessment form* – after completing a task, students write down what they learned by doing the task, where they had difficulties and how they could improve with the task in the future.

Classroom instructions

We have used the polite form (てください). Teachers may choose to use the plain form, leaving out ください or using なさい.

- Let's start.
  はじめましょう。
- Are you ready?
  いいですか。
- Listen carefully.
  よくきいてください。
- Take out your homework.
  しゅくだいをだしてください。
- Take out your notebook.
  ノートをだしてください。
- Take out your textbook.
  テキストをだしてください。
- All together.
  みんなで。*or* いっしょに。
- Repeat after me.
  あとについていってください。
- This side.
  こちらがわ。
- This row.
  このれつ。
- Boys only.
  おとこのこだけ。
- Girls only.
  おんなのこだけ。
- I'll say it again for you.
  もういちどいいます（よ）。
- Ask the person next to you.
  となりのひとにきいてください。
- Well done.
  よくできました。
- Let's play a game.
  ゲームをしましょう。
- Start the game.
  ゲームをはじめてください。
- Good luck!
  がんばって！
- Whose turn is it?
  だれのばんですか。
- Next.
  つぎ／つぎのひと。
- Put up your hand.
  てをあげてください。
- If you know, put up your hand.
  わかるひと、てをあげてください。
- Find a partner.
  パートナーをみつけてください。
- Get into pairs.
  ペアになってください。
- Get into groups of six.
  六人のグループになってください。
- Get into two lines.
  二れつにならんでください。
- Form two groups.
  ふたくみにわかれてください。*or*
  ふたつのグループをつくってください。
- Time is up.
  もうじかんです（よ）。
- Come to the front.
  まえにでてきてください。
- Go back to your seat.
  せきにもどってください。
- Take one each.
  いちまいずつとってください。
- Pass this down.
  これをわたしてください。
- Make up a dialogue.
  かいわをつくってください。
- Swap (papers) with someone.
  こうかんしてください。
- Let's correct it.
  なおしましょう。
- Please clean the board.
  こくばんをけしてください。
- Please turn on the light.
  でんきをつけてください。
- Please turn on the fan.
  せんぷうきをつけてください。
- Please turn on the heater.
  ヒーターをつけてください。
- Please turn off the light.
  でんきをけしてください。

- Please turn off the fan.
  せんぷうきをけしてください。
- Please turn off the heater.
  ヒーターをけしてください。
- I'll collect your homework.
  しゅくだいをあつめます。
- The homework is for tomorrow.
  しゅくだいはあしたまでです。
- Copy this into your book.
  ノートにうつしてください。
- Are there any questions?
  なにか、しつもんがありますか。
- Bring ... tomorrow.
  あした... をもってきてください。
- The bell has gone.
  ベルがなりました。
- Pack up.
  かたづけてください。
- That's all (for today).
  （きょうは）これでおわります。

Overview

Unit objectives

Students will be able to:

- greet and farewell people at school and at home
- check someone's name
- introduce themselves and say I'm pleased to meet you
- ask someone's name
- use appropriate titles after people's names
- talk about a day in the life of a high school student
- understand the principles of the Japanese writing system and differentiate between hiragana, katakana and kanji
- read and write eight hiragana and three katakana
- recognise some familiar words and names in hiragana and katakana
- understand how the parts of an obentoo are used in this book

Functions and language exponents

1 Greeting and farewelling
(たかこさん)、おはようございます。
(ケイトさん)、こんにちは。
(ハジョーノくん)、さようなら。
(なかむらせんせい)、またあした。

2 Checking someone's name and responding
(エマさん)ですか。
(はい)、(わたし)は(エマ)です。どうぞよろしく。
(ハジョーノくん)ですか。
(はい)、(ぼく)は(ハジョーノ)です。どうぞよろしく。

3 Asking someone's name and introducing yourself
おなまえは？。
(わたし)は(たかこ)です。どうぞよろしく。
(ぼく)は(ゆうすけ)です。どうぞよろしく。

Key vocabulary and expressions

たかこさん	こんにちは	はい
ケイトさん	おはようございます	いいえ
ゆくさん	さようなら	わたしは ... です
ハジョーノくん	またあした	ぼくは ... です
なかむらせんせい		どうぞよろしく
エマさん		おなまえは
ゆうすけくん		

Script

Students are expected to be able to read and write the key characters and recognise the associated words.

Key characters	*Associated words*
お	おはようございます、おなまえは
き	ゆき
こ	こんにちは
さ	さようなら
た	たかこ
な	なかむら
ま	またあした、おなまえは？
ゆ	ゆうすけ
エ	エマ
ケ	ケイト
ハ	ハジョーノ

Script understandings

- There are three writing systems used in Japanese.
- Hiragana is used for writing Japanese words.
- Katakana is used for writing words borrowed from other languages.
- There are 46 hiragana characters and 46 katakana characters; some look similar.
- Hiragana and katakana characters represent sounds.
- For each hiragana character there is a katakana character with the same sound.
- Kanji are like words and have meaning; many kanji look like pictures.
- Furigana are small characters (usually in hiragana) written above other characters to show how they are read.

Learning how to learn

- Developing good listening skills; what to listen for
- Listening and using clues to guess what is being said
- Developing strategies for coping when you don't fully understand something

Cultural elements

- How the parts of an *obentoo* are used in this book.
- *A day in the life of Izumi*: a series of photos with captions in English about school life in Japan. Issues covered include family routine, getting to school, homeroom, classes, cleaning, lunch at school, club activities, *juku*.

Other incidental language introduced

おはよう。
わたし？
すみません。
ごめんなさい。
えーと。
はやく！
えっ！
はい、そうです。
ちがう！
あっ！
がんばって！
またね。
いいなー。
いきたいなー。
もうバレーボールのじかん。

Extension material

Taking the class roll
しゅっせきをとりましょう。
しゅっせきをとります。
... さんはけっせきです。
... さんはしゅっせきです。
おそくなってすみません。

Need some extra words or expressions? Ask your teacher!

おはよう。	*Good morning.*
またね。	*See you later.*
じゃね。	*See you!*
バイバイ。	*Bye-bye.*
よろしく。	*Pleased to meet you.*
はじめまして。	*How do you do?*
がんばって。	*Good luck./Do your best.*
はい、そうです(ええ、そう)。	*That's right.*
いいえ、ちがいます(ちがう)。	*That's not so.*

Teaching suggestions

The following suggestions are provided as a guide to lesson planning and should be adapted to suit your teaching style and the learning styles of your students. These tasks are specific to this unit. For more information on general strategies for each section, refer to *Using Obentoo* on pages 3–8.

Pre-unit warm-up

- Show a picture of an *obentoo* or a real one and talk about the sections in the Student Book. Go through the information presented in *Welcome to Obentoo!* on pages vi–vii in the Student Book.
- Introduce the *Obentoo* students. See *Let's meet the Obentoo students* on page viii in the Student Book. There are a few suggested activities to support this section on page 1 in these Teacher Notes.

いただきます

S 59–62 2A

Warm-up

Show the OHTs and ask students what they think the cartoon is about. Write their ideas on the board. *Note:* students should not refer to their Student Books at this stage.

Listen and discuss

- *Listen and guess*: students look at the cartoon on the OHTs while listening to the recording and make guesses about what is being said and who is speaking.
- *Find the frame*: students listen to sections of the recording and find the matching frames in the cartoon story.

(Refer to *Listen and discuss* on pages 4–5 in these Teacher Notes for more information on presentation.)

Follow-up

- Using flashcards of the *Obentoo* students, ask ... さん／くんですか。Students answer はい、... さん／くんです or いいえ、... さん／くんです。To make the task more interesting, you could cover the card so that only a small part of the person is visible.
- *True/false game*: the teacher holds up flashcards of the *Obentoo* students (or enlarged copies of the cartoon panels) and says ... さん／くんです。Students write true or false. Alternatively, students could write a circle and call it まる *(circle)* for true and write a cross and call it ばつ *(cross)* for false.

べんきょうのベン

S 4–5 1A

Warm-up

- Explore the page: ask students what they can pick up from the page. Points to discuss could include the menu, the prices shown by the numbers before the character 円 en (yen = Japanese currency), and other details, for example the fox saying いただきます.
- *Discussion*: before playing the dialogue, you could ask students about differences they notice in the shapes of the characters.

Listen and discuss

Students look at the Student Book, listen to the narration and discuss.

Audio script

SPEAKERS: Ben, Emma

B: Hi! I'm Ben. I'm here to help you read and write Japanese. Some of the Japanese students call me *Benkyoo no Ben*, which is like 'Brainy Ben', because I ask a lot of questions about Japanese writing. The Japanese students think you're smart if you know *anything* about how to write Japanese! Yuusuke calls me *Fuben no Ben*, meaning 'Nuisance Ben', but we won't go into that just now.

...

E: This is great! A menu without a word of English! I'll starve before I can understand it!

B: Do you want a hand?

E: Can you read Japanese?!

B: I know a few things.

E: Well, I'm really hungry, so can we get on with it?

B: I suppose you can recognise the numbers on the right?

E: Yeah. They're obviously the prices. But how can I read what there is to eat?

B: See the round, wiggly characters in number 1? They're called hiragana.

E: Hiragana? What do they say?

B: There are three characters which make three sounds: U-DO-N, which means 'noodles'.

E: U-DO-N. Sounds good to me. The same characters, I mean, hiragana, are in the next one! What sort of noodles are they?

B: They're KI-TSU-NE-U-DO-N.

E: KI-TSU-NE-U-DO-N. So you mean each one of those hiragana is a separate sound?

B: はい。

E: Number three is U-DO-N too, but the three characters in front of it look a bit different!

B: Yeah, those first three characters are katakana.

E: Oh, katakana? They look more like straight lines with pointy bits.

B: That's how you can tell katakana from hiragana.

E: So what does it say?

B: It says KA-RE-E udon.

E: Don't tell me: curried noodles!

B: You're right! KA-RE-E means 'curry'!

E: That doesn't sound like Japanese. It's more like English!

B: Right again, Emma! In fact, all words written in katakana come from other languages. That's why they're written in katakana and not hiragana. Have a look at number 13. It says O-RE-N-JI-JU-U-SU.

E: Orange juice! What's the next one? Come on! I'm on a roll!

B: Number 14. That's A-PPU-RU-JU-U-SU.

E: A-PPU-RU-JU-U-SU. That's apple juice, right? And the last four characters, JU-U-SU, they're in number 13 too! So each katakana has a sound just like hiragana, right?

B: Yeah. For each hiragana sound, there is the same katakana sound.

E: So how many of these am I going to have to learn?

B: Only 46!

E: Sorry I asked!

E: What are the ones in 11 and 12, with lots of lines?

B: They're called *kanji*; and they've got strokes, not lines, Emma.

E: What sounds do they have?

B: Well, before we get onto that, the thing about kanji is that they're like words. They mean something.

E: They look a bit like little pictures.

B: That's how you tell what they mean. Have a look at the ones at the top of the menu. Nakayama Gakuen, the name of our school. The first character, NAKA, means 'inside' or 'middle'.

E: Ah yes, there's a line down the middle of the box.

B: And the next one, YAMA, means mountain, because it looks like three mountains.

E: Funny looking mountains!

B: Well, the shape of the character has changed over the years to make it easier to write. So, Nakayama ...

E: ... means 'in the mountains'. And those little hiragana on top of the kanji tell you how to say the kanji, right?

B: Yeah. They're called *furigana* and they're there to help you read the characters below them.

E: Now let me get this straight. Japanese people use three different writing systems: hiragana, katakana and kanji. Hiragana is used for writing Japanese words. Katakana is used for writing words borrowed from other languages. Both of these are just sounds. Kanji are like words and mean something. Oh, and they look like pictures.

B: You've got it.

E: Isn't that furigana stuff great for helping you figure out the kanji.

B: Yeah, it's pretty handy.

E: So how many lifetimes will it take me to learn all this?

B: Not that long, really. It only took me a few days to learn the hiragana. But the good thing is that, once you know the sounds, spelling in Japanese is easy.

E: That's a relief. Hey! I'm starving! If we don't order soon, we'll miss out altogether.

B: Well what do you want?

E: I'm going to try some of this *karee udon!*

Some students may take longer than others to understand how three writing systems can be used simultaneously in one language. You could reinforce this by:

- using different colours to write hiragana, katakana and kanji on the board and using the same colours for any word cards you might put up around the room
- asking students what they remember from the narration and focusing on these points to begin with. You could return to the rest of the narration later
- letting each student 'adopt' a number of hiragana and katakana characters and be responsible for reminding the class what they are and what words contain them.

Follow-up

- **2/T1** Using coloured pencils or highlighters, students indicate four examples of hiragana, katakana and kanji on this Japanese magazine cutting. Discuss with students the shape of each set of characters and ways of distinguishing them from each other.
- *Japanese character search*: if you have samples of authentic materials such as magazines, newspapers, Japanese food labels and wrappers, ask students to look through these to find examples of hiragana, katakana and kanji characters and furigana. Each student could choose one character and find five examples of that character in use.
- *Retell the story*: students take the parts of Emma and Ben and retell the dialogue in their own words, for example using different names.
- *Itadakimasu revisited*: students refer again to *Itadakimasu* in the Student Book and find examples of hiragana, katakana, kanji and furigana.
- *Exploring the writing systems of other languages*: invite students who are familiar with the writing systems of other languages to write examples of these on the board. Discuss any similarities with English or Japanese.

You may choose to go to the next *Benkyoo no Ben* section (pages 9–10) which presents the key hiragana and katakana characters for the unit **before** you start the *Donna aji?* section. Most students will be keen to learn some characters, and it will make the second part of *Donna aji?* (listen, read and repeat) much easier.

どんなあじ？

6–8 1A

1 Greeting and farewelling

Warm-up

- Replay *Itadakimasu* to refresh students' memories. Select key words and expressions, and ask students to repeat them after you.
- *Explore the page*: check that students are familiar with the expression どんなあじ？ You may also need to explain the numbering of the illustrations and sentences on the page. (Numbers are formally introduced in Unit 3.) Ask students what they think is happening in the pictures. You could draw the students' attention to Takako's kendo outfit.
- Ask students what words they remember for greeting and farewelling people.

Presentation

- Students look at the pictures, listen to the tape and repeat. If students have difficulty repeating after the speaker, you may choose to pause the tape between the name and the greeting. After listening and repeating, discuss what was said. Next see if the students can repeat the dialogues by themselves.
- Students could then look at the sentences below the pictures, listen to the tape and see if they can point to each word as they repeat. Then stop the tape and see if students can 'read' the sentences as they point.
- If you have not already done so, go to *Benkyoo no Ben* (Student Book pages 9–10) to introduce the new hiragana and katakana characters.
- Explain the *Practise with a partner* section at the bottom of the page and ask students to move around the room using the greetings. Points which could be discussed before or after this task: the use of commas and which dialogues contain hiragana, katakana and furigana.

Refer students to *Gohan to okazu* (p. 11) for useful vocabulary.

Avoid passive parroting! To increase the likelihood that students will listen actively, encourage them to think of actions or gestures to be performed as they say the key words in each sentence, e.g. rubbing the eyes for おはようございます and waving for さようなら.

Follow-up

- **4/T4 4A** Students listen to the tape and complete the table. They need to write down the names of the people Kate is talking to, and tick the appropriate box to show if she's greeting them in the morning, greeting them after 11.00 a.m., or farewelling them.

Audio script

SPEAKERS: **Kate, Emma, Takako, Yuki, Yuusuke, Nakamura Sensei, Harjono**

a Kate: エマさん、こんにちは。たかこさん、こんにちは。

Emma & Takako: こんにちは。

b Kate: たかこさん、さようなら。ゆうすけくん、コンピューターゲームがんばってね！さようなら！

Takako & Yuusuke: さようなら。

Takako: またあしたね！

c Kate: エマさん、さようなら。

Emma: Bye Kate! Oh, sorry ... さようなら。

Kate: なかむらせんせい、さようなら。

N.Sensei: あっ！ケイトさん、ケイトさんはニュージーランドからでしたよね。

Kate: はい、そうです。

N.Sensei: いいなあー。いきたいなー。さようなら。

Kate: さようなら。

d Kate: ハジョーノくん、エマさん、おはようございます。

Harjono & Emma: ケイトさん、おはようございます。

Yuki & Takako: ケイトさん、おはようございます。

Kate: ごめんなさい！ゆきさん、たかこさん、おはようございます。

e Yuki: ケイトさん、はやく！

Kate: はい、はい、じゃ、ゆうすけくん、またあした。

Yuusuke: ケイトさん、またあした。

Vocabulary notes

コンピューターゲームがんばってね！
Good luck with your computer game!
またあしたね！
See you tomorrow, OK?
ケイトさんはニュージーランドからでしたよね。
Kate, you come from New Zealand, don't you?
はい、そうです。
That's right.
いいなあー。いきたいなあー。
That's great. I want to go there!

ごめんなさい！
Sorry!
はやく！
Hurry up!

- 6/T7 With a partner, students act out the situations, using the appropriate Japanese phrases.
- *Pick-a-card*: make up two packs of cards using the flashcard images; one pack with greetings and another with the *Obentoo* students. Students then pick one card from each pack and make up a sentence using the information/picture clues on each card, for example たかこさん、こんにちは。
- *Role-play*: write greetings on cards and place them in a box. Give students another card each and ask them to draw two *Obentoo* students on it. When completed, place these cards in another box. Two students then take a picture card and a greeting card from the boxes and role-play that situation in front of the class. *Alternative:* write the names of the *Obentoo* students on each card instead of using pictures. You could use this task to introduce the correct way to bow:
  – students generally don't bow when greeting their friends
  – students generally use a polite nod of the head instead of stopping and bowing when greeting or farewelling someone 'on the run' (for example, a teacher in the corridor at school).
- *Fast talkers*: students move around the class and see how many people they can greet and farewell in a given time limit.

2 Checking someone's name and introducing yourself

Warm-up

Listening comprehension: without looking at their books, students listen and make notes about who was speaking and what they said.

Presentation

- Students look at the pictures in their Student Book, listen to the tape and repeat. Remember to pause the tape if students are finding it difficult. For example, for responses 1 and 3 you could pause the tape between sentences. After this first listen-and-repeat phase, students could come to the front of the class, taking the parts of the *Obentoo* students.
- As the class then listens and reads the sentences below the pictures, students at the front could hold up key hiragana characters to prompt each sentence.

Follow-up

6/T8 4A Students listen to the tape and tick the square if the answer is *yes* or cross if the answer is *no*. Students also give the correct (verbal) response in Japanese. You may like to do this task in two parts. First, students listen to the tape and tick or cross according to the information given. Then, choose students to answer the questions. For example:
a はい、ハジョーノです。どうぞよろしく。
b いいえ、エマです。

You may like to use the picture flashcards of the *Obentoo* students and do this task as a whole-class oral activity.

Audio script

a ハジョーノくんですか。
はい、ハジョーノです。どうぞよろしく。
b ゆきさんですか。
いいえ、エマです。
c ケイトさんですか。
d ゆうすけくんですか。
e たかこさんですか。
f ケイトさんですか。
g ハジョーノくんですか。、
h エマさんですか。
i ゆうすけくんですか。
j ゆきさんですか。

- *Pick-a-card II*: Student A picks up a card with one of the *Obentoo* students on it (as for the *Donna aji? 1* follow-up activity on this page) and hides the picture from Student B. Student B tries to guess who is depicted on the card and asks, for example ... さん／くんですか。 Student A responds appropriately by saying はい、... です。どうぞよろしく or いいえ、... です。どうぞよろしく。Students do not swap roles until Student B receives a positive answer.
- *Blindfold game*: one student stands at the front of the class and puts on a blindfold. Five other students then come to the front. The blindfolded student touches the face and head of the other five students one at a time and identifies them by asking ... さん／くんですか。If the name is wrong, the other students say いいえ。When the person is identified correctly s/he says はい、わたし／ぼくはです。*Extension:* you could get the students to say いいえ、ちがいます when the blindfolded student gives an incorrect name. This is more polite than いいえ。

You could ask your students to think of a way to remember that さん and くん are not used when people say their own names; for example, you could set up a モンスター・まちがい！*(Monster mistakes)* list on the pin-up board and add serious errors as they emerge.

- Check students' names by asking ... さん／くんですか。Students answer はい or いいえ、ちがいます。*Note:* the expression ちがう！(used in the cartoon on p.1 in the SB) is for informal use only and should not be used when responding to a teacher's question.

- *Guessing game*: a student comes to the front of the class and shows a picture of a famous person's face (or part of a face), and takes on this person's identity. The other students try to guess the person's identity by asking ... さん／くんですか。If they guess incorrectly, the student at the front answers いいえ or いいえ、ちがいます。If it is correct, s/he says はい、わたし／ぼくは ... です。The student who guessed the name correctly comes to the front of the class and chooses the next famous-face picture, and so on.

3 Asking someone's name and introducing yourself

Warm-up

See if students can recognise any of the words before playing the recording.

Presentation

- To vary the way the three sections of the page are used, ask students to make up gestures for each question and answer (to perform as they listen and repeat). Carry the gesture theme through the *Practise with a partner* section too. Remember to pause the tape if students are finding it difficult to repeat; for example, for responses 1–4, pause the tape between sentences.
- Students then look at the sentences and listen to the tape, as for Student Book pages 6-7.
- After the tape has been played, students could take turns 'conducting' by holding up one, two, three or four fingers to show which dialogue is to be recited by the class.

Follow-up

- *The name game*: the class is divided into two or four teams with each team standing in a line or circle. In each team, Student 1 (S1) turns to Student 2 (S2) and says おなまえは？ S2 replies わたし／ぼくは ...です。どうぞよろしく。S1 then says どうぞよろしく。S2 asks おなまえは？ and S3 replies わたし／ぼくは ...です。どうぞよろしく。S2 then responds with どうぞよろしく, and so on. The game is played as a relay race with the first team to finish being the winners.

> Watch out for students who mispronounce おなまえは？ as the more English-sounding おねーむは？

- *I'm famous!*: using pictures of famous people from magazines, students introduce themselves as the person in the picture. Students may wish to use よろしく instead of どうぞよろしく when talking to people their own age.
- **W 7/T9 S 4A** Students listen to the *Obentoo* students introduce themselves. They write their names in English in the order in which they hear them.

Audio script

SPEAKERS: Takako, Yuki, Kate, Emma, Yuusuke, Harjono, Nakamura Sensei

Takako: わたしはたかこです。どうぞよろしく。おなまえは？

Yuusuke: ぼくはゆうすけです。どうぞよろしく。

Yuki: ええと、わたしはゆきです。

Kate: わたしはケイトです。どうぞよろしく。

Harjono: あっ、こんにちは。ぼくはハジョーノです。どうぞよろしく。

Emma: わたしはエマです。どうぞよろしく。

N. Sensei: ぼくはなかむらです。どうぞよろしく。

- **W 7/T10** Students form circles of five. Using the conversation pattern in the Workbook, students go around the circle asking the person next to them who they are.
- **W 5/T6** Students fill in the empty speech bubbles in these pictures with the number of the appropriate response from the list.

Extension task

B 1.1 ろくおんしましょう *(Let's record it)*: students are presented with a number of situations in English and need to respond appropriately in Japanese. Students could record their conversations on tape, or could perhaps act out the situations in groups. You can vary the conversations by changing the names of the characters.

べんきょうのベン — ひらがな

S 9 S 1A

Characters introduced: お、き、こ、さ、た、な、ま、ゆ

- Before playing the tape, ask students to look at the page and suggest what information is being given, for example the alphabet, the consonants at the top, the vowels on the right, and that the large characters are taken from the alphabet.
- Play the tape while students look at the Student Book. Pause the tape whenever you hear a 'ding'.

Audio script

SPEAKER: Ben

Hi! Ben here! You remember that hiragana is used for writing traditional-sounding Japanese words. You can see the hiragana chart at the top of the page.

Traditional Japanese writing is arranged in columns, from right to left. Your teacher will help you say the characters in each column. See if you can work out the pattern.

…

Look at the group of eight large characters on the page. Point to each character as I say it, and repeat after me.

1 お

2 き

3 こ

4 さ

5 た

6 な

7 ま

8 ゆ

Try to recognise some of the words in *Itadakimasu* and *Donna aji?* See if you can find a word with one of these characters in it. Start with お.

…

おはようございます。

Well done. よくできました。

Now see if you can find words which contain the other characters you have learnt.

See you later! またね！

You will need to explain how the pronunciations of し、ち and つ (hiragana) and シ、チ and ツ (katakana) vary slightly from the pattern. The two special hiragana characters を (for marking words as objects) and ん (the only Japanese consonant) will also need to be explained.

- Use the word flashcards to practise students' recognition of the key words. (See point 6 on page 4.)
- **W 1–2** かきかた *(How to write)*: students practise writing the new hiragana characters in the boxes, using the correct stroke order.

Follow-up

- *Printing and handwriting differences*: if students have not discovered these already, you could draw their attention to the way the last strokes of さ、き and な are joined to the previous stroke in most printed Japanese fonts, whereas they are not joined when written by hand. This is similar to the way lower-case alphabetic letters such as *a* and *g* vary according to whether they are printed or handwritten.
- **S 9** *Find the odd sound*: students select the odd sound in each group of three presented. A sound is considered odd when it doesn't come from the same column or row as the other two sounds. *Solutions*: 1c, 2a, 3b, 4a, 5c, 6b.
- **S 9** Students look at the two photos of signs and see whether they can recognise any of the characters. For your info:
  どうぞお入(はい)りを *Please enter*
  (photo taken outside a tea shop in Uji)
  やきそば *Fried noodles*
  (sign on a food stall at a festival)
- *Hiragana-ercise*: students choose one of the characters studied and 'write' it in the air with their finger. The other students watch and try to guess the character. You could highlight correct stroke order by giving students bonus turns if they identify someone writing a character with the wrong stroke order.
- *Hiragana captain ball*: teams of eight students line up behind each other with each person holding a card showing one of the new hiragana. The first student (the captain) turns and reads out the hiragana the next student is holding and the student holding that card bobs down. The captain reads the next card and so on. After the last student's card has been called, the captain joins the line and the last student runs to the front and becomes the new captain. The first team finished is the winner.

べんきょうのベン — かたかな

S 10 (8) 1A

Characters introduced: エ、ケ、ハ

- Recap the use of katakana for borrowed words.
- See if the students can work out the pronunciation of the large characters (from their study of the pattern in the hiragana alphabet).
- Play the tape while students look at the Student Book page. Pause the tape whenever you hear a 'ding'.

Audio script

SPEAKER: Ben

Hi everyone! It's Ben again.

Remember that katakana is used for writing words that are borrowed from other languages, usually because there aren't traditional Japanese words for them.

The sounds for the katakana characters follow the same pattern as for the hiragana characters. Your teacher will help you say the characters in each column.

…

You may have noticed already that some katakana characters look a bit like their hiragana cousins. See how many you can find that look similar.

…

Look at the group of three large characters on the page. Point to each character as I say it, and repeat after me.

1 エ

2 ケ

3　ハ

Now find out which of the *Obentoo* students write their names in katakana.

See you later! またね！

To help students acquire the concepts of *hiragana-for-Japanese-words* and *katakana-for-borrowed-words* quickly, they should be asked regularly if a particular word would be written in hiragana or katakana (even though they may not yet be able to read the word).

Follow-up

- Use the word flashcards to practise students' recognition of the key words.
- **W 2** かきかた *(How to write)*: students practise writing the new katakana characters in the boxes, using the correct stroke order.
- **S 10** *Find the odd sound*: students select the odd sound in each group of three presented. *Solutions*: 1b, 2a, 3c, 4a, 5c, 6c.
- **S 10** Students look at the photos of signs and see if they can recognise any of the characters. For your info:
  じゃがバター　*Hot buttered potato*
  (sign on food stall at a spring festival)
  ロープウエーのりばは、この坂(さか) 15m 上(うえ)です。
  ベビーカーは左(ひだり)をご利用(りよう)下(くだ)さい。
  The cable car is 15 m up this hill. If you have a pram, use the path to the left. You could discuss the interesting borrowed words ロープウエー *(ropeway)* and ベビーカー *(baby-car).*
- *Katakana-exercise*: see *Hiragana-exercise* on page 17.
- **W 3/T2** Students use the key to colour in the picture and reveal the hidden image.
- **W 3/T3** Emma, Kate and Harjono have become human kana. Students write the kana they have become in the boxes provided.
- **W 4/T5** Students match up the names of the *Obentoo* students with their pictures.
- **W 7/T11** Students complete the characters and read them aloud. Then they write their favourite four hiragana and favourite two katakana. Teachers could then tally the results to determine the class's favourite characters so far.
- **W 8/T12** Students colour in all the squares containing katakana. Then they look for the hidden words in the chart and fill in the missing characters.

ごはんとおかず

S 11

Presentation

- *Any volunteers?*: students look at the tables in their Student Book and volunteers are asked to make sentences using the words shown. The rest of the class have to write down, in English, what the volunteers say. Other volunteers could be asked to use extension vocabulary covered during the unit.
- *Character count*: students are asked to find the most commonly used character they have studied among the words given in the tables.
- Make enlargements of the Japanese part of the tables and cut these into pieces. Students work in pairs to join the jumbled pieces. *Note*: if you want students to make up individual sentences you will need several copies of some pieces.
- *Hiragana/katakana sort*: students count the number of words in hiragana and the number of words in katakana.

Follow-up

- *Word and sentence grab*: write two sets of individual words or parts of sentences on cardboard. For example:

おなまえは？	わたしは	ゆき	です。
どうぞ　よろしく。			

  Fix the cards to a whiteboard or feltboard in random order. Divide the class into two teams. The teacher reads out a sentence and the first team to put the sentences together correctly wins. Alternatively, use one set of cards and time each team to see who is the quickest.
- *Word repair*: write words which have been taught on pieces of cardboard (of the same size) and cut each card in half. Place the word-halves in a pile and call out one or more of the words. Students compete in teams to see who can repair the words the quickest (by finding and matching the correct halves).

- *Gohan to okazu* contains the minimum amount of language which all students should be able to use in oral interaction and recognise in written script. You may wish to add to the vocabulary examples given and this is recommended.
- Students are not expected to be able to *write* all the language used in this section.
- *Grammar mnemonics*: students will generally find grammar study easier (and more enjoyable) if rules are presented using a simple mnemonic, for example *Cousin KA comes last and is always asking questions.* If you can't think of a mnemonic, your students may have some useful suggestions!

For further grammar explanation refer students to the せつめい section of the Student Book (pages 198–9).

Extension task

B 1.2 みなさん、しゅっせきをとりましょう *(Let's take the roll)*: call the class roll in Japanese, using

さん or くん after the students' names.
The students answer はい as their name is called.
For further extension, ask students to say ... さん／くんはけっせきです。*(... is absent)* when someone does not answer.

Go through the BLM with students and explain calling the roll in Japanese. Then choose a number of students to take part in a role-play as a listening task for the rest of the class. You hand out cards containing a name and a code – P for *present*, A for *absent* or L for *late* – to those students taking part in the role-play. You call the imaginary roll and students answer according to the information on their card. The rest of the class completes the class-roll on the BLM.

テーブルマナー

Ⓢ 12–13

Presentation

- Students look at the photos on the double-page spread in the Student Book and read the captions. Discuss the details in each of the photos: breakfast, school uniforms, shoe lockers, and so on. Give extra information about student life (see *Extra information* on this page). Discuss the similarities and differences with Australian school life. These may be recorded on a chart and used as a basis for further research or a class project.
- *On the buses (game)*: teams of students line up behind each other on chairs. You ask a question and the student at the head of each team must stand up as quickly as possible if s/he knows the answer. The first to stand up and answer correctly gains a point for his/her team. If the answer is incorrect, the team loses a point. All students move around one seat after each round.
- **Ⓑ 1.3** *Twenty questions about Japan*: you could use these questions in the *On the buses* game, or do it as a survey. Discuss what is generally known about Japan: the myths and the reality.

If you have access to a student from Japan, students could prepare a list of questions to ask him/her about Japanese school life.

After the survey, draw up a list of similarities and differences, between school life in Japan and Australia. Discuss your findings before a spokesperson reports back to the class. A summary of the survey could be presented at the school assembly.

- *The stereotyped 'uniqueness' of Japan*: you may need to ensure that students do not become focused only on the differences between their own culture and that of Japan by reminding them of the similarities as well.
- *Getting help with Japanese resources*: your nearest Japanese consulate, the Japanese embassy, the Japan Inform Japanese Language Teach (JLTA) or the Modern L Association (MLTA) sh give you details of providers of ... Japanese'.

Extra information (to support *Teeburu manaa* Ⓢ 12–13)

- School usually starts around 8.30 a.m. and goes until around 3.15 p.m. from Monday to Friday. Students go to school on Saturdays as well (two or three Saturdays per month) until about 1.00 p.m.
- Once at school students must change from their school shoes (usually black or brown) to soft, white slip-on runners to be worn inside or in the school grounds. Students place their school shoes in open shoe lockers (くつばこ). Students usually change their shoes again when going into the gymnasium.
- As soon as the morning bell rings, students go to their homeroom (ホームルーム). Here they are given information about school events, exams and daily organisation. Each class has a homeroom teacher who conducts the roll-call each morning. Students meet in their homeroom again at the end of the day. Homeroom gatherings usually last about 10 minutes. Some schools go to their homeroom again during the day, where students themselves conduct the lesson and discuss matters related to class and school organisation.
- There are usually six lessons of about 50 minutes with a 10-minute break between each lesson. Not all schools have a mid-morning break.
- At lunchtime (ひるやすみ) students may bring their own lunch (おべんとう), have lunch provided by the school in the classroom (きゅうしょく), or go to the school canteen (しょくどう),which is like a cafeteria and sells hot food and drinks.
- Just before the end of the day, teams of students (arranged in homeroom class groups) clean various areas around the school. This is known as おそうじ, and involves sweeping and wiping classrooms, corridors, locker areas and toilets. Each class must clean their own homeroom and usually one or two other designated areas.
- Following afternoon homeroom time, students participate in club activities (クラブかつどう). These are arranged by the school, and may be sports clubs or cultural clubs. They usually continue until 4.30 or 5.00 p.m. Club members may be required to attend sports matches or cultural exhibitions on the weekends as well.
- Because of the stiff competition to enter good schools in Japan most students attend some kind of cram school（じゅく）or have private tutoring after school.

…はし

…14 (tape) 1A

Presentation

Students listen to the conversation between Kate and Ben and discuss their answers to the questions on page 14 in the Student Book.

Audio Script

SPEAKERS: Kate, Ben

K: It's not fair! I'll *never* learn Japanese!

B: Don't worry. You will!

K: Huh! Who are you?

B: We haven't been introduced yet. I'm Ben. I've been living in Japan for a few years now, and I heard you were here, so I thought I'd see how you were getting on.

K: I've been better! How can I *ever* expect to learn Japanese?

B: I know what you mean, but it's not that bad! All you have to do is listen!

K: You sound like my mother! Anyway, I want to be able to *talk*! What good is listening! ... How did *you* learn Japanese?

B: Like I said. I just listened – otherwise I wouldn't know what the other kids were talking about, which made me feel pretty dumb. When I heard something I thought I'd heard before, I'd think 'Maybe *that's* what they're saying'. Then when I heard the word again I'd think 'Yeah! That's *it*!' Then I found I could say the word myself – automatically!

K: Did you write lots of things down?

B: Yeah, and I tried memorising words too. But when I heard something which sounded important I'd just have a guess! I was right a lot of the time, but if I wasn't, I would just pretend I understood and ask someone or think about it later.

K: Did you ever make a wrong guess?

B: Lots of times! But that just helped me make better guesses.

K: Are there still things you can't understand?

K: Yeah, all the time! But there's a lot I *can* understand and that's what counts!

K: It's weird! I find I'm saying Japanese words all over the place!

B: It was like that for me too. It's a good thing! I think it means you're listening!

K: Okay! I'll try to listen more! Just don't ever tell my mother I said that!

Follow-up

- *Panel interview*: record (on video or audio tape) several students being interviewed by another student taking the part of a TV or radio host. The host asks the questions in the Student Book. Keep the video or audio tape to play to students in their final year of high school!

> *The listening and speaking 'gap'*: you may need to reassure students that there will always be a gap between what they can understand and what they are able to say. Some students may need to be reminded that, in order to be able to say the words and sentences with ease, they will first need to have listened to and noticed them several times. The skills of listening attentively, guessing, noticing familiar words and forming 'hunches' can be discussed.

- *Let's talk about other languages*: invite students who speak another language to say several sentences, for example a greeting and a brief personal introduction, in front of the class. The other students try to guess what they are saying and talk about similarities with their own language(s) and/or Japanese.

おしょうゆ

(S) 14 (tape) 1A

Presentation

Students listen to the tape and repeat the new expressions. You could replay *Itadakimasu* and find where each one was used.

Follow-up

- *Focus on words*: write the following words on cardboard and attach them to the board – こんにちは、どうぞよろしく、すみません、はやく、またね、またあした、さようなら.

> You can use as many word cards in this task as you think your students can recognise. Remember that students will only need to recognise one or two characters to identify the word. You may need to read through the words with the students before doing the task.

Then write a short situation on cardboard in English to suit each word, for example *You're about to catch the train home. Your friend is waiting on the platform. What do you say?* A student selects a situation card, reads it to the class and then places it below the appropriate Japanese word. This task can be varied by having students make up their own situations, or asking them to select other Japanese words and make up situations for those. *Alternative*: you call out the words and students find the correct situation card.

- *Small group role-play cards*: write short situations on cards (in English) based on the language covered in Unit 1, for example *You are sitting in class and desperately need to go to the toilet. Your teacher is facing the blackboard. Attract her attention.* Each group selects a situation and chooses (or is given) two expressions from *Oshooyu* to include. The role-plays are performed in front of the class, after which each group give a brief explanation of how they used the expressions in their plays.

- おしょうゆ *board*: write the expressions in the Student Book on a chart (or on the pin-up board) and add other expressions as they are introduced.
- おしょうゆ *of-the-day*: students select one or more expressions for special attention during role-plays and dialogues.

おしょうゆ *incentives!*: you might find it helpful to establish an incentive scheme for students to use the *Oshooyu* expressions in their oral interaction tasks, for example *The* おしょうゆ *award of the week.*

おかし

15

Songs

- *Rounds*: sing the first song in rounds to the tune of *Row, row, row your boat.*
- *Actions*: make up actions to go with the key words in each line of the second song, which is sung to the tune of *Heads and shoulders, knees and toes.*
- *School assembly*: students might like to perform the songs, with actions, at a school assembly.

Craft activity

Screen printing names in katakana: you will need a screen printing set and ink (try your school art department), and newspaper. Ask students to bring their own T-shirt.

1 Cut out stencil of name or design using a knife or cutter.
2 Place newspaper inside T-shirt and around stencil.
3 Position stencil on T-shirt.
4 Print.

Students should cut out their own stencils and prepare for printing. The teacher should do all the printing. This activity should take two 40-minute lessons: one to prepare, one to print.

Putting it all together

- *AM or PM*: put two boxes at the front of the class. Label one box the *AM/PM* box and the other the *Famous person* box. Each person cuts out two pieces of paper. On one piece students write the name of a famous person they would like to meet, and put it into the *Famous person* box. On the other they write AM or PM and put it into the *AM/PM* box. Thoroughly mix the pieces of paper in each box. Each person takes one piece of paper out of each box and introduces him/herself to five people. Students must use the correct greeting according to whether it is AM or PM. See how many people students can remember afterwards.
- *National Aisatsu No Hi* (Greeting Day): arrange a National Greeting Day where all students learning Japanese in Year 7 or Year 8 must greet each other in Japanese if they see each other in the playground or around the school. Points are allocated for each correct greeting made: two points for initiating the greeting and one point for answering. If teachers so desire they may organise a 'sign sheet' whereby the names of both the greeter and the person receiving the greeting are recorded and initialled as proof of the exchange. Of course, prizes are awarded for the most points at the end of the day. The greetings may include: おはよう、こんにちは、さようなら、またね、またあした。
- *Role-play*: use dress-up clothes to enhance this activity. Students make hand-held face masks of celebrities' faces. They could paste the picture of the face onto cardboard, cut it out and attach it to a paddle-pop stick. (These can be used later as flashcards.) Students then imagine that they are at a Hollywood party. They make a grand entrance to the party and introduce themselves to as many people as possible.
- *Collage of things Japanese*: divide the class into groups of four. Each group collects newspaper and magazine clippings about Japan, labels and advertisements of Japanese products, anything Japanese, and brings them in every day for one week. Give the students five minutes at the beginning or end of each lesson to paste them onto a large sheet of cardboard. At the end of the week each group give a presentation of what they have found. You could laminate their work and display it on the classroom wall.
- *Class hiragana/katakana chart*: make class hiragana and katakana charts and fill in the characters as you learn them. Put them up in the classroom. Students can also make one of their own in their books or as a したじき.
- Encourage students to write their name in katakana on the top of every piece of work to be handed in. Allocating one extra mark for writing it correctly is a good incentive.

ごちそうさま

15

- 9 *Obentoo quiz*: students should check how much they have learnt by completing the *Obentoo quiz.*
- *Individual progress cards*: write the items listed in *Gochisoosama* onto the photocopiable student progress card on page 138 of the *Moshi Moshi Teachers' Handbook.* You may wish to add other items, for example other language points, other

script introduced, cultural understandings, completion of homework or assignment tasks.

- *Group/Class progress chart*: write the items on a large chart which the students in each group tick off as they are completed.

To save time when checking students' progress cards you could:

- check one student's card in each group and get that student to check another five or six students
- ask students to request checking by the teacher only when they are not sure about something
- ask students to work in groups checking each other's work while you walk around the class conducting spot checks and/or answering queries. To double-check the group's work, a spokesperson could report to the class at the conclusion of the session
- ask students to record examples for each item on the progress card at home on audio cassette. You could listen to the cassettes later and record a brief comment at the end of each student's work. This allows students to take as long as they need to demonstrate each item correctly.

Reference to *Yoroshiku National Curriculum Guidelines for Japanese (Moshi Moshi)*

The following is a list of the suggested language exponents presented in *Moshi Moshi* Module 1 よろしく *(How do you do?)* which have been introduced in Unit 1 of *Obentoo*. In some cases the example has been changed to correspond to the form introduced in *Obentoo*. Appropriate activities from *Moshi Moshi* are suggested below.

Language exponents

- Greeting others
  おはようございます。
- Leave taking
  さようなら。
  じゃまた。
- Modes of address
  ... さん
  ... くん
  ... せんせい
  ... ちゃん
- Introducing self and others
  (メリー)です。
  どうぞよろしく。
- Asking for and giving information about (name)
  おなまえはなんですか。
  わたしは(メリー)です。
  ぼくは(さぶろう)です。
- Asking for and giving confirmation
  (ケイトさん)ですか。
  はい、そうです。
  いいえ、エマです。
- Responding to class roll-call
  ... さん！
  ... くん！
  はい！
  (メリー)さんはけっせきです。
- Apologising
  ごめんなさい。
  おそくなってすみません。
- Attracting attention
  すみません。
- Expressing gratitude
  ありがとう。
  どうもありがとうございます。

Suggested activities from *Moshi Moshi*

- あなたのなまえは？
  Student Book page 4
- しゅっせきです
  Teacher Resources page 6

Unit 2

Overview

Unit objectives

Students will be able to:

- ask someone to do something
- respond to a request to do something
- ask where someone is from
- say where they come from
- read and write eight more hiragana and nine more katakana
- recognise some other key words in hiragana
- recognise five countries written in katakana
- read and write the kanji for Japan
- recognise the map of Japan and its major cities

Functions and language exponents

1 Asking someone to do something and responding
(みなさん)、(きい)てください。
はい／ちょっと まってください。
2 Asking where someone is from
(エマさん)、どこからきましたか。
3 Saying where you come from
(オーストラリア)からきました。

Key vocabulary and expressions

ちえこ
けんいち
しんご
ベン
トニー
カーラ
みなさん、...
さなえ
みせて(ください)
たって(ください)
すわって(ください)
きいて(ください)
みて(ください)
ドアをあけて(ください)
ドアをしめて(ください)
まどをあけて(ください)
まどをしめて(ください)
ちょっとまって(ください)
しずかに！
どこからきましたか。
オーストラリア
インドネシア
カナダ
アメリカ
ニュージーランド
にほん

Script

Students are expected to be able to read and write the key characters and recognise the associated words.

Key characters	*Associated words*
あ	あけて
け	けんいち
し	しんご、しめて、しずかに
す	すわって
せ	せんせい
ち	ちえこ
て	みて、みせて
み	みなさん
日本	
ア	アメリカ
イ	インドネシア
オ	オーストラリア
カ	カナダ
ト	トニー
ナ	カナダ
ニ	ニュージーランド
ヘ	ベン
ラ	カーラ

Script understandings

- Introducing nigori sound changes (katakana): ド (ドア) and ベ (ベン)
- Using the kanji 日本 for Japan
- Introducing the concept of stroke order

Learning how to learn

Talking about techniques for remembering and learning words

Cultural elements

- Identifying well-known images of Japan
- Locating cities and places on a map of Japan

Other incidental language introduced

やったー！
ああっ
もう！
あのうー。
みせて！
いいですねー。
はい
そうです。
...さん／くんは？
きりつ
れい
ちゃくせき
こちらは ... です。

Extension material

- Additional classroom expressions (*it is recommended that these expressions be taught for recognition only and introduced gradually as required)*
  ノートをみせてください。
  テキストをみせてください。
  しゃしんをみせてください。
  きいてください。
  テープをきいてください。
  せんせいをみてください。
  こくばんをみてください。
  ホワイトボードをみてください。
  テキストをみてください。
  テキストをあけてください。
  ノートをあけてください。
  テキストをとじてください。
  ノートをとじてください。
  てをあげてください。
  なまえをかいてください。
  ノートにかいてください。
  にほんごでかいてください。
  えいごでかいてください。
  もういちどいってください。
- Adding どうぞ at the front of a request to make it more polite
- Leaving off the ください to make it less formal
- Additional countries
  スペイン
  フランス
  イタリア
  ドイツ
  ベトナム
  オランダ
  スイス
  インド
  ちゅうごく
  かんこく

Need some extra words or expressions? Ask your teacher!

アフリカ
アラビア
ベルギー
ギリシャ
アイルランド
マラヤ
メキシコ
ポーランド
フィリピン
フィンランド
トルコ
タイ
ロシア

Teaching suggestions

The following suggestions are provided as a guide to lesson planning and should be adapted to suit your teaching style and the learning styles of your students. These tasks are specific to this unit. For more information on general strategies for each section, refer to *Using Obentoo* on pages 3–8.

いただきます

Ⓢ16–18 Ⓑ1A

Warm-up

Lesson starters: the teacher enters the room and says たってください (using a suitable gesture), greets the class, and says すわってください (also with a gesture). Discuss and practise with the class. Volunteers could then take the part of the teacher. A 'class captain' could be taught how to say きりつ、れい and ちゃくせき (*Stand!, Bow!, Sit!*). (Note, however, that these commands are seen as 'militaristic' by some teachers in Japan and are not used everywhere.) By using gestures, students will quickly pick up spoken classroom commands and requests. Students are only expected to be able to read those for which they know the first character/s.

Listen and discuss

- *Listen and guess:* students look at the cartoon on the OHTs while listening to the recording and make guesses about what is being said and who is speaking.
- *Find the frame:* students listen to sections of the recording and find the matching frames in the cartoon story.
- After going through the story focusing on meaning and key words and expressions, students answer the questions on page 18 of the Student Book in English, either in their notebooks or orally.

(Refer to *Listen and discuss* on pages 4–5 in these Teacher Notes for more information on presentation.)

Follow-up

- *Game:* けんちゃんがいった「たって！。」 This is a variation of 'Simon Says'. One person at the front of the group calls out an instruction preceded by けんちゃんがいった, for example, けんちゃんがいった「たって」('Everyone stands'). The leader continues to give instructions in the same way. If s/he gives an instruction without saying けんちゃんがいった the students should not respond. Those who do are 'out'. The winners are the students who remain 'in' until the end.
- まる／ばつ (*played as a true/false game*): the teacher holds up flashcards of the *Obentoo* students Tony, Shingo, Carla, Chieko, Sanae, Kenichi and Ben, and asks ...さん／くんですか。Students call out はい！and make a large まる (*circle*) with their hands for true; and call out いいえ！and make a large ばつ (*cross*) with their hands for false.
- わたし／ぼく *game:* students sit in a circle on the ground with one student as せんせい. S/he walks around the circle and touches the head of each player, saying わたし for girls, ぼく for boys and せんせい for one person. せんせい then chases the first student, who tries to get to the space left by せんせい. If the first student is tagged before getting back, s/he becomes せんせい and sits in the middle until another せんせい gets out. (This is a variation of 'Duck, Duck, Goose!').

The OHTs can be used in a number of different ways, for example:

- Copy the OHTs. Number each frame randomly, enlarge and cut up. The students form groups and are given one set each. The winning group is the first one to assemble the frames in the right order.
- Ask the students to act out each section, modifying or adding to the story where they can.

どんなあじ？

Ⓢ19–21 Ⓑ1A

1 Asking someone to do something and responding

Warm-up

- Replay *Itadakimasu* to refresh students' memories. Select key words and expressions, and ask students to repeat them after you.
- *Explore the page*: ask students what they think is happening in the pictures.
- Ask students what classroom instructions they remember.

Presentation

- Students look at the pictures, listen to the tape and repeat. After listening and repeating, discuss what was said. Next see if the students can repeat the dialogues by themselves.
- Students could then look at the sentences on Student Book page 20, listen to the tape and see if they can point to each word as they repeat. Then stop the tape and see if the students can 'read' the sentences as they point.
- Refer to *Benkyoo no Ben* (Student Book pages 22–3) to introduce the new hiragana and katakana characters.

Follow-up

- **Ⓦ16/T8 Ⓑ 4A** Students listen to the tape and match each instruction with the most appropriate picture.

Audio script

1 あのう、たってください。
2 あああ、まどをしめてください。
3 すみません、すわってください。
4 たなかくん、みせてください。
5 あっ、えーと、ドアをあけてください。
6 やったー、みてください。
7 しずかにしてくださいよ。

- **W 16/T9 ⑧ 4A** Students look at the picture of Mr Nakamura's classroom as he enters it. They listen to his instructions on tape, and then draw the classroom as it should be when he is ready to begin his lesson. Students may make notes in English as they listen.

Audio script

Shingo: きりつ。れい。
N.Sensei: みなさん、おはようございます。
Everyone: せんせい、おはようございます。
Shingo: ちゃくせき。
N.Sensei: みなさん、しずかにしてください。このへやはさむいね。トニーくん、まどをしめてください。
Tony: はい。
N.Sensei: カーラさん、ドアをしめてください。
Carla: はい。
N.Sensei: ゆきさん、しずかに、たってください。
Yuki: はい。
N.Sensei: ハジョーノくん、すわってください。
Harjono: はい。
Everyone: みなさん、ノートをあけてください。たかこさん、ノートをみせてください。
Takako: はい、どうぞ。
N.Sensei: ありがとう。さあ、はじめましょう。

Vocabulary notes

このへやはさむいね。
This room is cold, isn't it.
はじめましょう。
Let's begin.

- *Instruction relay*: the class is divided into two or more teams. They are lined up all facing in the same direction. Cards containing the instructions are placed in a box at the back end of each line. The person at the back of each line draws a card out of the box and acts out the instruction to the person in front of him/her. That person then acts out the instruction to the next person in front. This continues until the instruction reaches the front of the line, where that person says the instruction aloud. If the instruction is correct, the front person goes to the end of the line and draws another card from the box. If incorrect, the instruction is acted out again from the back. The game is won by the first team to correctly identify all of the instructions in the box.
- **W 17/T10** Students follow the path to the magic samurai sword, saying the instructions aloud as this go. As this is a speaking task, you might like to do this in small groups or as a class.
  Variations:
  1 Give students a list of the instructions, for example:
  - あけてください **(あ)**
  - みせてください **(み)**
  - きいてください **(き)**
  - ドアをしめてください **(し)**
  - すわってください **(す)**
  - たってください **(た)**

  Ask them to match each instruction with the appropriate situation on the workbook page by writing down each instruction's initial character in the appropriate situation box.
  2 Do it as a role-play, setting up the classroom as the path.

2 Asking where someone is from and responding

Warm-up

- *Look and guess*: before students listen to the tape, they look at the pictures and try to guess where the people are from.

Presentation

- Students look at the pictures in their Student Book, listen to the tape and repeat. After this, students could come to the front of the class and take the parts of the *Obentoo* students.
- Students listen to the tape and read the characters in the sentences below the pictures as they repeat.

Follow-up

- *Celebrity groups*: the class is divided into groups of 5–7 players, with each group researching a group of celebrities, for example, singers, TV personalities, sportspeople, historical figures and movie stars. Students collect pictures of their celebrities and introduce them to the class in this way: ...さんです。...からきました。 After the presentation, the other class members see who can remember the most information. This task can take place over several days, with one group presenting per day. The game can be made more challenging by getting each celebrity to also introduce a friend (with or without a picture).
- *Role-play*: each student chooses a name and a country of origin. Students then find out about

each other by asking the questions おなまえは？ and どこからきましたか。When everyone is finished, students return to their seats and try to list everyone they have met and their country of origin. The student who remembers the most names is the winner.

- W 17/T11 4A Students listen to the tape and write down the name of each student mentioned and where s/he comes from. You can have students write their answers in English or in Japanese if they can.

Audio script

a こんにちは。わたしはエマです。
オーストラリアからきました。
どうぞよろしく。

b みなさんこんにちは。ぼくはハジョーノです。
インドネシアからきました。
どうぞよろしく。

c きいてください。わたしはケイトです。
ニュージーランドからきました。

d あのう、ぼくはトニーです。カナダからきました。

e Shh しずかに！アメリカからきました。
カーラです。どうぞよろしく。

f はい。ぼくもオーストラリアからきました。
ベンです。

g ぼくはゆうすけです。日本のこうべからきました。

- W 18/T12 Students draw a line connecting each *Obentoo* student with the country s/he comes from. As extension, students could write the first character of the *Obentoo* student's name under each picture.
- W 18/T13 Students interpret for the famous visitors by translating the information given into Japanese. The answers can be recorded onto a tape as suggested in the Workbook, or performed as a role-play in front of the class.

べんきょうのベン—ひらがな

S 22 1A

Characters introduced: あ、け、し、す、せ、ち、て、み

- Before playing the tape, ask students to look at the page and see what characters they can remember from the previous unit.
- Play the tape while students look at the Student Book. Pause the tape whenever you hear a 'ding'.

Audio script

Speaker: Ben

Hi! Ben here again to bring you up to date with the hiragana and katakana you need to know for Unit 2. There are also some kanji on page 24 which will look impressive written in your Japanese notebook.

The hiragana you learnt in Unit 1 are printed in black in the chart at the top of the page. Point to each one as I say it and repeat after me.

お
き
こ
さ
た
な
ま
ゆ

よくできました。

Look at the characters in the yellow boxes in the chart. Use the pattern you learnt in Unit 1 to work out the sound of each one.

...

Now look at the group of eight characters on the page. Point to each one as I say it, and repeat after me.

1 あ
2 け
3 し
4 す
5 せ
6 ち
7 て
8 み

よくできました。

Look back to *Itadakimasu* and *Donna aji?* See if you can find words which contain the new characters. がんばって！

...

That's it from me for now.
またね。

Follow-up

- Use the word flashcards to practise students' recognition of the key words. (See point 6 on page 4.)
- W 10–11 かきかた (*How to write*): students practise writing the new hiragana characters in the boxes, using the correct stroke order.

Avoid stroke order 'overkill'. Although correct stroke order is very important, ensure that students have enough time to learn to recognise the characters before focusing on how to write them. It is easy to 'kill' students' interest in characters by treating stroke order too rigorously.

- **S 22** *Find the odd sound*: students select the odd sound in each group of three presented. *Solutions*: 1c, 2a, 3c, 4c, 5a, 6a.
- *Pass it on*: students form two teams and line up facing the board. The teacher shows the last student in each team a character. That student writes the character on the back of the person in front (with his/her finger). After the character is 'passed' up the line, the first person writes it on the board. The first team to pass the character to the front correctly is the winner. This game can be made more challenging by getting students to write two characters, or words. You may need to review correct stroke order after each round.
- *Mystery Message*: the class devises a series of codes for Japanese words using the first character of each sentence, for example:
  お = おはようございます。
  こ = こんにちは。
  さ = さようなら。
  おなま = おおなまえは？
  みて = みてください。
  あ = ドアをあけてください。
  し = ドアをしめてください。
  き = きいてください。
  ち = ちょっとまってください。
  しず = しずかに！ Students write messages to other members of the class, giving them instructions which they perform in front of the class. The other students then try to decode the message in Japanese, for example: こ、た、みて、し、す、さ.
- **B 2.1** ごきぶり (*cockroach*): students draw ten cockroaches on the grid. The teacher (or a student) then calls out pairs of characters. If a student has a cockroach drawn in the square where the two characters meet, that cockroach is eliminated. The first student to 'kill' all ten cockroaches is the winner. To ensure that students don't cheat, the winning student can be asked to call out the characters the teacher has read out. Teachers may prefer to play this game with a smaller number of characters. If so, adapt the grid on **B 2.1** or redraw it.
- *Wall displays*: if possible, display pieces of Japanese writing in your classroom, to help students become accustomed to seeing Japanese script.
- **W 15/T6** Students complete the words with the correct hiragana. They should use their hiragana chart to work out the unknown characters.

You may choose to leave the workbook activities until students have learnt the katakana characters for this unit. They can then work through the first seven workbook tasks in the order they are presented.

- **W 20/T17** ことばさがし: students colour in all the squares containing katakana. Then they look for the hiragana words and phrases in the chart and fill in the missing characters. Students may like to make up their own ことばさがし.
- Students look at the two photos of signs on page 22 and see whether they can recognise any of the characters. For your info:

電池(でんち)あります	*We have batteries.*
カメラ	*Cameras*
ありがとうございました	*Thank you very much.*

- **S 24** *Extra reading task*: students look at the photo of the class caricatures. First they have to find the names listed. Then they use the hiragana chart to find out the names of all the students, and write them in English in their notebooks. Discuss the use of family names first, of family names at school and even amongst friends, and of names with くん、ちゃん、さん、せんせい, for example たざきくん、えみちゃん.

べんきょうのベン — かたかな

S 23 B 1A

Characters introduced: ア、イ、オ、カ、ト、ナ、ニ、ヘ、ラ

- Recap the use of katakana for 'borrowed' words. Ask students how many words they know which are written in katakana.
- Play the tape while students look at the Student Book page. Pause the tape whenever you hear a 'ding'.

Audio script

SPEAKER: Ben

Remember the katakana from Unit 1? Point to the characters printed in black as I say them and repeat after me.

エ

ケ

ハ

よくできました。

Look at the characters in the yellow boxes. Use the pattern you learnt in Unit 1 to work out the sound of each one.

...

Now look at the group of nine large characters on the page. Point to each character as I say it, and repeat after me.

1 ア
2 イ
3 オ
4 カ
5 ト
6 ナ
7 ニ
8 ヘ
9 ラ

よくできました。

Katakana sound changes

You have probably noticed that the first character of my name, ベ, has two small marks next to the ヘ. These marks are called *nigori*. Nigori is a type of shorthand which changes the sound of ヘ *(he)* to ベ *(be)*. Nigori also changes the sound of ト *(to)* to ド *(do)*. Nigori can change the sound of hiragana characters too.

Have a look at the charts inside the front and back covers and see how many you can find.

See you later! またね。

Follow-up

- Use the word flashcards to practise students' recognition of the key words. See point 6 on page 4.
- **W 11** かきかた (*How to write*): students practise writing the new katakana characters in the boxes, using the correct stroke order.
- **S 23** *Find the odd sound*: students select the odd sound in each group of three presented. *Solutions*: 1c, 2c, 3c, 4a, 5a, 6b.
- Students look at the two photos of signs on Student Book page 23 and see if they can recognise any of the characters. For your info:

アイスクリーム	*Ice-creams*
バニラ	*Vanilla*
チョコレート	*Chocolate*
抹茶 (まっちゃ)	*Green tea*
ラムレースン	*Rum 'n' raisin*
チョコミント	*Choc-mint*
コーヒーアーモンド	*Coffee-almond*
チョコマーブル	*Choc-marble*
ストロベリー	*Strawberry*
メロンシャーベット	*Melon sherbet*
オレンジシャーベット	*Orange sherbet*
テレホンカード	*Telephone cards*

- **W 12/T1** Students find as many hiragana, katakana and kanji as they can hidden on the treasure island and colour them in different colours (for example the hiragana red, the katakana blue and the kanji green). They then write the characters in the spaces provided. Students might like to try making up their own たからさがし puzzle.
- **W 13/T2** Students match the *Obentoo* students with their hosts.
- **W 13/T3** Students repair the name tags by completing the stained characters.
- **W 14/T4** Students write the kana in the boxes provided.
- **W 14/T5** Students write the name of each *Obentoo* student under that person's めいし.
- **W 15/T7** Students complete the words with the correct katakana. They may use their katakana charts to work out the unknown characters.
- **W 21/T18** Students colour in all the squares containing hiragana. Then they look for the katakana words in the chart and fill in the missing characters. Students may like to make up their own ことばさがし.

べんきょうのベン—かんじ

S 24

Read and discuss the information on kanji on this page. Discuss the origins of kanji, readings, stroke order and shape. Students trace the strokes of 日本 with their finger and then practise writing them in their Workbook on page 12 (かきかた).

ごはんとおかず

S 25

Presentation

- *Any volunteers?:* students look at the tables in their Student Book and volunteers are asked to make sentences using the words shown. The rest of the class have to write down, in English, what the volunteers say. Other volunteers could be asked to use extension vocabulary covered during the unit.
- *Character count*: students are asked to find the most commonly used character they have studied among the words given in the tables.
- Make enlargements of the Japanese part of the tables and cut these into pieces. Students work in pairs to join the jumbled pieces. *Note*: if you want students to make up individual sentences you will need several copies of some pieces.
- *Hiragana/katakana sort*: students count the number of words in hiragana and the number of words in katakana.

Follow-up

- *Sentence scrabble* (for 4–6 players): write parts of sentences on cards, for example みせて、たって、すわって、ください、ドアを、あけて、ちょっと、まって、きこえません、and put them face down on the table. Each player picks up three cards and looks at them. If players can make a sentence with their cards when it is their turn, they put the cards in front of them and read out the sentence. If a player cannot make a sentence, s/he can throw back one card and take another. The winner is the student with the most sentences when all the cards in the middle have been used.

- *Introducing the small* っ: you could draw students' attention to the small っ used in たって、すわって、ちょっと and まって and its effect on pronunciation. This is covered later in the course by *Benkyoo no Ben* in Unit 5 (S 2A, Katakana section).
- To consolidate important grammatical points, try to use exercises in which students use the language to do something active; for example, use gestures for て-form verbs, words which contain the small っ sound or long vowel sound, and 'funny faces' for question words.

- **W 18/T14** Students conduct a survey to find students in the class can say the phrases indicated. Allow students four minutes to do this task.
- **W 19/T15** Students introduce soccer teams by saying where they come from.
- For further grammar explanation refer students to the せつめい section of the Student Book (pages 199–200).

Extension tasks

- **B 2.2** どこから? Introduce some extra countries and the structure ...さんは ...からきました。Students write the English for the countries listed and then circle the kana they have already learnt. They then practise the examples orally and play the game. If you have fewer than six students playing the game, select identities so that there is only one per student.
- **B 2.3** べんりなひょうげん Introduce some extra classroom expressions. Go through the BLM, with students repeating the new expressions. They then do part C in pairs.

テーブルマナー

S 26–7

Presentation

- Students look at the photographs on the double-page spread in the Student Book and try to identify the places or Japanese images in them. They then look at the map and try to match the small drawings on the map to each photograph. These pages should stimulate discussion of:
  - major cities in Japan
  - geography of Japan
  - the size of Japan compared with the size of Australia
  - distances within Japan
  - places of interest
  - images of Japan (*daruma*, *maneki neko*, etc.).
- Students spend two minutes looking at the photographs before closing their books. They then take turns completing the sentence 'Five things I learnt from the page are ...'
- Each student prepares three questions about the pictures (in a given time limit). Students then ask their questions while everyone has their books closed.
- Students choose a photo, research the topic in the school library and prepare a one-minute 'elevator speech', for example answering these questions: *Who (or what) am I? Am I young or old? What am I like? Where would you find me? Why am I important?*
- A student is selected to choose a detail in one (or more) of the photos. The other students ask him/her questions which the student can only answer with はい or いいえ.
- Students each prepare two quiz questions about Japan (based on the photos or related to them) which are placed in a hat and used for a team game.

Follow-up

- **B 2.4** *A look into Japan jigsaw*:
  1 Students cut out the jigsaw map and paste down the pieces in the correct positions to make a map of Japan. Thy then cut out the city and island signposts and paste them onto the map in the correct positions, before colouring the map.
  2 Students choose one of the eight cities and research it in the school library, finding information on its population, history, geography, places of interest, festivals, etc. Students could produce a poster introducing the city and its attractions. Travel brochures, magazines and travel guides would be useful for this activity; examples of travel guides are C. Taylor *et al.*, *Japan: A Lonely Planet Travel Survival Kit* (Lonely Planet Publications, 1994) and J.Kinoshita, *Gateway to Japan* (Kodansha, 1992).
- にほんについて *(About Japan) collage*: in groups, students collect material about places of interest in Japan from travel brochures, newspapers and magazines and paste them onto cardboard to make a collage. At the end of the week each group present their collage to the class.
- にほんせい *(Made in Japan)*: students list items in their home which are manufactured in Japan or made by a Japanese company. Follow up with a class discussion of the impact of Japan in the world since World War II.

Extra information (to support *Teeburu manaa* S 26–7)

- Japan has a land area of 377 435 square kilometres, more than 80% of which is mountainous.
- Japan consists of some 1000 islands. There are four major ones: Hokkaido (ほっかいどう), Honshu (ほんしゅう), Shikoku (しこく) and Kyushu (きゅうしゅう). The island of Okinawa (おきなわ) in the south-west of the country is the largest of the small islands.
- Japan has more than 40 active volcanoes, and experiences frequent earthquakes and *tsunami* (tidal waves).
- Japan has a population of around 123 million, 75% of its population living in the cities.

- **List of photographs and icons**

1 ゆきまつり Sapporo Snow Festival. This festival is held in Sapporo on Hokkaido in early February and is a huge display of snow sculptures by snow artists from all over the world.

2 キタキツネ The northern fox. This animal is popular in traditional Japanese stories (むかしばなし). The fox is said to be able to change its form and trick people.

3 アイヌ The Ainu are native people, thought to be descendants of the inhabitants of the islands of Japan from prehistoric times. Now they live mainly in Northern Hokkaido. The Ainu had their own language and customs, which were passed from generation to generation. Nowadays very little of the language and culture has survived due to past governments' policies to assimilate the Ainu. The young Ainu people have renewed interest in learning about their ancestors and recently exhibition villages and museums have been established in Hokkaido where tourists can learn a little of the lifestyle of the Ainu people.

4 ツキノワグマ The white-collared bear. This bear is unique to Japan. It is black with a distinctive white collar around its neck. White-collared bears are often referred to in traditional stories.

5 かまくら A hut made of snow. This is also a festival observed in the middle of January in Akita Prefecture, featuring snow huts in which children play house.

6 なまはげ Namahage is a demon often seen in festivals in Akita Prefecture. He is not evil but is said to punish lazy people.

7 こけし *Kokeshi* dolls are wooden, cylindrical dolls with hand-painted patterns. They are found throughout Japan; however, the Sendai area is most famous for them.

8 たなばた Tanabata or the Star Festival is held on 7 July. According to legend, on this day the weaver princess (Vega) and the cowherd (Altair) cross the Milky Way and express their love for each other. Children decorate bamboo trees with streamers and other decorations for たなばた (the Star Festival) and often write their wishes on colourful paper and attach them as well.

9 だるま *Daruma* or wish dolls. *Daruma* are round red dolls which come in many sizes. They are sold at festivals throughout Japan and are a sign of good luck. If Japanese people want to make a special wish, they paint in one of the eyes of the *daruma,* if the wish comes true, they paint in the other as a sign of gratitude. (*See* おかし *notes in Unit 7 on how to make your own daruma.*)

10 あかとんぼ Akatonbo, the red dragonfly. These are often seen in autumn in Japan. Children love to try to catch them.

11 ディズニーランド Tokyo Disneyland is located in Chiba Prefecture, only about 15 minutes by train from Tokyo Station.

12 とうきょうタワー Tokyo Tower is 330 metres high and towers over the city of Tokyo.

13 だいぶつ The Great Buddha in Kamakura. A bronze statue of Buddha, it weighs 850 tonnes and is 11.4 metres tall.

14 ふじさん Mt Fuji, the symbol of Japan, is Japan's highest mountain and stands 3776 metres.

15 まねきねこ The *manekineko* or beckoning cat is thought to bring good business to shops.

16 しんかんせん The Bullet Train. This super express train reaches speeds of up to 270 km/h and travels from Tokyo north-east to Morioka, south-west to Fukuoka/Hakata on the island of Kyushu, and north to Niigata.

17 きんかくじ Kinkakuji, the Golden Pavilion Temple. Originally constructed in 1397, it was burnt to the ground in 1950 by one of its monks. It was rebuilt in 1955. The Kinkakuji is one of Japan's most famous tourist attractions.

18 まいこ *Maiko san*: young women trained in the art of Japanese music and dance. They are employed to entertain clients in restaurants and tea houses with witty conversation, music and dancing.

19 ごじゅうのとう pagodas in Nara.

20 とうだいじ Todaiji Temple in Nara is the largest wooden structure in the world and houses a huge bronze statue of Buddha. The temple has been destroyed many times since its construction in the eighth century. The current reconstruction is two-thirds the size of the original.

21 おおさかじょう Osaka Castle. Originally built in 1583, the castle was destroyed in 1615. Rebuilt by 1626, it was burnt to the ground again in 1868. The current reproduction was completed in 1931.

22 ひなまつり Dolls' Day Festival is the festival for girls in Japan. On this day ひなにんぎょう (*hina* dolls) and peach blossoms are displayed in the houses of female children. Some children have parties with special food such as ひしもち (diamond-shaped rice cakes), しろざけ (sweet rice wine) and あられ (rice crackers).

23 あきまつり Autumn Festival is celebrated at different times throughout autumn in different parts of Japan. It is a festival of thanksgiving to the gods for a good harvest. おみこし (portable shrines) are carried around the town by members of the community.

24 せとおおはし Seto Ohashi. Opened in April 1988, this bridge links the island of Honshu with the island of Shikoku. At 12.3 kilometres long it is the world's longest double-decker bridge.

25 たぬき The badger. An animal made famous in Japanese traditional stories, the badger is said to be able to change its form to trick people.
26 へいわこうえん Hiroshima Peace Park is situated in the centre of Hiroshima on the Otagawa River and contains the museum, cenotaph and eternal flame.
27 みやじま Miyajima is a famous island off the coast of Hiroshima. The Torii Gate to the Itsukushima Shrine is one of the most famous landmarks in Japan.
28 ぼんおどり *Bon Odori* are summer dances which take place around the middle of August throughout Japan.
29 こいのぼり *Koinobori* are carp kites which are flown from flagpoles around 5 May each year for the Boys' Festival (こどものひ).
30 はなみ A pastime where Japanese people go flower viewing every year in spring (April).
31 くまもとじょう Kumamoto Castle. Originally built between 1601 and 1607, it was destroyed in 1877 during the Satsuma Rebellion. It is one of the great castles of Japan.
32 さくらじま A volcanic land mass off the coast of Kyushu at Kagoshima, Sakurajima was originally an island until a massive eruption in 1914, when it became joined to the mainland. The volcano is still active today, with almost constant eruptions of smoke and ash.

- **Cities**

Sapporo — The largest city in Hokkaido, with a population of 1.6 million. It is a modern city with a cosmopolitan flavour. Sapporo is famous for its Snow Festival in February each year, where huge ice sculptures are displayed in おおどうりこうえん。

Aomori — Situated on the coast of Northern Honshu, it is the gateway to Hokkaido. It has a population of 287 000, is the capital of Aomori Prefecture and is an important fishing and shipping centre.

Sendai — Situated on the coast of Honshu north of Tokyo, it has a population of 918 000. It is famous for it's *kokeshi* dolls and its Tanabata festival, which is held here from 6 to 8 August (later than the rest of Japan).

Tokyo — A sprawling metropolis with a population of approximately 12 million. It is the capital of Japan, the home of the Imperial Family and a centre of fashion, business and tradition.

Kanazawa — The capital of Ishikawa Prefecture, with a population of 442 000. It has many fine museums displaying examples of Japanese arts and crafts.

Kyoto — A city of 1.4 million people, with over 2000 temples and shrines that attract nearly 40 million visitors from Japan and overseas annually. It became the capital of Japan in 794 and was the home of the Imperial Family until 1868. During that period it was not always the capital; Kamakura was capital in the years 1185–1333 and Edo in the period 1600–1867.

Nara — The capital of Japan from 710 to 784, Nara is famous as a tourist destination. Particularly noteworthy is the Todaiji Temple, the largest wooden structure in the world. Nara's population is 349 000.

Osaka — A bustling modern city with a population of 2.6 million, it ranks second (after Tokyo) in economic importance in Japan.

Kobe — With a population of 1 477 000 it is a popular tourist destination for the Japanese. In 1995, Kobe was the site of Japan's worst recent earthquake.

Hiroshima — Situated on the Otagawa River in Western Honshu, it is famous for being the site of the world's first atomic bombing on 6 August 1945. The Hiroshima Peace Park and Museum are memorials to those who died on that day and attract visitors from all over the world. Hiroshima's population is 1 085 000.

Matsuyama — The largest city in Shikoku, with a population of 443 000. It is famous for Matsuyama Castle and the Dogo hot springs.

Nagasaki — Situated on the west coast of Kyushu, with a population of 450 000, Nagasaki is famous as the first place of contact with the West (the Dutch and the Portuguese) in the sixteenth century. In more recent history it was destroyed as the second atomic bomb target in World War II.

Kagoshima — The southernmost major city in Kyushu, with a population of 536 000. Its main attraction is Sakurajima.

(Populations are 1994 figures.)

おはし

⊖ 28

Presentation

Students read the *Obentoo* students' suggestions for making learning Japanese easier. Then they form small groups and write their own suggestions on butcher's paper. These can be presented to the whole class and condensed into a class list of suggestions to be displayed in the classroom.

As an alternative, students could take the parts of the *Obentoo* students and answer the class's questions.

Follow-up

- *Learning skills project*: students form groups. Each group selects one of the learning techniques given in the Student Book (or makes up its own) and uses the technique for a week or so. The groups discuss their findings and report back to the class. The 'Best 7' ideas could be put on a chart on the pin-up board.
- *Internet link-up*: using the Internet, students make contact with students from another school who are learning Japanese and compare the techniques

they use. Alternatively, for students without Internet access, a hands-free telephone could be placed in the classroom and voice contact made with students from another school.

おしょうゆ

S 28 CD 1A

Presentation

Students listen to the tape and repeat the new expressions.

Follow-up

- *Swap and tell*: students make up situations in English where these expressions could be used. Others then try to identify the appropriate word.

> *Don't encourage word-for-word translations.*
> Discourage students from translating expressions word-for-word into English. Monolingual students often think that languages function in similar ways and they may need to be shown that this is not the case. Some students also believe that some languages are 'superior' to or more important than others, asking questions like 'What does that mean in real language?' This section could let students see that languages help people see the world differently.

- **W 19/T16** *Oshooyu quiz-time*: students read the situations and circle the correct answer. As a follow-up, they could make up their own multiple-choice questions and ask them in a TV gameshow role-play.

おかし

S 29

Song

Sing the song to the tune of *I met a bear* (もりのくまさん). It should be sung in two groups, the second echoing the first for the first four lines. After that the groups come together for the last two lines.

Craft activity

いもはん *Potato stamp*: students should be practising writing their own names in katakana by now, so you could explain to them the use of the はんこ or personal seal. (はんこ is a personal name stamp used instead of a signature on legal documents and letters, and is always stamped in red ink.)

Students can make their own はんこ with a raw potato (or a sweet potato or large carrot):

1 Cut the potato in half so that a large smooth edge is exposed.

2 Write your name (or the first character of your name, if it is too long) *back to front and inside out* onto the cut surface of the vegetable.

3 Cut around the shape of the characters with a lino cutter or knife, and cut away the background so that the characters are raised.

4 Dip your stamp in ink or paint and sign your work with your personal seal.

Rap

Practise your aerobics to this Japanese rap, using the following actions. The stressed syllable is bold.

Actions:

たって	stand up
すわって	sit down
まどをあけて	two arms up, opening window
まどをしめて	two arms down, closing window
ドアをあけて	two arms out, opening door
ドアをしめて	two arms inward, closing door
せんせいをみて	hands to eyes like binoculars
テープをきいて	open hands behind ears, listening
しずかにしずかに	finger to mouth: quiet

たって、す**わ**って
まどをあけて、まどをしめて
たって、す**わ**って
ドアをあけて、ドアをしめて
たって、す**わ**って
せんせいをみて、テープをきいて
たって、す**わ**って
しずかに、**し**ずかに、**shhhhhhh**

Putting it all together

- Students take turns to lead the class at the beginning and end of each lesson. Try this:
  - When the teacher enters the room, the 'leader' tells everyone to be quiet and stand up.
  - Then s/he leads the class in the greeting to the teacher.
  - Then s/he tells everyone to sit down (if anyone is still talking, s/he tells them to be quiet).
  - At the end of the lesson, the leader tells everyone to stand.
  - S/he leads the class in saying goodbye to the teacher.

  (The teacher should talk about the system used in Japan, where students stand and greet the teacher when s/he enters the room.)
- けんちゃんはいった: Kenichi's nickname is けんちゃん and there is a game named after him called けんちゃんはいった。It's like 'Simon Says'. To play けんちゃんはいった:
  - Students decide who will be けんちゃん.
  - They make up gestures or actions for each of the commands they've learnt, for example, pointing their hands down and lowering them as if they're closing a window.
  - If the person who is けんちゃん says けんちゃんはいった「たって」or けんちゃんはいった「たってください」or けんちゃんはいった「きりつ」the players should stand up (or obey the command given).
  - If けんちゃん says たって or たってください or きりつ the players should ignore the command.

– The winner can call out やったー！！

- Put magazine cut-outs of famous people on the board. Students choose one of them and perform a simple role-play, saying:
  – A greeting
  – Where s/he is from
  – Who s/he is
  – Something else, for example, an instruction to the audience.

  Students may like to use props or costumes. You could video the role-plays to show students at the end of the year.

ごちそうさま

S 29

- W 22 *Obentoo quiz*: students can check how well they have learnt the unit by trying the *Obentoo quiz* themselves or teachers can use it as an assessment task.
- *Unit review*: ask volunteers to give examples of each outcome in the list and the mistakes that people are likely to make with each one.
- *Individual progress cards*: write the items listed in *Gochisoosama* onto the photocopiable student progress card on page 138 of the *Moshi Moshi Teachers' Handbook*. You may wish to add other items, for example other language points, other script introduced, cultural understandings, completion of homework or assignment tasks.

Be wary of over-emphasising 'difficulties' in the unit or errors which have been made, as this can easily undermine students' confidence. Some students need to be reminded that the world's best tennis players lose games because they make mistakes. This issue could be pursued in a class discussion.

Reference to *Yoroshiku National Curriculum Guidelines for Japanese* (*Moshi Moshi*)

The following is a list of the suggested language exponents presented in *Moshi Moshi* Module 1 よろしく (*How do you do?*) which have been introduced in Unit 2 of *Obentoo*. In some cases the example has been changed to correspond to the form introduced in *Obentoo*. Appropriate activities from *Moshi Moshi* are suggested below.

Language exponents

- Nationality
  どこからきましたか。
  （ニュージーランド）からきました。
- Following classroom instructions
  みなさん、すわってください。
  （ほんをあけて）ください。
  （きいて）
- Asking for repetition
  もういちどいってください。

Suggested activities from *Moshi Moshi*

きいてください　Teacher Resources page 3

Unit 3

Overview

Unit objectives

Students will be able to:

- count up to 20
- ask someone's age and respond when asked their age
- ask for someone's telephone number and respond when asked for their number
- wish someone a happy birthday
- say thank you
- recognise kanji numbers up to 20 and write kanji numbers up to 10
- read and write five more hiragana and three hiragana sound changes
- identify different people in Japanese society
- discuss different lifestyles

Functions and language exponents

1 Counting up to 20
一、二、三、四、五、六、七、八、九、十、
十一、十二、十三、十四、十五、十六、十七、
十八、十九、二十

2 Asking someone's age and responding
(けんいちくん)はなんさいですか。
(十二)さいです。(エマさん)は？
(わたし)も(十二)さいです。

3 Asking for someone's telephone number and responding
(ちえこさん)、でんわばんごうは？
(773 0210)です。カーラさんは？
(わたし)は(763 2966)です。

Key vocabulary and expressions

はじめ！
おわり！

一、二、三、四、五、六、七、八、九、十、十一、十二、
十三、十四、十五、十六、十七、十八、十九、二十

いっさい／一さい
はたち／二十

Script recognition

Students are expected to be able to read and write the key characters and recognise the associated words.

Key characters	*Associated words*
い	なんさいですか
か	なんさいですか
は, ば	でんわばんごうは
ほ, ぼ	ぼく
わ	わたし

一、二、三、四、五、六、七、八、九、十、十一、十二、
十三、十四、十五、十六、十七、十八、十九、二十

Script understandings

- Introducing *nigori* sound changes (hiragana):
で(でんわ)、ば(ばんごう)、ぼ(ぼく)
- The use of は (*ha*) as *wa*, e.g. わたしは、でんわばんごうは、おなまえは、こんにちは
- Lengthening sounds in hiragana using う and in katakana using ー(ぼう)
- The use of kanji numbers to count (up to 20)
- Different ways to say zero: ゼロ (0) when writing Arabic numerals and まる(〇) when writing kanji numerals

Learning how to learn

A 'star quiz' takes a light-hearted look at attitudes towards learning, learning goals, approaching unfamiliar words, making mistakes, comparing yourself with others, doing classwork.

Cultural elements

Looking at photographs of Japanese people with different lifestyles (for example, traditional versus contemporary), and guessing their age.

Other incidental language introduced

もういちど！
ありがとうございました。
どうもありがとう。
ありがとう。
なあに？
おたんじょうびおめでとう！
どうぞ。
わあああ！
いただきます。

Extension material

- Counting from 20 to 99
- Talking about ages from 21 to 99
- Writing kanji numbers up to 99
- The alternative form でんわばんごうはなんばんですか。

Need some extra words or expressions? Ask your teacher!

もしもし。
おでんわですよ！
おたんじょうびおめでとうございます。
おめでとう。
おめでとうございます。
なんですか。

Teaching suggestions

The following suggestions are provided as a guide to lesson planning and should be adapted to suit your teaching style and the learning styles of your students. These tasks are specific to this unit. For more information on general strategies for each section, refer to *Using Obentoo* on pages 3–8.

いただきます

Ⓢ 30–2 Ⓢ 1B

Warm-up

- *Revision:* recap the identity of the *Obentoo* students using flashcards: おなまえは？わたし／ぼくは ... です。どうぞよろしく。... さんですか。はい／いいえ、わたし／ぼくは ... です。
- *Host families:* talk about student exchange programs and host sisters/brothers. Match the *Obentoo* students to their hosts, for example ... さん／くんのホスト・シスターは ... さんです。
- *Cultural points:* you could ask the students to find:
  - the name of the sport featured in the cartoon (kendo)
  - the items used by kendo players: bamboo sword, face mask, chest protector, thigh protector quilts and padded mittens to protect hands
  - how kendo players thank each other after a game or training session
  - the use of いただきます
  - how people often point to their noses when referring to themselves

Listen and discuss

- *Listen and guess* and *Find the frame*: as in Units 1 and 2.
- Students answer the questions on page 32 in the Student Book.
- Refer to *Listen and discuss* on pages 4–5 in these Teacher Notes for more information on presentation.

Follow-up

- '*Stand Up/Sit Down' game:* the class is divided into two teams: 'Stand up/sit downers' (SSers) and 'Guessers' (G'ers). SSers each choose two numbers from 1 to 20 and write them down. The teacher then calls the numbers at random and the SSers stand up on their first number and sit down on their second. G'ers have to identify the two numbers of each SSer without writing anything down. G'ers get points for identifying SSers' numbers. There are two winners: the SSer who goes standing up and sitting down the longest (without being caught) and the G'er who guesses the most pairs of numbers correctly.
- *Kana relay:* divide the class into four teams. Using the kana introduced in Units 1 and 2, place cards with single kana in ice-cream containers about 2 metres from the front of each line of students. Place four empty containers about 4 metres further away. When the teacher says はじめ！, the first student in each team runs to the first container, takes out a card, reads it out, says a word containing that kana, puts the card in the second container, runs back to the team and tags the next player, and so on. The game continues until a team has moved all its cards to the second container (or the teacher says おわり！).
- *Role-play:* (based on the cartoon frames at the bottom of Ⓢ 31): students act out this section of the story, taking the parts of each of the *Obentoo* students so that each person is asked his or her age, for example ... さん／くんはなんさいですか。 The students can make up their own answers.
- *Two versions of 4 and 7:* students will find it easier if they learn *one* way of counting 4 and 7 to begin with, for example 4 = よん and 7 = なな. The alternative pronunciations (4: し and 7: しち) could be introduced when the students start to learn how to count ages. You could explain that many Japanese people avoid using し because it also means 'death'.
- *Thanking people:* you will need to explain the different ways of thanking people introduced in the cartoon:
  ありがとう, used among friends, usually to thank someone for a gift or present
  どうもありがとう, a more polite way of thanking someone for a gift or present
  ありがとうございました, a semiformal way of thanking someone, for example a sporting opponent
  どうもありがとうございました (not used in the cartoon), a still more formal way of thanking someone.
- *Kanji numerals:* you will also need to explain that kanji numerals are generally only used in formal documents such as certificates, in newspapers (for the date), in restaurants where traditional dishes are served, in vertical writing and on name cards. Arabic numerals are used on most other occasions.

どんなあじ？

Ⓢ 33–5 Ⓢ 1B

1 Counting up to 20

Warm-up

- Replay *Itadakimasu* and explore the page as in Units 1 and 2.
- *Number actions:* make up actions to suit each of the numbers and perform them as the students learn to count. Counting can be varied: loud/soft, forwards/backwards, quickly/slowly, etc. Suggested actions:
  いち、に = scratch the knee
  さん = point to the sun

よん = have a yawn
ご = point to the door
ろく = playing the guitar (rock band)
なな = shake head (nah nah nah)
はち = make roof with hands (rabbit hutch)
く = tickle the neck (coochie coochie coo)
じゅう = make a dew drop with fingers.

Presentation

- Students look at the pictures, listen to the tape and repeat. After listening and repeating, discuss what was said. Next see if the students can repeat the dialogues by themselves.
- Students then look at the sentences below the pictures, listen to the tape and repeat, as in Units 1 and 2.

Follow-up

- うんどう (*Exercises*): take the students outside for this task and choose five pairs of students to be sports instructors. Each pair makes up an exercise for the rest of the class to do. When the pairs of instructors are ready, one person says みなさん、みてください。and the class watches (and counts) while the other instructor demonstrates the exercise. The instructor then says みなさん、たってください and the whole class then joins in (doing the exercise and counting) until the instructor says おわり！ Encourage the students to make up imaginative exercises!
- *Number bunches:* the teacher (or a student) calls out numbers and the class forms groups of that number of people. Left-over students are 'out'.
- *Human number sequence:* the class is divided into two teams. Team 1 make up a number sequence (e.g. 2, 4, 6) and present it to the other team by forming lines of the numbers they want to represent. Team 2 continue the sequence and count aloud for two more numbers (i.e. 8 and 10).
- *Correcting pronunciation:* you could go on はつおん (pronunciation) duty; moving around the class listening for pronunciation errors.
- *Keeping everyone involved:* for active counting practice (when students are not using the 'number actions' from the warm-up above) they could count with their fingers. The Japanese method uses one hand only and begins with the palm held open:
  1 = cross palm with thumb
  2 = cross thumb with index finger
  3 = cross thumb with middle finger
  4 = cross thumb with ring finger
  5 = cross thumb with little finger
  6 = uncross little finger
  7 = uncross ring finger
  8 = uncross middle finger
  9 = uncross index finger
  10 = straighten thumb
- *Using Japanese numbers in other subjects:* ask students how they could use Japanese numbers or Japanese counting in other subjects or activities.

2 Asking someone's age and responding

Warm-up

Look and guess: before students listen to the tape, they look at the pictures and try to remember where each of the students is from.

Presentation

Present first with the tape as suggested in earlier units. Then have students take the parts of the *Obentoo* students, with everyone else repeating after them.

Follow-up

- *Gameshow* おぼえていますか: students bring a photo of a famous person, a member of their family or someone they know (under 20 years of age). Each student then introduces his/her person, saying who they are and their age, for example ... さん／くんです。... さいです。Three contestants are then chosen. It is their task to remember the name or age of the person in each photo. (The names and ages should be written on the back of the photos.) The teacher then collects the photos and asks either おなまえは？ or なんさいですか。The contestants get one point for a correct answer and lose one for an incorrect answer.
- わたしです。*(It's me!):* students bring photos of themselves (at any age) and introduce themselves to the group, e.g. わたし／ぼくは ... です。わたし／ぼくは ... さいです。(To be accurate, でした should be used here. You can teach this structure if you wish.) The teacher then collects the photos then asks the class おなまえは？ and なんさいですか／でしたか。The students have to remember the information given and answer correctly.
- *Role-play:* a casting agency is looking for actors for a TV soap opera. The agency (a group of students) writes down the ages of the characters being sought (without showing the other students). People are then interviewed until the characters with the right ages are found.
- **W 27/T9 8 4A** Students listen to the interviews on tape to find out where the people pictured come from and how old they are. They write their answers in the table.

Audio script

SPEAKERS: Sanae, Harjono, Kate, Ben, Carla

a

S: みなさん、こんにちは、きょうのwelcome interview にようこそ。わたしはDJのかとうさなえです。どうぞよろしく。では、さいしょに、ハジョーノ・スダーガーくんとはなしてみましょう。ハジョーノくん、こんにちは。

H: こんにちは。

S: ハジョーノくんはインドネシアからですね。

H: そうです。
S: なんさいですか。
H: ぼくは１２さいです。
S: １２さいですか。
H: ええ。
S: 日本はどうですか。
H: とてもたのしいです。
S: それはいいですね。

b
S: そして、オーストラリアのケイトさんですね。
K: いいえ、わたしはニュージーランドからきました。
S: あっ、そうですね。ニュージーランドですね。すみません。
K: いいえ。
S: ケイトさんはなんさいですか。
K: わたしは１１さいです。
S: そうですか。じゃ、がんばってくださいね！
K: はい、ありがとう。

c
S: じゃ、ベン・サマーズくん、こんにちは。
B: こんにちは、さなえさん。
S: ベンくんはオーストラリアからですね。
B: はい、そうです。
S: ベンくんはなんさいですか。
B: ぼくは１２さいです。
S: そうですか、わたしも１２さいです。日本はどうですか。
B: とてもたのしいです。
S: いいですね。

d
S: じゃ、さいごにカーラ・トリードさんとはなしましょう。カーラさん、こんにちは。
C: こんにちは。
S: どこからきましたか。
C: アメリカからきました。アメリカ人です。
S: カーラさんはなんさいですか。
C: わたしは１３さいです。
S: なかやまがくえんはどうですか。
C: とてもたのしいです。
S: それはいいですね。
じゃ、みなさん、ハジョーノくん、ケイトさん、ベンくんとカーラさん、きょうはどうもありがとうございました。では、またあいましょう。

Vocabulary notes

日本はどうですか。
How is Japan?
とてもたのしいです。
It's really fun.
それはいいですね。
That's good.
きょうはどうもありがとうございました。
Thank you for today.
じゃ、
Well then.
では
Well then.
またあいましょう。
We'll see you again.

- Ⓦ **28/T12** Students go around the class to find six students who are the same age as they are, and write their names and ages in the chart. Students are to use the question なんさいですか？ When they find them, they say: あっ、わたしも or あっ、ぼくも.
- *Useful abbreviations:* show students how わたしも。and ぼくも。can be used as alternatives to わたしも ... さいです。and ぼくも ... さいです。
- *Pronunciation points!:* you may need to highlight the pronunciation of ages with the double-consonant (or small っ): いっさい (1 year old), はっさい (8 years old), じゅっさい (10 years old), じゅういっさい (11 years old) and じゅうはっさい (18 years old).
- はたち *Coming of age:* せいじんの日 (Coming-of-age Day) is a national holiday held in Japan on 15 January for people who reach 20 years on any date between 2 April of the previous year and 1 April of the current year.
- わたしはくさいです！ (I am smelly!): you could point out to the students that, although く is sometimes used for 9, if you want to say you are nine years old, the correct way is わたし／ぼくはきゅうさいです。not わたし／ぼくはくさいです。

3 Asking someone's telephone number and responding

Warm-up and presentation as for previous units.

Follow-up

- *How well do you know your friends?:* students write their telephone numbers on paper and put them in a box. The teacher (or a student) selects a number and reads it out. The rest of the class see if they can identify whose telephone number it is. Students get points for each person's number they correctly identify.
- じこしょうかい *(personal introduction):* five students are chosen to introduce themselves (or a mystery identity), giving their name, age,

telephone number, country of origin and any other information they have learnt to say. The teacher then asks questions about the people who have spoken.

- *Song:* (sung to the tune of 'London Bridge'):
  もしもし、あのね、あのね、あのね。
  もしもし、あのね、ああ、そうですか。
  さようなら、みなさん、みなさん、みなさん。
  さようなら、みなさん、さようなら。
- しりとり *('Number Tennis'):* the class is divided into two teams and one person 'serves' to the other team by saying his/her telephone number. Anyone from the other team whose telephone number starts with the last digit of the number just called can 'return' by saying his/her telephone number. The two teams try to keep the 'rally' going for as long as possible. Alternatively, they play against each other and win a point every time they 'serve' a number which the other team cannot respond to (or respond quickly to). If the prefix is the same for all students, have students just quote the last four or five digits.
- **W 29/T14 8 4A** Students listen to the messages on Takako's answering machine and match the callers with the correct phone number.

Audio script

SPEAKERS: Carla, Ben, Chieko, Harjono, Yuusuke, Nakamura Sensei

a

Answering machine: もしもし、もりやまです。いま、るすにしています。るすばんでんわにメッセージをのこしてください。あとででんわします。

(This is repeated before each item below)

Carla: もしもし、わたしはカーラです。でんわばんごうは763—2966です。どうぞ、でんわしてください。

b

Ben: もしもし、たかこさん、ベンです。おたんじょうびおめでとう。ねー、なんさいですか。でんわして。でんわばんごうは、864—0492です。じゃーね。

c

Chieko: あ、ちえこですけど、773—0210にでんわしてね。バイバイ。

d

Harjono & Yuusuke: 「おたんじょうびおめでとう。おたんじょうびおめでとう。おめでとう、たかこさん。おたんじょうびおめでとう。」

Harjono: ハジョーノです。

Yuusuke: ゆうすけです。でんわばんごうは、764—8011です。

e

N.Sensei: たかこさん、こんにちは。なかむらです。がっこうまででんわしてください。でんわばんごうは670 — 2244。

Vocabulary notes

もしもし、もりやまです。
Hello, this is the Moriyama residence.
いま、るすにしています。
We are not here right now.
るすばんでんわにメッセージをのこしてください。
Please leave a message.
あとででんわします。
We'll phone you later.
でんわしてください。
Please phone me.
ねー！
Hey!
でんわして！
Phone me!
じゃーね！
See ya!
けど
but
でんわしてね。
Phone me, OK?
バイバイ。
Bye-bye.
がっこうまで
to school

- **W 29/T15 8 4A** Students listen to the directory assistance information and write the correct telephone numbers in numerals.

Audio script

SPEAKERS: Operator, Person 1, Computer, Persons 2, 3 and 4

a

O: もしもし、104のすずきでございます。

P1: すみません、でんわばんごうをしりたいんですが。

O: はい、どうぞ。

P1: なまえはたなかさぶろうです。

O: たなかさぶろうさんですね。

P1: はい、そうです。

O: かしこまりました。たなかさぶろうさんごあんないいたします。ありがとうございました。

C: でんわばんごうは764—3987です。でんわばんごうは764—3987です。

b

O: もしもし、104のすずきでございます。

P2: すみません、でんわばんごうをしりたいんですが。

O: はい、どうぞ。

P2: なまえはかわかみかおるです。

O: かわかみかおるさんですね。

P2: はい、そうです。

O: かしこまりました。かわかみかおるさんごあんないいたします。ありがとうございました。

C: でんわばんごうは487—6363です。でんわばんごうは487—6363です。

c

O: もしもし、104のすずきでございます。おなまえおねがいします。

P3: なまえはやまだひとみです。

O: やまだひとみさんですね。

P3: はい、そうです。

O: かしこまりました。やまだひとみさんごあんないいたします。ありがとうございました。

C: でんわばんごうは194—8220です。でんわばんごうは194—8220です。

d

O: もしもし、104のすずきでございます。

P4: ふじもとよしおおねがいします。

O: ふじもとよしおさんですね。

P4: はい、そうです。

O: かしこまりました。ふじもとよしおさんごあんないいたします。ありがとうございました。

C: でんわばんごうは255—9071です。でんわばんごうは255—9071です。

Vocabulary notes

104のすずきでございます。
This is 104, Suzuki speaking. (*104 is the number for directory assistance.*)
すみません、でんわばんごうをしりたいんですが。
Thank you, I'd like to know a phone number, please.
はい、どうぞ。
Yes, go ahead.
... ですね。
It's ... isn't it?
かしこまりました。
Certainly.
たなかさぶろうさんごあんないいたします。
Finding the number for Mr Saburo Tanaka ...

- **W 30/T16** Students interview five people in the class to find out their names, ages and telephone numbers and record the details, in English, in the table provided. Practise the questions first with students.
  おなまえは？
  なんさいですか。
  でんわばんごうは？
- *Pronunciation point:* you may need to highlight the extended vowel う at the end of ばんごう, which can easily be 'clipped'. You could also point out how the vowel *sounds* like 'o' but is written as う.
- *Telephone numbers:* take particular note of the use of の between the area code and the number. When written in numerals it is represented by a dash or a space, but it is read 07 の 236 の 4125. This 'sound' makes it easier to remember a telephone number, and it's very important in Japan, for it shows the telephone exchange numbers, which are omitted by local callers.

べんきょうのベン — ひらがな

S 36 C 1B

Characters introduced: い、か、は、ほ、わ

Warm-up

Before playing the tape, ask students to look at the page and see what characters they can remember from the previous unit.

Presentation

Play the tape while students look at the Student Book. Pause the tape whenever you hear a 'ding'.

Audio script

SPEAKER: Ben

Hi! Ben here again with the new hiragana you'll need for Unit 3. I'm also going to tell you about some more nigori sound changes and a hiragana character which has a special use. I'll be telling you about kanji numbers too.

The hiragana you learnt in Units 1 and 2 are printed in black in the chart. Point to each one as I say it and repeat after me.

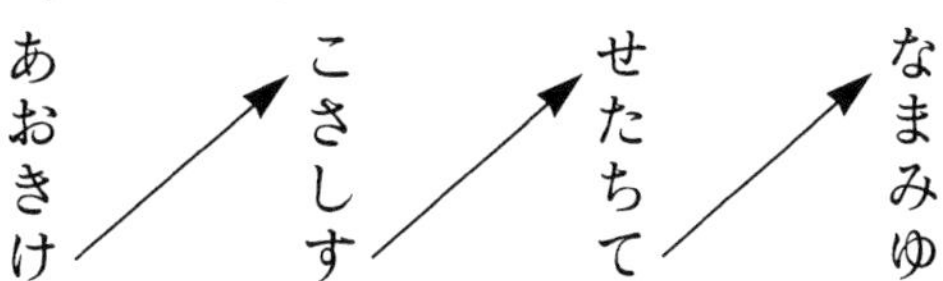

よくできました。

Look at the characters in the yellow boxes in the chart. Use the pattern you learnt in Unit 1 to work out the sound of each one.

...

Now look at the group of five large characters on the page. Point to each one as I say it and repeat after me.

1 い
2 か
3 は
4 ほ
5 わ

よくできました。

Look back to *Itadakimasu* and *Donna aji?* See how many words you can find which contain the new characters. がんばって！

Hiragana sound changes

Remember what you learnt about nigori in Unit 2? Now you will learn about three hiragana characters which can be used with nigori. Can you find which character in the chart is used with nigori to make the sound で?

Right, it's て.

Try another one! Which character in the chart goes with nigori to make ば?

Yes, it's は.

よくできました。Finally, which character goes with nigori to make ぼ?

Right, it's ほ. So remember the rule: each character in the 'H' column は, ひ, ふ, へ and ほ, takes a 'B' sound when used with nigori and becomes ば, び, ぶ, べ or ぼ.

In the 'T' column, the characters most often used with nigori are た, て and と and these become だ, で and ど.

You might have noticed that the hiragana は is sometimes pronounced 'wa'. This happens when it appears at the end of a word. For example, after words like わたし and ぼく to make わたしは and ぼくは.

は as 'wa' can also be used to ask a question like ハジョーノくんは？ (*What about you, Harjono?*) or エマさんは？ (*What about you, Emma?*).

See how many times you can find は used as 'wa' in *Itadakimasu.*

If you're wondering whether は is ever pronounced 'ha' — well it is: when it's used *within* a word or at the beginning of a word, like はい or おはようございます.

またね！

Follow-up

- Use the word flashcards to practise students' recognition of the key words.
- **W 23** かきかた (*How to write*): students practise writing the new hiragana characters in the boxes, using the correct stroke order.
- **S 36** *Find the odd sound:* students select the odd sound in each group of three presented. *Solutions*: 1c, 2a, 3b, 4a, 5b, 6b.
- **S 36** Students look at the photo of the sign on a food stall at a spring festival in Tokyo. For your info: いか焼 (やき) barbequed squid.
- *Hiragana snap:* students sit in a circle and two sets of hiragana cards (using the characters from Units 1 to 3) are shuffled and dealt to all players. Students take turns turning over their cards one at a time onto a pile in the middle, saying the characters as the cards are turned over. If two consecutive cards are the same, players call 'Snap' and put their hands on the pile of cards. The person whose hand is at the bottom keeps the cards and the game continues. The person with the most cards at the end is the winner.
- *Hiragana hopscotch!:* place 8 to 10 large hiragana cards face up on the floor in a line between two teams. On はじめ！, the first person from each team 'hops' over the first card (with legs apart) and says the hiragana on it. When players meet, they play じゃん・けん・ポン (Jan Ken Pon: this game is used to determine turntaking. To begin the game, two or more players wave a closed hand in the air three times, calling out *Jan! Ken! Pon!* as if to beat time, and on the third count they form their hand into *paper* (open hand), *scissors* (closed hand with index and middle fingers extended) or *stone* (fist). Winning is based on the following three rules: paper wins over stone (paper will wrap stone), scissors win over paper (scissors will cut paper) and stone wins over scissors (stone will break scissors). When two people play and both show same forms, or when three people play and they show different forms, the game is undecided and players try again.). The winner continues forward over the remaining cards. The loser goes to the back of his/her team. The winning team is the first to get all players to the opposite side.
- *Combination concentration:* make up two sets of cards: one for each hiragana character and combination, and the other with the equivalent sounds in roomaji. The cards are turned face down and students take turns turning over two cards at a time — one from each set. If they make a matching pair, they keep the cards and have another turn. The winner is the one with the most pairs at the end. You can make the game more challenging by teaching the equivalent katakana for each hiragana introduced, making three matching cards required for a set!
- *Rhyming sounds:* the class is divided into teams of 5–6 which line up in front of the board. The teacher calls one kana and the first person from each team runs to the board and writes another character with the same vowel sound (as the one called by the teacher). The teacher sets a time limit by counting in Japanese up to an agreed number.
- **W 25/T1** Students identify the non-Japanese names by circling them.
- **W 25/T2 and 3** Students write the Japanese names in hiragana.
- **W 25/T3** Students use hiragana and katakana charts to work out the names of the *Obentoo* students and complete the names with the characters they already know.
- *Nigori mnemonics:* see if the students can think of 'silly stories' to remember the *nigori* sound changes, for example that *ha, hi, hu, he,* and *ho* plus *nigori* make *ba, bi, bu, be* and *bo*. Alternatively, present the kana with *nigori* and ask the students to guess the sounds of other kana in the same line. Present a series of words (with *nigori*) and get students to guess the sound(s) using the charts in the Student Book.

> Avoid too much pre-practising! Games are generally more effective when they are used to practise hiragana (and katakana) as soon after the new characters have been introduced as possible. Their value can diminish if there is too much pre-practice.

べんきょうのベン — かんじ

37 IB

Characters introduced: 一、二、三、四、五、六、七、八、九、十

Warm-up

- Recap the numbers. See which ones students can read already.

Presentation

- Play the tape while students look at the Student Book page. Pause the tape whenever you hear a 'ding'.

Audio script

SPEAKER: **Ben**

There are two ways of writing numbers in Japanese. One way is numerals as in English. The other way is kanji. You can use either way.

Kanji numbers are generally used in formal writing, for example in certificates and namecards.

Look at the kanji numbers from 1 to 10 on the page. Point to each one as I say it, and repeat after me.

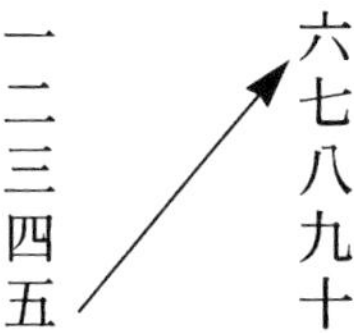

Look at the kanji numbers from 1 to 20 at the top of the page. See if you can work out the pattern for writing 11 to 20.

...

In Japanese, there are two pronunciations for zero; depending on whether it's a numeral or a kanji. Numeral 0 is pronounced ゼロ. Kanji zero is pronounced まる which actually means *circle*.

That's it for me until Unit 4. またね。

Follow-up

- **23–4** かきかた *(How to write)*: students practise writing the kanji numbers in the boxes, using the correct stroke order.
- **37** *Find the odd numbers!*: students have to distinguish between the odd and even numbers. *Solutions*: 1a, 2c, 3b, 4a, 5c, 6a.
- Students look at the photograph on page 37 of the Student Book and answer these questions:.
  1 What kind of sign is this?
  2 What do the kanji represent at the bottom?
  3 What number is 〇?
  4 How many kinds of そば are sold?
  5 How much is やまかけ？
  6 How much is とろろそば？

For your info: the photograph was taken in a noodle restaurant in Tokyo. The prices are written in kanji. Notice the use of the kanji 〇 (まる).

- *Kanji shuffle:* flashcards of kanji number sequences are shuffled and turned upside down in piles. A group of students wait beside each pile. On はじめ！the winning group are the first to turn over their cards and arrange them in the correct order.
- *Human kanji:* students form groups and devise ways of forming the kanji numerals with their hands or bodies. The rest of the class try to identify the numbers formed.
- *Kanji relay:* the class is divided into teams of 5–6 players, who line up in front of the board. The teacher shows or calls a kanji number and each team must write that number on the board one stroke at a time in relay. The first team to write the character correctly (using the correct stroke order) is the winner.
- *Kanji mnemonics:* students make up their own mnemonics to remember either the meaning of the kanji (i.e. the number) or the sound. The best suggestions can be made into cards and put on display.
- *Kanji maths:* students make up maths problems using kanji numerals and write them on cardboard. These can be used as 'fillers' when students finish work early, etc.
- *Beat the clock:* prepare a set of simple maths problems (with 5–7 questions per set) using kanji numbers, or get the students to prepare them. Give each group two or three sets and see which is the first team to finish.
- *Using まる correctly:* remind students that まる should be used for 'zero' when kanji numbers are being used. ゼロ (zero) can be used for Arabic numerals.
- **37** *Vertical writing:* students look at Yukiko's address and telephone number written in kanji. Ask students what they notice about vertical writing. Possible answers: it is written from right to left, furigana is placed on the right of the kanji and zero is written as 〇. Discuss how kanji numbers are always used for vertical writing, for example on name cards or documents. Show students how larger numbers, for example 千九百九十七 (*1997*) and 一 (*no*) are written vertically. You might also like to discuss how punctuation and 一 in katakana words are written vertically.
- **26/T5** Students follow the kanji numbers

from 1 to 10 through the beehive maze, then tally up how many of each kanji are left in the maze and write the totals in kanji.

- Ⓦ **26/T6** Students count the specified items in their classroom and write the correct kanji number next to each item. (This can be a speaking as well as a writing task.)
- Ⓦ **27/T7** Students carry out the additions and write each answer in kanji.
- Ⓦ **27/T8** Students write the next numbers in the sequences given.
- Ⓦ **28/T11** Students match the people to their correct ages.
- Ⓦ **28/T12** Students write the ages that come immediately after the ages given.
- Ⓦ **29/T13** Students give the ages according to the candles on the cake. This can be done as a written task: students just write 六さいです or copy from the example. Alternatively, it can be done as a speaking task.
- Ⓦ **30/T17** Students complete the sentences with the correct kana.
- Ⓦ **30/T18** Students write in their notebooks every possible combination of the numbers 四、五 and 六. How many combinations are there? Then students do the same using the numbers 七、八、九 and 十.
- Ⓢ **44** *Extra reading task:*
  1 でんわばんごうは〇三の九六八五の四一五一です。
  ありがとうございました。
  The number is 03–9685–4151.
  Thank you very much.
  2 おたんじょうびおめでとう！
  Happy Birthday!

Extension Task

- Ⓑ **3.1** レストランでたべましょう*:* students look at the menu on the page and answer questions about the numbers that appear in it.

ごはんとおかず

Ⓢ **38–40**

Presentation and follow-up

- *Find the match!:* enlarge the boxes on the *Gohan to okazu* pages and attach them to the board. Prepare a set of single word cards and put these in a container. Students choose cards from the container and find a pattern which suits the word they have drawn. This can be played as a team game, with two sets of pattern boxes and two sets of word cards. The first team to fill all spaces is the winner. Patterns from previous chapters can also be added.
- *Unjumble the sentences:* cut up the sentence patterns into pieces and see how quickly students can reassemble the correct pieces.
- For further grammar explanation refer students to the せつめい section of the Student Book (page 200).

Understanding before production: be wary of using too many number-production games and activities before students have had sufficient exercises in which they practise recognising (or understanding) the numbers without needing to say them, for example:

- listening to telephone numbers and writing them down
- listening to the teacher saying two ages, with students holding up one hand or two, depending on which one is older
- listening to three or four sentences about people and their ages and writing down the person who is the oldest, youngest and so on.

Extension tasks

- Ⓑ **3.2** てがみをかきましょう *(Let's write a letter)*: students read and respond to notes passed across the classroom seeking information about other students. Then they write one of their own.
- Ⓑ **3.3** すうじ・スープ *(Numbers soup)*: students try to work out the numbers from 20 to 99 and read and write the kanji for some of these numbers.
- Ⓑ **3.4** 九十九さい: students are introduced to ages from 21 to 99, with some reading and writing tasks.
- Ⓑ **3.5** *Draw and guess!*: students try to guess the age of the people drawn by their partners.
- Ⓑ **3.6** *Pairwork*: students practise asking someone's age and telephone number. Each student asks his/her partner for the missing information and writes it down.

テーブルマナー

Ⓢ **41–2**

Presentation

- Students look at the pages in the Student Book (you can do one page at a time if you like) and try to guess the ages of the people. Use the pattern なんさいですか with students answering ... さいです. Discuss in English what kinds of people are shown — their occupation, clothing, lifestyle and what they are doing in each picture. These photographs can be used as a stimulus for further discussion of a range of issues such as traditional Japan versus modern Japan, the changing role of women in Japan, education in Japan, the aged in Japan, geisha, and sport and leisure in Japan. Students can be encouraged to find pictures of Japanese people in different occupations and social situations as a project or to stimulate further discussion. Magazines such as *Pacific Friend* and *Japan Pictorial* are very useful for this.

- **List of photographs (with ages)**
  1 ちゅうがくせい (junior high school students) ages 12, 12, 13. These boys are in

ちゅうがくいちねん (Year 7) at a public high school in a country area of Japan. Notice the summer uniform worn by the boys, much less formal than the black military-style uniform worn in winter.

2 A doctor aged 32 in a large university hospital in Sendai.

3 ゆみちゃん — age 2. Children of this age often have their names shortened and ちゃん added.

4 こうこうせい (senior high school students) — ages 15,16. These girls are in 高二 or 高校二年 (Year 11). The photo was taken in an elective sewing class.

5 These men (aged 65, 63, 62, 70) come to this park every day to play gate-ball (ゲートボール, a type of croquet popular among senior citizens in Japan).

6 A rock'n'roller aged 16 from Harajuku in Tokyo. Many young people come to Harajuku on Sundays dressed in outrageous clothing to sing and dance in the area between the Olympic Stadium and the Meiji Shrine.

7 A dental nurse from Matsuyama — age 22.

8 A family living in Osaka — ages 34, 32, 20.

9 Actors at えいがむら in Kyoto dressed up as samurai — ages 19, 22.

10 えみちゃん (age 3) eating おべんとう.

11 Many housewives in Japan study tea ceremony and attend tea ceremonies organised by the various schools. Ages of ladies in photograph are 44, 73 and 76.

12 The elderly are very well respected in Japan. Traditionally, the eldest son in the family looks after his parents in their old age. Today, in a large number of families, the grandparents live with the family. The lady in the photograph is 81.

13 Children aged 4 and 5 at a ようちえん (kindergarten).

14 A boy and his older sister — ages 11 and 18.

15 Policemen in Hiroshima — ages 36 and 41.

16 Boy aged 4 playing on the steps.

17 Two dentists in their surgery — ages 40 and 38.

18 Sumo wrestler — age 20.

19 A girl who works in a department store in Tokyo — age 19.

20 しょうがくせい (primary school student) aged 10, having lunch at a school picnic.

21 まいこさん (apprentice geisha) aged 28 and 32, entertaining visitors to the Byodoin near Kyoto.

22 わたなべせんせい (PE teacher) aged 52 at a high school.

- Ⓑ **3.7** *Test your memory!*/An information sheet with some interesting facts about Japanese people and their lifestyle. Students read and see how much information they can remember using keyword clues.

おはし

Ⓢ **43**

Presentation

Students answer the 'star quiz'. See Ⓑ **3.8** for answer key.

Follow-up

- *Out and about:* the class prepare a list of places where they can:
  - buy Japanese food
  - eat Japanese food
  - see Japanese movies
  - buy Japanese magazines and/or books
  - buy Japanese gifts
  - buy (or rent) Japanese CDs
  - hear Japanese spoken
  - see or learn Japanese martial arts or traditional arts, e.g. the tea ceremony, ikebana
  - get posters and information about Japan.
- *More lists!:* make a list of the names of Japanese people the students have met.
- *Links with other schools:* students may be able to exchange their names and addresses with students from other (nearby) schools who are learning Japanese.

おしょうゆ

Ⓢ **44** Ⓣ **1B**

Presentation

- Students listen to the tape and repeat the new expressions.

> Note the use of the various words for 'thank you': ありがとう、どうも、どうもありがとう、ありがとうございます、ありがとうございました、どうもありがとうございます(ました)

Follow-up

- フルーツ・バスケット *(Fruit Basket):* choose three of the expressions on the *Oshooyu* page. Students sit on chairs in a circle. Each student is allocated one of the expressions. A student stands in the middle (without a chair) and calls out one of the expressions. All the students who were given that expression must quickly find another chair (which cannot be the one next to them). The last person misses out on a chair and stands in the middle. If the person in the middle calls おしょうゆ, then all students must stand and find another chair. If anyone is caught in the middle more than three times, s/he has to sing the *Obentoo* song!

おかし

Ⓢ **45**

Song

にほんご *Rap:* students perform the song as a rap, for example at the beginning and end of class.

Students could make up their own raps using the key patterns in *Donna aji?*

Craft activity

わしにんぎょう *birthday card*: students make a Japanese birthday card.

Putting it all together

- Have students produce a directory of the students in their class, with their names, ages and telephone numbers written in Japanese, so that it can be given to Japanese exchange students who visit your school.
- Make some kanji number charts to decorate the classroom.
- Play a game of ばんざい:
  1. Each student draws a grid of 3 squares by 3 squares.
  2. Students choose nine numbers between 1 and 20 and write one kanji number in each square.
  3. Teacher reads out numbers at random.
  4. Students cross out numbers as they are called.
  5. When all numbers in a line or diagonal have been crossed out, the student calls out やたー！ ('I've made it'). The first person to cross out all of his/her numbers calls out ばんざい！ The person who calls out ばんざい should then call the numbers back to check. To make the game longer, use a 4 by 4 grid.
- *Mystery Babies:*
  1. Students bring their favourite (or least embarrassing) baby photo to class.
  2. On the back of the photo, students write their name, their age, when the photo was taken, and where they come from.
  3. Without letting anyone else see it, they put it in a box.
  4. Someone takes one photo out of the box and shows it to the class. Students take turns asking questions which can only be answered with はい、or いいえ until someone guesses the information and the identity of the baby. Age and nationality must be guessed before the name. *Suggested questions:*
     五さいですか。
     オーストラリアからきましたか。
     なまえは ... ですか。
- おたんじょうびおめでとう: list everyone's birthdays on a calendar and display it on your classroom wall. When it's someone's birthday, students say おたんじょうびおめでとう！ The birthday person answers ありがとう。
- *Role-play (three students, school principal, school office assistant)*: you are a new student who is just beginning school in Japan. Two other students are asked to take you to meet the principal. They introduce themselves to you and you to them. They then take you to meet the principal, who asks you your name, where you are from, and your age. You are then taken to the school office where you are asked again your name, where you are from, your age and your telephone number.

ごちそうさま

Ⓢ 45

- Ⓦ 31 *Obentoo quiz.*
- *Individual program cards:* write the items listed in *Gochisoosama* onto the photocopiable student progress card on page 138 of the *Moshi Moshi Teachers' Handbook.* You may wish to add other items, for example other language points, other script introduced, cultural understandings, completion of homework or assignment tasks.

Reference to *Yoroshiku National Curriculum Guidelines for Japanese (Moshi Moshi)*

The following is a list of the suggested language exponents presented in *Moshi Moshi* Module 1 よろしく (*How do you do?*) which have been introduced in Unit 3 of *Obentoo*. In some cases the example has been changed to correspond to the form introduced in *Obentoo*.

Language exponents

- Asking for and giving information about age
  なんさいですか。
  (...)さいです。
- Asking for and giving information about telephone numbers
  でんわばんごうは？
  でんわばんごうはなんですか。
  (400-2143)です。
- Asking for repetition
  もういちど。
- Expressing gratitude
  ありがとう。
  どうもありがとう。
  ありがとうございました。
- Suggested kanji for recognition:
  一　二　三　四　五
  六　七　八　九　十

Overview

Unit objectives

Students will be able to:

- say their nationality
- ask where someone's home is and respond when someone asks them
- ask someone's year at school and respond when someone asks them
- read and write twelve more hiragana
- make three more hiragana sound changes
- read and write the kanji 人
- understand the Japanese education system
- talk about what a Japanese high school looks like and what activities students do there
- recognise patterns in the structure of Japanese and other languages

Functions and language exponents

1 Saying your nationality
Asking and saying where someone's home is
(わたし)は(オーストラリア)人です。
うちはどこですか。
(シドニー)です。

2 Asking someone's year at school and responding
(カーラさん)はなん ねんせいですか。
(ちゅうがく)(二)ねんせいです。

Key vocabulary and expressions

シドニー
パース
こうべ
ジャカルタ
マディソン
オークランド
ヴァンクーバー
...人
オーストラリア
日本
インドネシア
アメリカ
ニュージーランド
カナダ
...ねんせい
しょうがく
ちゅうがく
こうこう

Script

Students are expected to be able to read and write the key characters and recognise the associated words.

Key characters	*Associated words*
う	うち
え	おなまえは
く	くん、しょうがく、ちゅうがく
と、ど	どこ
に	こんにちは
ね	ねんせい
ひ、び	おたんじょうびおめでとう
む	なかむら
め	おめでとう
よ、ら	さようなら
ん、じ	じん
人	日本人

Script understandings

- Introducing nigori sound changes (hiragana): じ (じん)、ど (どこ)、び(おたんじょうび)
- The use of kanji (人) as a 'shortcut'
- Noticing the difference between similar kanji, for example, 人 (じん: *person*) and 入口 (いりぐち: *entrance*)

Learning how to learn

The skill of noticing patterns in sentences is developed through an imaginary language, Farnii-go (on Mars). Students have to then look for patterns in familiar Japanese sentences.

Cultural elements

Looking around a school in Japan: facilities, customs and etiquette, school activities, club activities

Other incidental language introduced

わたしのともだちです。
かわいい！
きれい！
そうですか。
いいえ、...
そして、...
またね。

Extension material

- Additional nationalities
  イギリス人
  フランス人
  ドイツ人
  イタリア人
  スペイン人
  ギリシャ人
  サウジアラビア人
  インド人
  ベトナム人
  ちゅうごく人
  かんこく人
- Speaking specifically about where you come from
  (オーストラリアのシドニーからきました。)
- Capital cities in Australia and New Zealand
  メルボルン
  ホバート
  アデレード
  パース
  ダーウイン
  ブリスベン
  オークランド
  ウエリントン
- Asking where someone lives and responding
  どこにすんでいますか。
  ...にすんでいます。

Need some extra words or expressions? Ask your teacher!

マレーシア	Malaysia
パプアニューギニア	Papua New Guinea
フィジー	Fiji
アフリカ	Africa
南アフリカ	South Africa
南アメリカ	South America
ロシヤ	Russia

Teaching suggestions

The following suggestions are provided as a guide to lesson planning and should be adapted to suit your teaching style and the learning styles of your students. These tasks are specific to this unit. For more information on general strategies for each section, refer to *Using Obentoo* on pages 3–8.

いただきます

46–8 1B

Warm-up

Revision of numbers (あかパジャマ: *'Red pyjamas' game*): students form groups of 10 and sit in a circle. Students go around the circle counting from 1. If a student's number includes a 3 or is a multiple of 3, s/he must say あかパジャマ. If someone makes a mistake (by saying an incorrect number or not saying あかパジャマ, s/he is 'out'. The winner is the last student left 'in'. Some students may mispronounce these words by lengthening the ジャ or clipping the パ (as they might do in English). All the sounds in these words should have equal stress: あ-か-パ-ジャ-マ.

Listen and discuss

- *Listen and guess* and *Find the frame:* as in Units 1 and 2.
- Students answer the questions on page 48 in the Student Book.

Follow-up

- *'Who Am I?' game*: using a set of 'famous people' cards, students choose a person and the rest of the class must guess who it is by asking *yes/no* questions related to age, nationality, and (finally) name. You can search for data on famous people on the Internet by entering the person's name and conducting a search.
- *How well do you know your schoolmates?*: the class is divided into two teams who line up facing each other and linking arms. The teacher makes a list of students in each year who study Japanese and asks students to guess which year a particular student is in. Students in a team then decide on the answer and say ...ねんせいです。(all together). If they are incorrect, they lose a student to the other team. If they are correct, they take a student from the other team. The winning team is the one that has more players at the end of the game. The game could be made more interesting by copying pictures of students in other years from old school annuals and using these as reference material.
- *Obentoo students flashcard review*: the teacher shows a picture of one of the *Obentoo* students and asks ...さん／くんはなんねんせいですか。The students answer ...さん／くんは ...ねんせいです。You may need to decide on a standard system for giving information about year levels at school. Your students may become confused between using the Japanese school system and the system in your area. It may be easier to talk about all students as if they were at school in Japan or as if they all attended school in your area.
- *Obentoo students* まる／ばつ: the teacher holds up flashcards of the *Obentoo* students and gives a true or false piece of information about each one, for example なまえは ...さん／くんです。...さいです。...人です。うちは ...です。...ねんせいです。Students then indicate if the sentence is true or false by making a large circle (まる) with their hands or crossed-arms (ばつ). The teacher can make all or part of the information true or false. However, if any piece of information is false, the response is 'false'. So that students decide independently, they can close their eyes (after looking at the flashcard), then listen to the teacher's sentence(s) and make their response. This game provides a good opportunity to use slightly more demanding sentences (for listening/understanding only), for example この人のなまえは ...さんです。日本人で、...さいです。うちはとうきょうです。
- *Unjumble the cartoon*: make a copy of the cartoon OHTs, cut up the frames and arrange them in the wrong order. Students then listen to the story and try to put the frames in the correct order.

どんなあじ？

49–50 1B

1 Saying your nationality/Asking where someone's home is and responding

Warm-up

- Replay *Itadakimasu* and explore the page as in Unit 1 and 2.
- うちはどこ？(*oral interaction game*): the teacher begins by saying わたし／ぼくは ...じんです。Students take it in turns to reply うちは ...です。For example:
  Teacher: わたしはアメリカじんです。
  Student 1: うちはニューヨークです。
  The teacher continues around the class and students are not allowed to give an answer used by someone else. (To practise geography skills, place a large map of the world on the board.) This can be played as a team game. To help students pronounce place names correctly, it might be useful to practise this task as vocabulary 'pairs' first, for example イギリス／ロンドン、イタリア、ローマ、オーストラリア／アデレード.
  Alternatively, you could play the game first (knowing that students are likely to mispronounce the place names) and then use the place names which the students mention for practising/correcting afterwards.

Presentation

- Students look at the pictures, listen to the tape and

repeat. After listening and repeating, discuss what was said. Next see if the students can repeat the dialogues by themselves.

- Students then look at the sentences below the pictures, listen to the tape and repeat, as in Units 1 and 2.

Follow-up

- **W 34/T2 8 4B** Students listen to the *Obentoo* students and write down the nationality of each one next to his/her name.

Audio script

SPEAKERS: Sanae, Tony, Emma, Harjono, Kate, Carla

a S: かとうさなえです。にほん人です。
b T: トニー・クルーズです。
カナダじんです。
c E: エマ・ジェニングズです。
オーストラリア人です。
d H: ハジョーノ・スダーガーです。
インドネシア人です。
e K: ケイト・ヘンダソンです。
ニュージーランド人です。
f C: カーラ・トリードです。
アメリカ人です。

- **W 34/T3 8 4B** *Who's talking?*: students find out the identity of each speaker by listening to the clues (age and home town).

Audio script

SPEAKERS: Harjono, Tony, Kate, Sanae, Emma, Carla

a H: こんにちは。ぼくは十二さいです。
うちはジャカルタです。
b T: こんにちは。ぼくはなかやまがくえんのいちねんせいです。うちはバンクーバーです。
c K: わたしは十一さいです。うちはオークランドです。
d S: みなさん、こんにちは。わたしは十二さいです。うちはこうべです。
e E: こんにちは。わたしは十一さいです。
うちはシドニーです。
f C: こんにちは、みなさん。わたしは十三さいです。うちはマディソンです。

- **W 38/T10** Students take turns introducing themselves in Japanese using the information on the student ID cards.
- **W 35/T4** Students match each country's name to its flag and then add the character 人 to change it to the nationality.
- **W 35/T5 8 4B** *Famous ghosts*: students listen to the tape and write where each of the ghosts comes from.

Audio script

SPEAKERS: Madame X and Famous Persons 1, 2, 3, and 4

a
MX: こんにちは。
FP1: こんにちは。
MX: なんさいですか。
FP1: ７６さいです。
MX: ああ、そうですか。うちはどこですか。
FP1: アメリカです。
MX: おなまえは？
FP1: Albert Einstein です。
MX: どうもありがとうございます。

b
MX: こんばんは。
FP2: こんばんは。
MX: どこからきましたか。
FP2: アメリカからきました。
MX: うちはどこですか。
FP2: Gracelands です。
MX: おなまえは？
FP2: わたしは Elvis Presley です。
MX: どうもありがとう。さようなら。

c
MX: こんにちは。
FP3: こんにちは。
MX: なんさいですか。
FP3: 二十五さいです。
MX: うちはどこですか。
FP3: オーストラリアです。
MX: おなまえは？
FP3: Ned Kelly です。
MX: どうもありがとうございます。

d
MX: こんにちは。
FP4: こんにちは。
MX: どこからきましたか。
FP4: アメリカからきました。
MX: うちはどこですか。
FP4: ハリウッドです。
MX: おなまえは？
FP4: わたしは Marilyn Monroe です。
MX: どうもありがとう。

- **W 37/T8 8 4B** Students listen to the speakers introduce themselves. They match each speaker to the city where s/he lives, and then match the English signposts with the Japanese ones on the map.

Audio script

Interviewer: うちはどこですか。
1 Hanako: こんにちは。はなこです。

うちはきょうとです。

2 Daisy: モー。うちは、さっぽろです。なまえは、デージーです。

3 Kitanoumi: おっす。きたのうみです。うちはとうきょうです。

4 Shikako: うーん。ムシャムシャ。わたしはしかこです。うちはならです。

5 Hiroshi: こんにちは。ぼくはひろしです。うちはまつやまです。まつやまはいいですよ。

6 Tanaka: いらっしゃい、いらっしゃい。たなかです。うちはくまもとです。

7 Wakako: はー。わかこです。うちはひろしまです。

8 Yuki: さむい。さむい。わたしはゆきです。うちはあおもりです。またね。

Vocabulary notes

モー。	Moo.
きたのうみ	Kitanoumi (name of sumo wrestler)
いらっしゃい。	Welcome.
さむい。	It's cold.

As a follow-up to this task you may like to look again at the map of Japan and discuss Japanese people whom your students may know, and where in Japan they come from. You could put up a map of Japan in the classroom and label it with the names of the people you know.

An alternative task is to have students mark on a map of Australia places where they have friends or relatives and give an oral presentation to the class using the map and photos, for example ともだちです。なまえはフィリップです。フィリップさんはオーストラリア人です。うちはメルボルンです。Of course, they could give additional information about age or year at school if they like.

- **W 36/T6** Students match each *Obentoo* student with the appropriate speech bubble.
- **W 36/T7** *Nationality quiz*: Student A reads out the first nationality in Japanese. Student B responds, in Japanese, with what country these people come from. For example:
  Student A: 日本人
  Student B: 日本人は日本からきました。
  Students swap roles after each one.
- *Japan all over*: students make small pictures (or stick figures) of various people and place them on a large map of Japan. Each person is also given a name. Students then choose an identity (either all choose their own or all choose someone else's) and introduce themselves to the class, for example わたし／ぼくは ...です。日本じんです。うちは ...です。This task could also be used to introduce the pattern ...さんは(日本)じんです。To make students aware of place-name words which have long sounds and/or short *tsu*, they could use gestures to show when words contain these 'sounds', for example an outstretched arm to signify a long sound, and a clenched fist to signify a short *tsu*.
- *Australia all over*: as for *Japan all over*, above, except that students refer to a large map of Australia. This task would be good for practising the pronunciation of Australian place names.

2 Asking someone's year at school and responding

Warm-up

- *Rap*: students join in the following 'rap' (with underlined characters indicating the beat): なんねんせいですか、ですか。なんねんせいですか、いちねんせいです、です。いちねんせいです。The rap could be performed in groups, with one group asking the question and other group(s) answering. Students can take turns in providing the numbers for the answers; alternatively, they can be cued by a conductor, who stands at the front holding number cards, or uses some other means of signifying which number is to be used in the answer. You may need to remind students that the second character せい is pronounced as え even though it is written as い. You could also mention that in a number of areas of Japan, for example, around Kyoto, it is common to pronounce です as で・す rather than 'des' where the 'u' is almost silent.

Presentation

As in earlier units.

Follow-up

- *Magazine talent search*: students cut out pictures of children from magazines and paste them on cardboard. The class has to decide what year they are in and their age. Expressions which might be useful in this task include:

ちがいますよ。	*You're incorrect!*
そうですね。	*That's right, isn't it?*
そうですか。	*Is that right?*

  This task could be extended by using newspaper cutouts of older people. Japanese newspapers and airline magazines would provide plenty of suitable material.
- **W 39/T11** **4B** Students listen to the tape and complete the table in the Workbook with the names of the *Obentoo* students' friends and their years at school.

Audio script

a **Chieko:** ともこさんです。ともだちです。
Emma: ともこさんはなんさいですか。
Chieko: 十一さいです。
Emma: なんねんせいですか。
Chieko: わたしたちとおなじちゅうがくい

ちねんせいです。

b Ben: このひとはピーターさんです。
Shingo: ピーターさんはなんさいですか。
Ben: 十三さいです。
Shingo: なんねんせいですか。
Ben: 九ねんせいです。

c Carla: ソフィーさんです。ペンフレンドです。オーストラリア人です。うちはアデレードです。
Sanae: なんさいですか。
Carla: 十五さいです。
Sanae: なんねんせいですか。
Carla: 十一ねんせいです。

d Tony: このひとはデービッドです。ともだちです。
Yuusuke: うちはどこですか。
Tony: ヴァンクーバです。
Yuusuke: なんねんせいですか。
Tony: 八ねんせいです。

e Emma: トレーシーさんです。ともだちです。
Takako: オーストラリア人ですか。
Emma: いいえ、フランス人です。
Takako: なんねんせいですか。
Emma: 八ねんせいです。

Vocabulary note

わたしたちとおなじ	the same as us

- **39/T12** Students read the captions underneath the pictures and write what they say in English.
- **40/T14** Students write two sentences in Japanese about each of the students, according to the information given.

べんきょうのベン — ひらがな

51 1B

Characters introduced: う、え、く、と、に、ね、ひ、む、め、よ、ら、ん

Warm-up

Before playing the tape, ask students to look at the page and see what characters they can remember from the previous unit.

Presentation

- Play the tape while students look at the Student Book. Pause the tape whenever you hear a 'ding'.

Audio script

SPEAKER: Ben

Hi! Ben here again to bring you up to date with the hiragana you need to know for Unit 4. There are no new katakana this time, but there is a new kanji.

The hiragana you learnt in Unit 3 are among the ones printed in black in the chart. Point to each one as I say it and repeat after me.

い
か
は
ほ
わ

よくできました。

Look at the characters in the yellow boxes in the chart. Use the pattern you have learnt to work out the sound of each one.

...

Now look at the group of 12 large characters. Point to each new character as I say it, and repeat after me.

1	う	**5**	に	**9**	め
2	え	**6**	ね	**10**	よ
3	く	**7**	ひ	**11**	ら
4	と	**8**	む	**12**	ん

よくできました。

See how many words you can find in *Itadakimasu* and *Donna aji?* which contain the new characters. がんばって！

...

Hiragana sound changes

There are three more hiragana sound changes in Unit 4. Which characters in the chart are used with nigori to make the sounds じ, ど and び?

...

よくできました。They're , し, と and ひ. Point to each one and repeat after me.

し、じ
と、ど
ひ、び

Making sounds longer

You may have noticed that the words ばんごう, おはようございます and さようなら contain a long 'o' sound. However, the hiragana used to lengthen the sound is not お, it's う.

Katakana words, on the other hand, like to be individual and have their own system for lengthening sounds. They use a dash, which we call ぼう. See how many katakana words you can find with ぼう in *Itadakimasu*. がんばって！

Katakana ぼう is also used when writing furigana!

That's it from me for now. Be sure to have a look at the kanji shortcut on page 52. またね！

- Notice the sound changes listed on page 51. You may like to talk about the sound changes for the whole of the S, T and H lines.

Follow-up

- Use the word flashcards to practise students' recognition of the key words.
- **32–3** かきかた (*How to write*): students

practise writing the new characters in the boxes, using the correct stroke order.

- **S 51** *Find the odd sound*: students select the odd sound in each group of three presented. *Solutions*: 1a, 2a, 3b, 4c, 5b, 6c.
- Students look at the photos of signs on page 51. Discuss with students what they say and where they might be found. *For your info*: 味一番(あじいちばん)おべんとういま売れています *The best tasting lunch boxes, on sale now!* そば・うどん町田(まちだ) The sign on a noodle stand on a railway station at Machida (Tokyo)
- **W 34/T1** Students find the characters hidden on the island, colour them in different colours and then write them in the spaces provided.
- **W 44/T18** Students colour in all the squares containing katakana, then look for the hidden words and phrases in the puzzle and fill in the missing hiragana in the spaces provided.
- *Hiragana captain ball*: see Unit 1, page 17.
- *Hiragana bingo*: this could be played using all the hiragana covered so far.
- *Hiragana word write*: the teacher calls out words containing the hiragana learnt so far and students write down as many characters (contained in the word) as they can, in the quickest possible time. This task does not need to be restricted to familiar words. If students require additional dictation practice, you could write out several sentences with which the students are familiar and leave a number of spaces (or lines) where the students have to write in the missing characters after listening to the sentence being read out. This task serves as a gradual introduction to 'free' dictation.
- *Consonant call*: the teacher calls out a consonant from one of the hiragana/katakana lines, e.g. S, and students write down as many of the characters from that line as they have learnt, e.g. さ, し, す, せ, as quickly as possible. The first student to write the characters correctly (and the most neatly) is the winner. The task can be varied by playing it as a board game, with students standing in two, three or four lines in front of the board and writing the characters on the board. This enables stroke order to be closely monitored.
- *What's missing?*: the teacher calls out a 'line' of hiragana characters in sequence, with one character missing from the sequence, for example, あ、い、う、え、_?_ or い、き、_?_、ち、に. The students have to correctly identify the missing character and write it down. Once students are familiar with the hiragana alphabet, they could be asked to make up and call out the sequences. At first, it might be helpful to have the hiragana chart on display.
- にごり watch: make flashcards of words which contain にごり or combination sounds. Students have to identify the 'special' features in each word. This task provides a good opportunity to include a range of script variations. Students do not need to be able to understand every feature contained in the words chosen, so you might like to emphasise particular features, for example, words containing the small っ. Katakana word features could also be introduced, even though the students may not be able to read the words completely.

べんきょうのベン — かんじ

S 52

Character introduced: 人（じん）

Warm-up

Recap the characters the students have covered so far. You could also talk about the origin of the kanji 日本 (origin of the sun; the land of the rising sun). Whether students can read the kanji or not, you could look at other examples and discuss their (possible) origin, for example 日 = sun, 月 = moon; 明るい = sun+moon = bright.

> At this stage, it is important to focus students' attention on the shape and meaning of kanji, and how they are different from hiragana and katakana, rather than giving too much emphasis to the various pronunciations of a particular kanji.

Presentation

Students read the page.

Follow-up

- **W 33** かきかた (*How to write*): students practise writing the new kanji character in the boxes, using the correct stroke order.
- **W 45/T19** Students complete the sentences with the correct kanji and kana.

ごはんとおかず

S 53–4

Presentation and follow-up

- Students look at the boxes on pages 53–4 and explain to a partner the meanings and usage of the language presented there. Students explain to their partner about the Japanese education system. They then ask their partner a few questions to see if s/he has really understood!
- *For your info*: the photographs on page 54 of the Student Book show (above) three junior high school boys (Notice the black military-style uniforms, which are the winter uniforms of a junior high school in Tokyo. The boys are studying hard to enter a good senior high school.) and (below) a group of ようちえん (kindergarten) students going on an excursion.
- **W 40/T13** Complete the conversion chart showing ages and school years.
- **W 41/T15** Students identify the mixed-up parts of each of these sentences by colouring the components of each a different colour. They then

put the components of each sentence in the correct order by numbering them in the empty squares.

- Ⓦ **43/T17** Students fill in the blanks in each of the letters and write a letter of their own, using the examples as a guide.
- *Cloze test*: using the passage below as a guide, leave out words which contain key details such as countries, cities, and names. Students complete the blanks and see how many alternative versions they can make. For example, こんにちは。... は ... です。... さいです。... ねんせいです。... は ... 人です。うちは ... です。どうぞよろしく。When completed, the passages could be read out to the class.

> If students have not worked with cloze tests before, you might like to start by using short passages with only a few details left blank. As students' confidence and vocabulary grow, longer and more complex sentences could be used. It may also be helpful to remind students how particles refer to the words which precede them (and are therefore also known as post positions).

- *Picture this sentence (sentence pattern building)*: in small groups, students draw pictures or symbols to represent the words in a sentence. On completion, the cards are held up in front of the class, who 'read' the group's sentence. Words like です、は、の can be written in hiragana, or left as blanks or 'wild cards' which the class have to figure out. To make the task more challenging, after the students have gone through the task as suggested, pictures in each sentence could progressively be replaced with blank cards, forcing students to guess/remember the correct words. Sentences could be joined to give the students more to recite.
- *Beat the buzzer*: students have to convert school years in the Japanese system to school years in the Australian (or other) system, in the shortest possible time. For extra challenge, make up a set of students in each year of school in Japan and allocate each a name, age and other details. Give each student an international pen pal in the equivalent school year (and give them other details as well). Once students have studied the information about the students for three minutes, it is covered up. The teacher then calls out a student's name and the class compete to see how much information about that person's pen pal they can remember and give in Japanese. Points are deducted from a student's score for errors made.
- For further grammar explanation refer students to the せつめい section of the Student Book (page 201).

Extension tasks

- Ⓑ **4.1** Use this BLM to introduce extra countries.
- Ⓑ **4.2** Use this BLM to introduce the structure どこにすんでいますか。... にすんでいます。
- Ⓑ **4.3** *Pairwork*: students practise asking what year at school someone is in and where s/he comes from. Each student asks his/her partner for the missing information and writes it down.

テーブルマナー

Ⓢ **55–6**

Presentation

- Have students look at the map and brainstorm any information (types of classrooms, activities, etc.) they can find on the page.
- Have the names of the places on cards on a feltboard or on an overhead, and see if students can recognise any of the characters. You could then read them out and have students try to explain them in English, referring to the map (page 55) and photographs (page 56).
- Use the map and photos as stimulus for discussion of issues relating to school, such as:
  - classrooms and school subjects
  - sports
  - uniform
  - school routine (changing shoes, home room, 50-minute classes with 10-minute break in between, cafeteria lunch, きゅうしょく (provided lunch), おべんとう, club activities)
  - うんどうかい
  - ぶんかさい
  - すいえいたいかい
- For extra writing practice, students could use the list on page 56 to make labels for all the rooms around the school, especially if you are expecting Japanese visitors. (This can also help to promote Japanese within the school.)
- *For your info*:
  1. こうもん School gate/entrance
  2. いりぐち Entrance
  3. ロッカー Students' lockers. Students leave their bags and books in the lockers in the morning and go back to the lockers during the 10-minute break between each class.
  4. じむしつ School office
  5. ほけんしつ Clinic
  6. しょくいんしつ Staffroom. In Japan all teachers of a particular year share the same staffroom. There may be up to 50 teachers in the staffroom.
  7. としょかん Library
  8. じてんしゃおきば Bike racks
  9. しえぶつのきょうしつ Biology room
  10. ちゃしつ Tea ceremony room (used for tea ceremony club)
  11. きょうしつ Classrooms
  12. くつばこ Shoe lockers. Students change from their school shoes into soft runners or

slipper-type shoes to be worn within the school buildings and grounds. Students usually change their shoes again on entering the gym.

13 こうてい School grounds. There are often covered walkways which enable students to go from building to building.
14 ちゅうしゃじょう Carpark
15 たいいく PE area
16 うんどうじょう Sports ground
17 かがくじっけんしつ Science laboratory
18 ぎじゅつきょうしつ Technology room
19 ちりのきょうしつ Geography room
20 おんがくきょうしつ Music room
21 ちょうりしつ Cooking room
22 かていかのきょうしつ Home science room
23 びじゅつしつ Art room
24 バスケットボールコート Basketball court
25 テニスコート Tennis court
26 バレーボールコート Volleyball court
27 たいいくかん Gymnasium
28 けんどうじょう Kendo hall
29 じゅうどうじょう Judo hall
30 シャワー Showers
31 プール Pool
32 じどうはんばいき Vending machines
33 しょくどう Cafeteria
34 ちょうりば Kitchen

> This list can also be used for hiragana reading practice and vocabulary extension later in the course.

- Using the information provided, students interview a Japanese student about his/her school life in Japan and then write a report based on the interview.

Follow-up

- *Survey*: students make up a survey to ask Japanese people to whom they might have access about their daily life in Japan. This data could form the basis of an ongoing ひゃく人にききました, which in turn could be used to form quiz questions for students in other years. If you do not have access to Japanese people to interview, your students could post questions on the Internet for Japanese students to answer.
- *Similarities and differences*: using the information presented in the *Teeburu manaa* section, students make a list of similarities and differences between their own school life and that of a Japanese student.
- **Ⓑ 4.4** *Fact or fiction?*: students read the information bubbles and colour them green for fact and red for fiction.

おはし

Ⓢ 57

Presentation

Students work through the pattern-identification exercises on Student Book page 57.

Follow-up

- *Your own language*: students form small groups and make up their own written language, using 10 items of vocabulary. Each group then makes rules for creating questions, making statements (in answer to the questions) and making negative statements. The group then presents (in writing) a sentence to the class to illustrate each rule and the other members of the class try to 'crack the code' and 'translate' the sentence.
- *Your own language (follow-up)*: if there are speakers of other languages in the class, they could then give the equivalent sentences to the ones made up by the students. Students should then try to distinguish the words in the sentences and see if they can identify the patterns. The task could be concluded with a brief discussion of the similarities between languages.

> When students are *speaking* languages which the other students have not heard before, they will need to be reminded to speak extremely slowly so that the other students can distinguish the sentence patterns used. For extra challenge, each group could make up further pairs of sentences and the other students have to try to guess the pattern they used. This might lead into a discussion about features such as sentence order, the use of tense, and subject and object markers. The discussion might also address how intonation can aid comprehension during oral interaction.

おしょうゆ

Ⓢ 58 Ⓑ 1B

Presentation

Students listen to the tape and repeat the new expressions.

Follow-up

- **Ⓦ 45/T20** Students circle the correct answer.
- *Theatre sports*: the teacher calls out an expression from the *Oshooyu* section in Units 1–4. A small group of students is then given two minutes to make up a situation in which that expression might be used and act it out (or mime it, saying only the particular expression) in front of the class. The other students then have to guess the situation being mimed or acted out. This game can be used to introduce expressions which the students have not heard or used before. The performing group is the only one to be given an English equivalent of the new expression; the rest of the class have to work it out for themselves.

おかし

58

Song

- Sing the song to the tune of *Ten little Indians.*
- *Variety rap*: students select sentences from *Donna aji?* or *Gohan to okazu* and make up their own rap. The students could experiment by introducing 'creative' features such as words which are spoken correctly and then backwards.

Craft activity

Calligraphy: you may be able to show students how kanji are written with a brush and ink on special paper. To do calligraphy with students you will need:
- calligraphy brushes (brushes with pointed bristles, both large and small sizes)
- black ink called ぼくじゅう (liquid ink) or すみ (solid ink sticks, which need to be rubbed in water to make the ink — a very time-consuming process)
- white calligraphy paper called はんし. An alternative to はんし, at least for students to practise on, is old phone books. The paper is about the same thickness and absorbency.

These materials are all available from Japanese or Chinese supermarkets at reasonable prices.

Refer to the cultural notes on Student Book pages 120–1 for more information about calligraphy (しょどう). You could also show students how the art of *sumi-e* developed from しょどう.

While it may be stating the obvious, it is very easy for calligraphy 'first-timers' to accidentally spill or splash black ink on their school clothes or on school property, and the ink can be difficult (and expensive) to remove. We suggest that, before any calligraphy activity:
- Desks are covered with newspaper, several layers thick.
- Desks are put together and ink placed in the middle to minimise the risk of accidental spills on the floor.
- The number of students having access to each すずり (ink well) is controlled/monitored.

Afterwards, we suggest that:
- Aprons are used by students who are washing down ink wells and brushes.
- Students are shown how to hold the ink well away from them as it is washed, to minimise splashing, and taps are turned on to a 'gentle' flow.
- The hair on the brushes is drawn together while still slightly wet, so that the hairs do not curl.

Putting it all together

- **42/T16** Students make up a new identity and fill in their personal ID card. Then they survey five people in the class and record their imaginary details in the chart. For this task you can direct students to use any questions they have dealt with up to now or use the suggestions given.
- **38/T9** Have students make up introductory speeches for these two students and record them on tape. Then have students make up their own self-introduction. This can be used when Japanese exchange students come to visit or can be recorded on tape and sent to a school in Japan, together with a class photo.
- **46** *Obentoo quiz.*
- *Penfriend pic*: have students bring in a photo of their penfriend (or a friend or relative from overseas). Students show the photo to the class and give some information about that person. *Suggestions*:
ペンフレンド／ともだちです。
なまえは ... です。
... さいです。
... 人です。
うちは ... です。
... ねんせいです。
でんわばんごうは ... です。
Teachers may like to make up a listening comprehension sheet for students to fill in as they listen to their classmates, or follow up with a game of おぼえていますか to see if students can remember information later. (For the latter, you may need to allow students to take notes while they are listening.)
- *Celebrity heads*: have students bring a picture of their favourite celebrity with information about him/her and put the pictures on the board.
  - As a class, practise asking and saying each celebrity's nationality, age and home.
  - Then write each celebrity's name on a headband and put the headbands in a box.
  - Each student takes a headband from the box and puts it on his/her partner's head. You must not see the name of the celebrity you are wearing.
  - Students then asks their partner a question about the celebrity on their head, such as
オーストラリア人ですか。
うちはニューヨークですか。
十九さいですか。
to which their partner must truthfully answer はい or いいえ。
  - The first three students to guess their celebrity win.
- *Finger puppets*:
  - With a partner (or group of three people), draw the backdrop for a finger puppet play, for example, the city or place where the play will be set.
  - Draw a face on your hand above your middle and index fingers. (Don't forget to hold your fingers downwards as you draw.)
  - The setting is ten years from now; you are travelling somewhere in the world, when you run into one or two old school friends.
  - Ask them: 'Are you...?' (because they look quite

different now), where their home is, their age, their telephone number (for this activity you may like to teach ひさしぶりですね).

- なんですか *game*:
  - Choose a question you have learnt, for example, うちはどこですか. One student then thinks of an answer, for example, シドニーです。
  - The other students try to guess the first student's answer by asking questions, for example, ニューヨークですか。The first student must answer truthfully はい or いいえ.
  - When someone guesses the correct answer, that person can choose another question which s/he must say aloud, then think of an answer, and so on.
- *On the buses*:
  - Students are divided into teams which sit in lines behind the first person in the team.
  - Someone in the class or the teacher asks questions in Japanese.
  - The first student in the front row of seats who thinks s/he knows the answer stands up.
  - If that student answers the question correctly, his/her team wins a point. If the answer is wrong, the team loses a point.
  - Everyone then moves one seat forward, with the students at the front going to the back, and the game continues.
  - The team with the most points at the end of the game are the winners.
- *Role-play*: have a series of different role-play situations written on cards, requiring students to give the same information. For example: *You are representing your scout group at an international scout jamboree in Japan. Prepare your introductory speech, giving the following information: your name, your age, your year at school, where you come from and where you live. Say you are pleased to meet everyone.* Students choose a card on their way into the room, have 5 minutes to prepare, and then have to perform the role-play in front of the class.

ごちそうさま

S 58

- *Self-assessment form and discussion*: after students have completed the unit they could assess their own general achievements using the form on page 137 of the *Moshi Moshi Teachers' Handbook*. The form provides space for the students to list what they have achieved, the difficulties they have encountered and strategies they could use for improvement. After students have completed the form, they could discuss the three headings and make suggestions about ways to improve their Japanese.
- Have pairs of students make up little quizzes for each other.

Reference to *Yoroshiku National Curriculum Guidelines for Japanese (Moshi Moshi)*

The following is a list of the suggested language exponents presented in *Moshi Moshi* Module 1 よろしく *(How do you do?)* which have been introduced in Unit 4 of *Obentoo*. In some cases the example has been changed to correspond to the form introduced in *Obentoo*.

Language exponents

- Asking for and giving information about year of schooling
  なんねんせいですか。
  ...ねんせいです。
- Asking for and giving information about place of residence
  うちはどこですか。
  うちはシドニーです。
  どこにすんでいますか。
  (アリス・スプリングス) にすんでいます。
- Asking for and giving information about nationality
  どこからきましたか。
  ニュージーランドのオークランドからきました。
- Suggested kanji for recognition:
  人

Suggested activities from *Moshi Moshi*

はなこさん、こんにちは
Teacher Resources pages 2 and 5
はじめました！
Teacher Resources page 3,
Student Book page 6
じこしょうかい
Teacher Resources pages 3 and 7
Hiragana World Letters
Teacher Resources pages 4 and 7
どこからきましたか
Teacher Resources pages 4 and 9–10

Overview

Unit objectives

Students will be able to:

- ask someone how many people there are in their family and respond when someone asks them
- count up to 10 people
- say the people in their family and find out about someone else's family
- ask someone what pets they have and respond when someone asks them
- recognise and write twelve more hiragana characters
- recognise and write one more katakana and one more sound change
- recognise and write the kanji for one person up to 10 people
- talk about family life in Japan

Functions and language exponents

1 Asking how many people in someone's family and responding
(エマさんは)なん人かぞくですか。
(六)人です。

2 Saying who is in the family
(おとうさん)と(... さん)とわたし/ぼくです。

3 Asking and saying what family and pets you have
(ハジョーノくん)、ペットがいますか。
はい、(いぬ)がいます。
はい、(いぬ)と(ねこ)がいます。
いいえ、いません。
カーラさん、おとうとがいますか。
はい、おとうとがいます。

Key vocabulary and expressions

なん人かぞくですか。
一人、二人、三人、四人、五人、六人、七人、八人、九人、十人

おじいさん/おばあさん、おとうさん/おかあさん、おにいさん/おねえさん、おとうと/いもうと、わたし/ぼく

... がいますか。
... がいます。
... と ... がいます。
... いません。

いぬ、ねこ、うま、とり、うさぎ、きんぎょ、おとうと、いもうと

Script

Students are expected to be able to read and write the key characters and recognise the associated words.

Key characters	*Associated words*
そ	かぞく
つ	つづけましょう
ぬ	いぬ
の	わたしの、ぼくの
ふ	ふたり
へ	
も	いもうと
や	はやく
り	とり
る	うるさい
れ	きれい
ろ	ろくねんせい
ツ	ペット
人	一人、二人、...、十人

Script understandings

- Introducing *nigori* sound changes (katakana): ペ (ペット)
- Further use of the kanji 人 (pronounced にん)

Note: all characters other than を will have now been presented.

Learning how to learn

A magazine format where students learning Japanese write in and ask questions about topics such as ways to remember にごり words, using/not using *roomaji*, the introduction of writing skills, and 'good habits' when learning to write

Cultural elements

Emma writes to her friend in Australia about life in Japan. Topics covered include the Japanese sport of kendo, family life with Emma's host family, the kimono, the bath, eating rice and sumo wrestling.

Other incidental language introduced

がんばります。
ざんねんです。
おめでとうございます。
はじめましょう。
じゃあ、...
つづけましょう。
はい、そうです。
いいえ、ちがいます。
ぜんぶで...
おねがいします。

Extension material

- Giving information about more than one brother or sister
いもうとが二人います。
- Expressing the *elder* and *younger* of two brothers
うえのおにいさん
したのおにいさん
- Saying you are a twin
わたしはふたごです。
- Saying you are an only child
わたしはひとりっこです。
- Giving information about more than one pet: counting animals

いっぴき	ろっぴき	ねこがさんびきいます。
にひき	しちひき	いぬがにひきいます。
さんびき	はっぴき	
よんひき	きゅうひき	
ごひき	じゅっぴき	

Need some extra words or expressions? Ask your teacher!

おばさん	aunt	モルモト	guineapig
おじさん	uncle	さかな	fish
いとこ	cousin	うし	cow
めい	niece	ひつじ	sheep
おい	nephew	カンガルー	kangaroo
こども	child	コアラ	koala
むすこ	son	やぎ	goat
むすめ	daughter	かえる	frog
おかあさん*		ウォンバット	wombat
おとうさん*		むし	insect
		くも	spider
		ねずみ	mouse
		さる	monkey

(*These words are also used for stepmother and stepfather. In Japan it is still uncommon for people to talk of divorced parents. To clarify the situation, students may refer to their あたらしいおかあさん or あたらしいおとうさん.)

Teaching suggestions

The following suggestions are provided as a guide to lesson planning and should be adapted to suit your teaching style and the learning styles of your students. These tasks are specific to this unit. For more information on general strategies for each section, refer to *Using Obentoo* on pages 3–8.

いただきます

59–62 2A

Warm-up

まるばつ *Make-a-line game* (noughts and crosses make a line): have 25 vocabulary items or questions in Japanese written on the back of kanji numbered cards. Attach them to a feltboard with Velcro or to a whiteboard with Blu-Tack with the number side visible in a 5 × 5 grid. Divide the class into two teams, ○ and ×. The teacher is the game compere. Teams take turns in choosing a number and trying to answer the question or translate the word on the other side of the card. If the answer is correct, the team gets a ○ or × in that position on the grid. The first team to get a row of three across, down or diagonally are the winners. Introduce the language which will appear in *Itadakimasu* and encourage students to play the game using it:

...さん、なんばんですか。
...ばんおねがいします。
がんばって！
がんばります！
はい、そうです。
いいえ、ちがいます。
ざんねんです。
おめでとうございます。

Further gameshow games can be played with students as comperes when they are familiar with the expressions.

Listen and discuss

- *Listen and guess* and *Find the frame:* as in Units 1 and 2.
- Students answer the questions on page 62 of the Student Book.

Follow-up

- *'Know your friends' gameshow*: students write a sentence saying how many people are in their family on a piece of paper and give it to the teacher. Three 'contestants' are chosen to play. The teacher asks the question ...さんはなん人かぞくですか。The contestants press a buzzer, ring a bell or raise their hand to answer. If the contestant answers correctly, s/he gets one point. Contestants lose a point for an incorrect answer. For this game, you could also introduce the question ...さんのかぞくはなん人ですか。
- *Family member charades*: the names of family members are written on a piece of paper and put into a hat or bucket. The class is divided into groups of 6–8 students who take turns miming an action to indicate a family member, according to the person on the piece of paper they draw from the hat. Each group then get one point for each family member they correctly identify from the action mimed. The winning group is the one which makes the greatest number of correct guesses. Other pieces of paper could be added giving other details, such as what pets the person might have, where s/he lives, or his/her year at school. When using other categories, place the items for each additional category in a separate hat or bucket.
- *Famous families*: make flashcards of well-known families from TV shows, cartoons, comics, movies, etc., and ask students questions about each family, for example:
  なんにんかぞくですか。
  おねえさんがいますか。
  ペットがいますか。
  ...人ですか。
  うちはどこですか。
  An alternative way to use the flashcards: give information about each family and the students have to guess which family you are talking about.
- *Itadakimasu revisited*: students take the parts of the people in the cartoon on pages 59–62 of the Student Book and act out the story, changing the details as they see fit.
- *Unjumble the cartoon*: students sort out the jumbled frames of the Student Book cartoon as they listen to the recording.

どんなあじ？

63–5 2A

1 Asking how many people in someone's family and responding

Warm-up

- Replay *Itadakimasu* and explore the page as in Units 1 and 2.
- *Song (sung to the tune of 'Ten Little Indians')*: 一人、二人、三人きました。四人、五人、六人きました。七人、八人、九人きました。十人きましたよ。

Presentation

- *Listen and repeat*
- *Listen, look at sentences and repeat* as in earlier units.

Follow-up

- なん人グループですか。The teacher (or group leader) calls out a number, for example 三人, and students form groups of that number. Any students who do not make the correct-sized group are 'out'.
- *Sign sheet*: students write sets of six numbers below 10, for example 4, 5, 6, 2, 7, 3. They then ask other students なん人かぞくですか, ticking off the numbers as they find a student with that number

of people in his/her family. The winner is the first student who has ticked all his/her numbers.

- **W 50/T3** Students look at the picture and answer the questions in Japanese, for example 三人です。

2 Saying who is in your family

Warm-up

- *Family tree*: the teacher draws a family tree on the board and asks the students questions about its members, for example:
  だれですか。
  ...さんですか。
  ...さんがいますか。
  ...人かぞくですか。
  Once students have completed this task, you may decide to introduce the system for identifying members of one's own family, beginning with ちち／はは、あに／あね. You might also like to point out that おとうとさん／いもうとさん can also be used to talk about someone else's younger brothers and sisters.

Presentation

As in earlier units.

Follow-up

- *Listen and draw*: students form pairs. S1 asks S2 questions about his/her family and then draws a picture of the information given.
- *Ask your partner*: students form pairs and find out about their partners by asking questions, such as:
  なん人かぞくですか。
  ...さんがいますか。
  ...さんのなまえはなんですか。
  ...さんはなんさいですか。
  Each person then draws a picture of his/her partner's family tree.
- *Sign Sheet II*: each student makes up family they would like to have (of up to six people) and writes their identity on a sheet. They then make up a list of five family members and go around the class asking ...さんがいますか。 until they find someone whose family has the next person on their list. After ticking that person off their list they can ask the same person about the next family member. Once the person they ask does not have the next family member on their list, that student must ask someone else.
- **W 51/T4 8 4B** Students listen to the conversations on tape and match up each dialogue with the correct family picture.

Audio script

1 **A:** なんにんかぞくですか。
B: 五人です。おとうさんとおかあさんとおとうとといもうととわたしです。

2 **A:** なんにんかぞくですか。
B: 六人です。おじいさんとおかあさんとおとうさんとおねえさんとわたしです。
A: えっ、一人、二人、三人、四人、五人です。五人かぞくですか。
B: ああ、それから、おとうとです。六人かぞくです。

3 **A:** かぞくのしゃしんですか。
B: はい、そうです。
A: 五人ですね。
B: はい、おかあさんとおねえさん二人とおとうととぼくです。

4 **A:** かぞくは？
B: 三人です。おかあさんとおとうさんとわたしです。
A: あっ、ひとりっこですか。
B: はい、そうです。

Vocabulary notes

かぞくのしゃしん	family photo
かぞくは？	How about your family?
ひとりっこ	an only child

- **W 51/T5 8 4B** Students listen to the tape and write down the members of Kyoko's family and any other information she gives.

Audio script

Speakers: Kyoko, Kyoko's mum and brother

K: 私はたなかきょうこです。十三さいです。
私のかぞくをしょうかいします。
あっ、おとうさんです。おとうさん、おとうさん。
あっ、ごめんなさい。
おとうさんのなまえはおさむです。42さいです。

M: きょうこ、すすむ、ごはんよ！

K: あっ。おかあさんです。おかあさん、おなまえは。

M: <お母さん>よ。

K: お母さん、もういちど。おなまえは。

M: 私はけいこです。

K: なんさいですか、お母さん。

M: 四十一さいです。

K: ありがとうございました。

M: どういたしまして。

...

B: やったー。

K: あっ、おとうとです。すみません、おなまえは？

B: えっ、なあに？

K: おなまえは？

B: しってるだろう。

K: いいの！　お．な．ま．え．は？

B: たなかすすむです。
K: なんさいですか。
B: 十さいです。
K: なんねんせいですか。
B: しょうがく五ねんせいです。
やったー。
K: ありがとうございました。

Vocabulary notes

私のかぞくをしょうかいします。	I'd like to introduce my family.
ごめんなさい。	Sorry!
ごはんよ！	Dinner's ready!
どういたしまして。	You're welcome.
なんだよ？	What do *you* want?
しってるだろう。	You know what it is!
いいの！	All right!
もういちど。	Once again.

- **W 51/T6** Students identify the family members by drawing a line from each word to the correct picture.
- **W 52/T7** Complete the puzzle to reveal the members of the family and then write the full words in the boxes provided.
- **W 53/T8** Students complete the words by filling in the missing kana to reveal the members of Sanae's, Tony's and Takako's families, then they write down who is in their own family. Students could also take on the role of one of the *Obentoo* students and talk about 'his/her family', or talk about their own family.

3 Asking and saying what family and pets you have

Warm-up

- *'Stand up/sit down' — pets*: refer to instructions in previous units, for example Student Book page 25.

Follow-up

- *Pet ESP*: the names of pets are written on cards and put into a box. The class is divided into two teams. A player from one team draws out a card and thinks about the pet written on the card for 5 seconds. The other students try to guess the pet on the card within a 10-second time limit by asking ...がいますか。 This task would be useful for introducing the names of other animals not covered in *Donna aji?*
- **W 56/T16** Students answer the questions in Japanese according to the picture clues. This can be done as an oral or written task.
- *Class survey*: students conduct a survey to find out which students in their class have pets and what they are. Results are then collated on a graph with the names of pets and other details written in Japanese. Questions to be asked in the survey could include:
おなまえは？
うちはどこですか。
ペットがいますか。
...ですか。(type of pet)
ペットのなまえは？
ペットはなんさいですか。
After students have done this task with truthful answers, each person could choose any two pets s/he would like to have and the questions could be repeated. To make the 'pretend' survey more interesting, all students could be asked to choose the two most popular and the two least popular pets, and write their answers on a piece of paper. Once the survey is completed, the results could be compared with students' prior predictions to find the winner.
- **W 53/T9** Using the questions as a guide, students find out as much as they can about their partner's family. Then they could draw a picture of their partner's family.
- **W 54/T10** Students fill in the chart with ticks according to the information on the tape about who has what pet.

Audio script

SPEAKERS: Interviewer, Nakamura Sensei, Sanae, Yuki, Yuusuke and Tony

I: すみません、なかむらせんせい。
N: なんですか。
I: ペットのアンケートですが。
N: はい。
I: ペットがいますか。
N: はい、とりとうさぎがいます。
I: はい、そうです。
N: はい、どうもありがとうございました。

I: あっ、さなえさん、まって。
S: えっ、なーに？
I: ペットのアンケートですよ。ペットがいますか。
S: はい、うさぎがいます。
I: うさぎですか、ありがとう。

I: ゆきさん、ゆきさん。
Y: えっ？
I: ペットがいますか。
Y: ペット？
I: ペットのアンケートですよ。
Y: ああ、えーと、きんぎょがいます。
I: きんぎょですね、はい、ありがとう、またね。
Y: ああ、あのう、それから、ねこがいます。
I: きんぎょとねこですか。
Y: はい、そうです。

I: ゆうすけくん！
Y: あっ、ペットのアンケートですね。
I: そうです。ねこがいますか。
Y: いいえ、いません、いぬととりがいます。

I: いぬととりですね。へえー、じゃ、ありがとう。
T: あっ、ぼくもいぬがいます。
I: あれ、トニーくんもペットがいますか。
T: はい、いぬとねこがいます。
I: あっ、トニーくんのペットはいぬとねこですね。じゃ、ありがとう、さようなら。

Vocabulary notes

ペットのアンケートです。	This is a pet survey.
なーに？	Whaat!
まって。	Wait!
えーと	um ...
それから	and also

- **55/T13** Students have three minutes to ask, in Japanese, as many students in their class as they can about their pets. They record their findings in the chart. If someone doesn't have any pets, they record his/her name and an X. For example:
  ペットがいますか。
  はい、います。いぬがいます。 or
  いいえ、いません。

べんきょうのベン ― ひらがなとかたかな

66–7 2A

Characters introduced: そ、つ、ぬ、の、ふ、へ、も、や、り、る、れ、ろ (page 66), ツ (page 67)

Warm-up

Before playing the tape, ask students to look at the page and see what characters they can remember from the previous unit.

Presentation

- Play the tape while students look at the Student Book. Stop the tape whenever you hear a 'ding'.

Audio script

Speaker: Ben

Hi! Ben here again. You'll be pleased to hear that you have now learnt most of the hiragana. In fact, after this unit, there is only one more.

The hiragana you have already learnt are printed in black in the chart. Say each one aloud as you point to it.

...

The new characters are in the yellow boxes in the chart. Use the pattern you have learnt to work out the sound of each one.

...

Now look at the group of 12 large characters. Point to each one as I say it, and repeat after me.

1	そ	5	ふ	9	り
2	つ	6	へ	10	る
3	ぬ	7	も	11	れ
4	の	8	や	12	ろ

Look back to *Itadakimasu* and *Donna aji?* See if you can find words containing these characters.

Katakana

Remember the katakana you learnt in Units 1 and 2? They are printed in black in the chart. Point to each one as I say it, and repeat after me.

ア イ エ オ
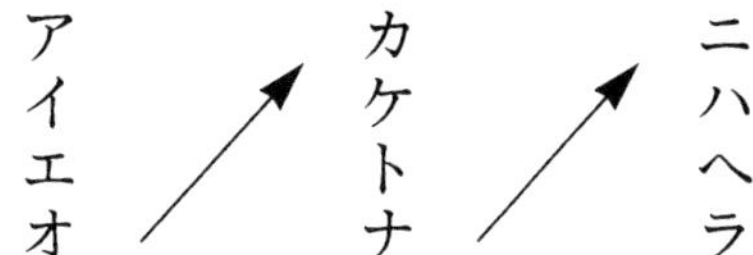
カ ケ ト ナ
ニ ハ ヘ ラ

Now look at the character in the yellow box in the chart. Can you work out how it is pronounced?

It's pronounced ツ. Say it again after me. ツ. Sometimes you will see katakana ツ written slightly smaller than normal, for example in the word ペット, pet. The small ッ is obviously not pronounced, so why is it there?

Words borrowed from English often end in a consonant, like pe<u>t</u> for example, but there is no katakana for the sound <u>t</u>. Look at the 'T' column in the katakana chart: タ, チ, ツ, テ, ト, but no <u>t</u>. So Japanese people use ト and *pet* becomes ペット.

Japanese people find it easier to say ペット with a short pause between the two sounds ペ and ト. Try saying it yourself. ペット..., ペット...

When writing ペット, this short pause is shown by a small ッ. It is not pronounced, it just means 'short pause here'.

Similarly, small hiragana っ is used in some hiragana words for the same reason, to indicate a short pause.

Katakana sound changes

More about the word ペット. You have seen it lots of times in this unit, and probably have noticed that the first character ペ has a small circle next to へ. This small circle is called まる.

Like にごり, まる is a type of shorthand which changes the sound of the character. にごり changes the sound of へ to べ. まる changes the sound of へ to ペ.

Look at the chart inside the back cover. See how まる changes the sound of the other characters in the 'H' column?

...

まる can change the sound of hiragana characters too. Look at the chart inside the front cover to see how まる changes the sounds of the characters in the 'H' column.

- Students read the new characters on page 66 as they point to them. Then they read the whole hiragana chart.
- Discuss the information on page 67 about kanji and focus on kanji compounds being based on a unit of meaning. You may like to present some other examples of compounds containing the

kanji 人. Tell students the meanings of the individual characters and have them guess the meaning of the compounds. Don't worry about the readings at this stage. Some examples:

大人 adult (*big person*)
人生 human life (*person-life*)
人形 doll (*person-shape*)
人魚 mermaid (*person-fish*)

- Have students look at the photos on pages 66 and 67. They should try to recognise as many characters as they can. For your info:
  のりば *Sign indicating where you can get on the train*
  千代田の さくらまつり *The Chiyoda Cherry Blossom Festival (Chiyoda is an area in Tokyo.)*
  ショッピング バッグ 1枚 100円
  Shopping bags 100 yen each

Follow-up

- Use the word flashcards to practise students' recognition of the key words.
- **W 47–8** かきかた *(How to write)*: students practise writing the new characters in the boxes, using correct stroke order.
- **S 66–7** *Find the odd sound*: students select the odd sound in each group of three presented. *Solutions*: (p. 67) 1b, 2a, 3c, 4a, 5b, 6c; (p. 67) 1b, 2c, 3b, 4c, 5a, 6a.
- ひらがな *practice*: by the end of this unit, students will have been introduced to all the hiragana characters except を. General hiragana practice could include:
  – writing each other's names in hiragana
  – writing other Japanese names in hiragana (have another look at the class board on page 24 of the Student Book; students should now be able to read the name of all of the students in Class 3-3).
  – making up and writing pet names in hiragana.
  You could also give the students practice at reading Japanese place names on a map, where the places are written in hiragana and/or kanji with furigana. Have another look at the map of Japan on pages 26–7 of the Student Book.
- *Calligraphy*: students could practise writing hiragana using the ふで (brush), すずり (traditional ink well), and すみ (brush).
- *Hiragana (and katakana) bingo*: refer to suggestions on page 44.
- ごきぶり: refer to suggestions on page 27. In brief, this game involves the teacher (or a student) calling out hiragana characters corresponding to coordinates on a grid. If the ごきぶり drawn on the student's grid crosses the coordinate called out, the student can register the coordinate as a 'hit'. The first student whose ごきぶり are all 'hit' is the winner.
- *Focus on small つ and ッ*: make flashcards of words containing small つ which the students may not have seen before. These could then be used for reading practice, for example: がっこう、ざっし、けっこう、けっこん、やっきゅう、いっしょ、ペット、ベスト・ヒット、ベット、カセット、ショッピングバッグ。
- **W 49/T1** Students colour the kanji balloons the same colour as the corresponding hiragana balloons.
- **W 49/T2** Tony has made a hiragana chart to help him remember the new kana but unfortunately his いぬ has walked all over it with his muddy paws. Students help Tony repair the chart by completing the missing kana.
- **W 55/T14** Students circle the odd one out.
- **W 54/T11** Jacquie's pets are lost in the jungle. Students look for the missing pets and colour them in. They also tick them off the list as they find them.
- **W 54/T12** Students fill in the missing kana to find out what the animals are.
- **W 58/T19** Students look for the hidden words and phrases in the chart. They colour them in when they find them and then write the words in the boxes.
- **B 5.1** Hiragana crossword.

ごはんとおかず

S 68–9

Presentation and follow–up

- *Jumbled sentence game*: the class is divided into two teams. The teacher writes a jumbled sentence on the board and one player from each team must identify the sentence and write it correctly on the board. The first team to correctly write the sentence receives one point.
- *Answer the question — quickly!*: students are asked the questions in the charts on Student Book pages 68 and 69. Each student must give an answer which no other student has used. *Variation*: ask students the questions given on the page and hold up a related flashcard. The students have to answer using any word *other than* the word represented by the flashcard.
- **W 57/T17** Students go around the class to find other students who match the information on the lotto grid. They fill in their names underneath the appropriate statements.
- **W 56/T15** Pairs of students ask and answer the questions for each of the families in the pictures.
- For further grammar explanation refer students to the せつめい section of the Student Book (pages 201–2).

Extension tasks

- **B 5.2** *More about brothers and sisters and pets*: use this BLM to introduce the concepts of more than one brother/sister or pet, twins and only children.
- **B 5.3** *How would you say …?*: gives extra practice of this extension material.
- **B 5.4** *Missing person!*: students work in groups of three to ask each other for missing information about the families of five Nakayama Gakuen students.
- **B 5.5** むしめがね *(Magnifying glass)*: students

read Jun's letter and answer the questions. Then they reply, telling Jun about their own family.

テーブルマナー

Ⓢ 70–1

Presentation

Students read Emma's letter and look at the photos. Use the letter as stimulus for discussion of these topics: host families, kendo, what to call family members, extended families in Japan, kimono/obi, gateball, Japanese bath, father working late, sumo.

Follow-up

- ようこそ、エマさん *(Welcome, Emma)*: as a variation on the theme of the letter from Emma, the students could take the part of one of the people in Takako's family and write to Emma, welcoming her to her new Japanese host family. In the letter, the person would introduce himself/herself and talk about his/her interests and lifestyle. Students may need to conduct some research in the library first or use information from Japanese people in their community.
- エマさんからのてがみ — *alternative*: in the sentences at the beginning of each paragraph, 'blank out' the places where key details are given. Students then write in their own information (based on their own research). Alternatively, the last half of each paragraph could be left blank, with students completing it in their own words.
- Ⓑ **5.6** *Japanese daily life quiz*: a quick quiz for students.

おはし

Ⓢ 72–3

Presentation

Students read the letters and responses.

Follow-up

- *How many questions?*: students write out all the questions they know how to ask in Japanese.
- *FAQ (Frequently Asked Questions) board*: each student writes a question s/he would like answered about ways to go about learning Japanese. The questions are 'posted' in a hat and each student writes an answer to the question s/he takes out. If the same question is asked more than once, it could be posted on the FAQ board (along with appropriate answers). FAQs and answers could be collected and made available to students in other classes (and in later years).
- *The easy way ...*: students make up mnemonics and/or actions for remembering the names of family members and pets, and people counters.
- Students may wish to write their own replies to the letters given on pages 72–3 of the Student Book and this may lead to a class discussion of the issues raised.
- Students may wish to write their 'letters' to the school newsletter (complete with answers from other students).

おしょうゆ

Ⓢ 73 Ⓖ 2A

Presentation

- Students listen to the tape and repeat the new expressions.
- *Theatre sports*: the teacher calls out an expression from the *Oshooyu* section in Units 1–5. A small group of students is then given two minutes to make up a situation in which that expression might be used and act it out (or mime it, saying only the particular expression) in front of the class. The other students then have to guess the situation being mimed or acted out. This game can be used to introduce expressions which the students have not heard or used before. The performing group is the only one to be given an English equivalent of the new expression; the rest of the class have to work it out for themselves.

おかし

Ⓢ 74

Song

- Sing the song to the tune of *Ten little Indians.*
- *Variety rap*: students select sentences from *Donna aji?* or *Gohan to okazu* and make up their own rap. The students could experiment by introducing 'creative' features such as words which are spoken correctly and then backwards.

Craft activity

Mothers' and Fathers' Day cards: make cards for 母の日 and 父の日 using coloured cardboard folded into a card, with an origami crane attached.

Putting it all together

- On a sheet of paper, students draw or attach a picture of themselves and their family. They then provide some information about themselves in Japanese, mentioning name, age, year at school, where they come from, telephone number, how many members in the family, who they are, pets. These can be displayed on the classroom wall.
- Conduct a gameshow quiz in your classroom similar to the one presented in *Itadakimasu*. Have students write their name and information about their family in Japanese on a card. Create a board on which you attach the cards. Number the cards and attach them to the board number side up. These are the quiz questions. Students can be timed to guess information about other class members, as in the *Itadakimasu* manga.
- *Family photos*: students bring a photo of their family and pet(s) to school. They should try to bring a photo which no one else in the class has seen, or a photo in which they look much younger so they won't be easily recognised. Put all

of the photos on a pin-up board and make sure there is a number below each photo. Each person tells the class about his/her photo, in Japanese, and the rest of the class have to write down the number of the photo being talked about.

- たのしいかぞく (*Happy Families*): Each person cuts up eight pieces of cardboard approximately 5 × 7cm. On six of the pieces, draw a different person from the family. Draw pets on the other two pieces. Write the name of the family below each picture. To play the game, form groups of four or five players. The families are put together and shuffled, and equal numbers of cards are dealt to each person in the group. One at a time, each person asks someone else おばあさんがいますか or いぬがいますか, for example. If that person has the card s/he *must* say はい、います。 and hand over the card. The first person to collect a whole family is the winner.
- **Ⓑ 5.7** *Population survey*: students find out the numbers of people in their family, the family of one of their parents, and the family of one of their grandparents. They bring the results back to school and conduct a survey of the results in Japanese in class.

ごちそうさま

Ⓢ 74

- Before you present students with the *Gochisoosama* section, see if *they* can tell *you* what they have learnt in this unit.
- **Ⓦ 59** *Obentoo quiz*.
- *Individual progress cards*: write the items listed in *Gochisoosama* onto the photocopiable student progress card on page 138 of the *Moshi Moshi Teacher's Handbook*. You may wish to add other items, for example other language points, other script introduced, cultural understandings, completion of homework or assignment tasks.

Reference to *Yoroshiku National Curriculum Guidelines for Japanese (Moshi Moshi)*

The following is a list of the suggested language exponents presented in *Moshi Moshi* Module 1 よろしく *(How do you do?)* which have been introduced in Unit 5 of *Obentoo*. In some cases the example has been changed to correspond to the form introduced in *Obentoo*. Appropriate activities from *Moshi Moshi* are suggested below.

Language exponents

- Family
  ... さんはなん人かぞくですか。
  かぞくはなん人ですか。
  (四)人かぞくです。
  (四)人です。
  おとうさんと...とわたしです。
- Pets
  ペットがいますか。
  はい、いぬがいます。
  いいえ、いません。

Suggested activities from *Moshi Moshi*

Who would I like to be?	Teacher Resources page 12, Student Book page 10
かぞくのはなし	Teacher Resources pages 12 and 16–17

Unit 6

Overview

Unit objectives

Students will be able to:

- ask what someone's pet is and respond when asked
- say what a pet's name is
- talk about at least eight animals
- describe a pet
- ask whose pet it is and respond when asked
- ask what a particular pet eats and respond when asked
- read and write all of the hiragana characters
- read and write all of the combination sounds using small や、ゆ and よ
- read and write words containing long vowel sounds
- read and write words containing small つ
- use Japanese punctuation
- talk about what sounds animals make in Japanese
- talk about the inside of a Japanese house

Functions and language exponents

1 Asking what someone's pet is and saying its name
(けんいちくん)のペットはなんですか。
(あひる)です。なまえは「(ガーコ)」です。

2 Describing a pet/Asking whose pet it is and responding
(うるさい)です。だれのペットですか。
(けんいちくん)のペットです。

3 Asking and saying what pets eat
(きんぎょ)はなにをたべますか。
(えさ)をたべます。

Key vocabulary and expressions

あひる
きんぎょ
へび
うま
いぬ
うさぎ
とり
ねこ
「ガーコ」
「ガーコちゃん」
「すし」と「てんぷら」
「サム」
「せいこう」
「ポチ」
「ミミ」
「ピーちゃん」
「タマ」

うるさい
かわいい
ちいさい
こわい
おおきい

パン
やさい
えさ
おべんとう
くさ
さかな
にく

Script

Students are expected to be able to read and write the key characters.

Key characters
を

きゃ、きゅ、きょ
ぎゃ、ぎゅ、ぎょ
しゃ、しゅ、しょ
じゃ、じゅ、じょ
ちゃ、ちゅ、ちょ
にゃ、にゅ、にょ
ひゃ、ひゅ、ひょ
びゃ、びゅ、びょ
ぴゃ、ぴゅ、ぴょ
みゃ、みゅ、みょ
りゃ、りゅ、りょ

Script understandings

- Using particle を, for example おべんとうをたべます。
- Introducing small や、ゆ and よ sound changes (hiragana):
  きゃ、しゃ、ちゃ、しょ、じょ、ちょ、しゅ、ちゅ、ぎゃ、etc.
- Writing long vowel sounds
- Introducing small つ
- Common forms of pronunciation

Learning how to learn

A '*Did you know...?*' feature including:

- An introduction to the sound of 'borrowed' words
- The use of ちゃん as an alternative to さん
- The correct pronunciation of です
- The use of う to lengthen hiragana sounds
- The use of あ、い、え and お to lengthen sounds
- The use of ー (ぼう) to lengthen katakana sounds
- The use of onomatopoeia for animal sounds
- Ending words with a small つ
- Common forms of punctuation

Cultural elements

さなえさんのうち — Introduction to the Japanese house. A floor plan and photos of the inside of a Japanese house are labelled with the names of the rooms and some household items. Discussion topics include rooms in the house, げんかん、スリッパ、こたつ、おふろ、トイレ、とこのま、おしいれ、ふとん, and the customs which surround these items.

Other incidental language introduced

わあ！
うそー！
ひどーい！
こどもがいます。
きょうはペットのはなしをしましょう。
おもしろいです。
じゃ、...
そして、...
どうぞ。

Extension material

- Extending the use of だれの to other contexts
  だれのうちですか。
  だれのせんせいですか。
  だれのノートですか。
  だれのうさぎですか。
  だれのかぞくですか。
  だれのおかあさんですか。
- Indicating possession in a shorter form
  わたしのです。
  ぼくのです。
  ピーターさんのです。
- Extending the use of ... のなまえ to other contexts
  ともだちのなまえは ... です。
  おとうさんのなまえは ... です。
  わたしのともだちのドナ(は十四さいです。)

Need some extra words or expressions? Ask your teacher!

See Unit 5 for extra pets.

おとなしい	gentle, tame
あぶない	dangerous
ふとっています	fat
やせています	thin

Teaching suggestions

The following suggestions are provided as a guide to lesson planning and should be adapted to suit your teaching style and the learning styles of your students. These tasks are specific to this unit. For more information on general strategies for each section, refer to *Using Obentoo* on pages 3–8.

いただきます

75–8 2A

Warm-up

Role-play: revise classroom instructions with a role-play task. One student takes the part of Nakamura Sensei and the others take the parts of the *Obentoo* students. The students make up a 'show and tell' using photos (or hand-drawn pictures) of family members and pets introduced in Unit 5.

Presentation

- *Using the OHTs*: see if students can work out the gist of the story by referring only to the pictures. Before playing the tape or reading the story, see if they can find out one (or more) pieces of information about each of the animals depicted in the cartoon. During the first 'look through', they might only be able to identify the animals and one or two names. You could lead in to the adjectives by seeing if the students can suggest an adjective (in English) which would describe each animal. Alternatively, you could get the students to look at the questions on page 78 before listening to the story and see how many answers they can guess.
- *Listen and discuss*: as in earlier units.

Follow-up

- *Now it's our turn!*: divide the cartoon into small segments and have small groups of students (up to 6) act out each segment. Remind students to use the key language from the cartoons in their role-plays. Other words could be added if the students can manage them. The role-plays could be videotaped.
- *Quick! Quick! guessing game*: the class is divided into teams of six players. Each player chooses a pet card from a basket (the basket should contain only one card per player). The students go to the front one at a time and the others try to guess what pet card the student is holding by asking the question ... さんの ペットは ... ですか。 The student can only reply はい、そうです。 or いいえ、ちがいます。 When someone has guessed the pet correctly, the next student goes to the front and the class try to guess his/her pet; this continues until all pets have been correctly guessed. The teacher may wish to impose a time limit; in this case, the number of pets correctly guessed within the time limit is a team's 'score'. This game can be played at different times by each group as part of a 'work stations' task, or all at once, timed by the teacher.
- *Our Japanese saga*: as extra reading practice, you could write a 'saga' about your class along the lines of the *Itadakimasu* stories, using the names of students in the class, with a title such as 'The Days of Year 8' or 'The Young and the Noisy'. The students could also be encouraged to write their own episodes.

どんなあじ？

79–82 2A

1 Asking what someone's pet is and saying its name

Warm-up

- Replay *Itadakimasu* and explore the page as in earlier units.
- *Pet questions*: using the flashcards of the *Obentoo* students, ask students questions with the following patterns:

  Question: ... さんの ペットは なんですか。
  Answer: ... です。
  Question: なまえは？
  Answer: ... です。

Presentation

- *Toss-the-てだま*: students listen to the dialogues and repeat. When listening for a second time, after the question is played, the tape is paused and the teacher throws a てだま (small bean-bag) to one of the students, who answers the question. The tape is restarted and the whole class repeats. After the next question is played, the tape is paused again; the student who has the bean-bag throws it to another, who must answer, and so on.
- Listen, look at the sentences and repeat, as in earlier units.

Follow-up

- ほんとうですか: going around the class, the teacher asks students the same questions, this time about themselves.
- *Question chain*: one student asks the next student: ... さん／くんのペットはなんですか。 That student answers and then asks someone else, making a chain. If a student doesn't have a pet, s/he can make one up.
- おぼえていますか *gameshow*: using the questions ペットがいますか。なんですか。なまえは？ students write answers, for example わたしのペットはねこです。なまえは「Felix」です。 Play the game according to the instructions for Unit 5 on page 57.
- **W 62 4B** Students listen to the tape and write down what pet each person has and to which area they have to take them to show them.

Audio script

SPEAKERS: P1 (registrar) and P2–6 (students)

a **P1:** こんにちは。おなまえは？
P2: けんいちです。

P1: はい、けんいちくんのペットはなんですか。
P2: あひるです。なまえはガーコです。
P1: はい、あひるですね。
P2: はい、そうです。
P1: にくみです、にくみにどうぞ。
P2: はい、ありがとう。

b P1: はい、おなまえは？
P3: まさおです。
P1: まさおくんのペットはなんですか。
P3: いぬです。
P1: いぬのなまえは？
P3: プティです。
P1: プティちゃんはかわいいですね。いちくみにどうぞ。
P3: いちくみですか。
P1: はい、いちくみです。
P3: ありがとうございます。

c P1: はい、つぎ。
P4: こんにちは。
P1: こんにちは。おなまえは？
P4: きみこです。
P1: ペットはなんですか。
P4: へびです。
P1: なまえは？
P4: へびのなまえですか。
P1: はい、そうです。
P4: あっ、ハリーです。
P1: さんくみです。
P4: さんくみですね、ありがとう。

d P1: おなまえは？
P5: しんです。ペットはフィンです。
P1: えっ、なんですか。
P5: きんぎょです。
P1: ああ、きんぎょのなまえはフィンですね。
P5: はい。
P1: さんくみです。
P5: はい、ありがとう。

e P1: おなまえは？
P6: さなえです。
P1: さなえさんのペットはなんですか。
P6: うさぎです。なまえはみみです。
P1: ええ！　かわいいですね。うさぎはにくみです。
P6: にくみですね。
P1: はい、そうです。

Vocabulary notes

にくみ	Group 2
いちくみ	Group 1
つぎ	Next.
さんくみ	Group 3

- **W 62/T5** Students find the words for the pets in the word puzzle and write them in the boxes provided.
- **W 63/T6** Students unjumble the words and use them to label the pictures.

2 Describing a pet/Asking whose pet it is and responding

Warm-up

Adjective mnemonics: draw flashcards to represent each of the new adjectives and ask students to think of an action mnemonic to suit each one, for example うるさい = 'Sigh! The rooster woke me up again!'

Presentation

- *Can you guess who it is?*: students listen to the tape (without looking at their books) and try to guess who is talking and what they're saying. Refer to clues from the cartoon story.
- *Listen and repeat* and *Listen, look at sentences and repeat* as in earlier units.

Follow-up

- *Flashcard review*: place all the pet flashcards in a box. Draw out the cards one at a time and ask だれのペットですか。Students reply: ... くん／さんのペットです。
- *Memory test*: students form groups and turn flashcards of the *Obentoo* characters and their pets upside down. They turn the cards the right way up and match each person to the correct pet, then say whose pet it is and what it is like, for example うるさいです。けんいちくんのペットです。
- **W 63/T7 8 4B** Students listen as なかむらせんせい tries to sort out which pet belongs to which person. Students draw lines to connect the pet owners with their lost pets.

Audio script

Nakamura: *(dog barking)* だれのペットですか。
Yuusuke: あきらくんのペットです。
Akira: はい、ぼくのです。サミ！サミ！
Nakamura: *(duck noise)* だれのペットですか。
Masaru: ぼくのペットです。
Nakamura: あっ、まさるくんのですね。
Masaru: はい、そうです。
Nakamura: *(horse noise)* だれのペットですか。だれのペットですか。
Yuusuke: スージーさんのペットです。スージー！　スージー！ Flicker が　いますよ！
Suzie: え、ああ、Flicker！わたしのペットです。どうもありがとう。
Nakamura: ああ！へびです。
All: こわい！
Nakamura: だれのペットですか。
Jane: わたしのへびです。
Nakamura: へえ！ジェーンさんのですか！
Jane: はい、そうです。わたしのペットです。
Kenji: バグズ！バグズ！
Nakamura: バグズ？
Kenji: はい、バグズはうさぎです。
Nakamura: けんじくんのペットはうさぎです

ね。なまえはバグズですね。あっ、みて！うさぎがいますよ。

Kenji: ああ、バグズ！はい、ぼくのペットです。

- **W 64/T8 4B** Students listen to the tape and write down the name of the pet's owner, the type of pet, and how the pet is described.

Audio script

a A: わー、ちいさいですね！だれのいぬですか。
B: ニックさんのペットです。

b A: ああ、うるさい、あのとりは。だれのペットですか。
B: あっ、すみません、わたしのとりです。わたしはスーです、どうぞよろしく。

c A: みて！あれは ... ねこですか？
B: ええ、そうですよ。
A: おおきいですねえ。だれのペットですか。
B: ほんださんのペットです。

d A: かわいいうさぎですね。だれのですか。
B: サリーさんのです。

e A: こわいです。いぬはきらい！だれのペットですか。
B: デービッドさんのいぬです。

- **W 64/T9** Students read the sentences to identify some of the pets in the pet care centre by description. After completing this task in the Workbook, students can write similar sentences in their notebooks for the pets not mentioned.
- **W 65/T10** Students read each paragraph, then complete the table and/or draw pictures to illustrate.
- **W 65–6/T11** Students find out which pet belongs to which *Obentoo* character by following the grid of the あみだくじ puzzle. When they have worked out which pet belongs to which person, and the pet's name, they complete the sentences in Japanese.

Amidakuji are used in Japanese companies to allocate tasks to employees. For example, if five people (A, B, C, D, E) are to work with five other people (F, G, H, I, J) on five tasks (1, 2, 3, 4, 5), instead of drawing names out of a hat, they draw up an *amidakuji*. The names of people A, B, C, D and E are written on the first line, the names of people F, G, H, I and J on the second line and tasks 1, 2, 3, 4 and 5 on the third line. All names and tasks are joined with vertical lines. Then horizontal lines are drawn connecting each of the vertical lines. One or more horizontal lines may be drawn. The puzzle is followed as described on page 65 in the Workbook and, magically, the people and tasks are randomly sorted!

- **W 67/T12** Students describe each picture by using the clues to fill in the blanks.
- **W 67–8/T13** Students write three sentences under each row of pictures to describe what they see. Teachers may choose to do this as a speaking task, or, using a set of flashcards, have students make up their own sentences.

3 Asking and saying what pets eat

Warm-up

Hands up!: without showing the flashcards (or pictures) to the students, call out the word for a pet food in Japanese; pause, then call out of the animals (again, without showing it to the class). If students think the animal eats the food called out they raise their hands; if not, they don't. Show the cards after everyone has made their guess.

Presentation

- *Actions galore!*: as students listen and repeat, get them to make up actions to suit the animals being talked about and the pet foods mentioned. They should perform both actions as they listen to and repeat each question and answer.
- *Listen, look at sentences and repeat,* as in earlier units.

Follow-up

- *Who eats what?*: put two sets of flashcards on the board — one of animals and one of food. You could introduce extra animals in this task, as students are only required to talk about the foods. Ask the question ... はなにをたべますか。Students answer ... をたべます。
- *Who eats what? (variation)*: divide the class into teams and have them answer as fast as possible for points. You could force the students to give correct or incorrect answers by saying ほんとう (*true*) or うそ (*false*) after asking the question but before students answer. For example:

  TEACHER: ねこはなにをたべますか。ほんとう！
  STUDENTS: さかなをたべます。
  OR
  TEACHER: ねこはなにをたべますか。うそ！
  STUDENTS: やさいをたべます。
- **W 68/T14 4B** Students listen to the clues given on the tape and guess which animal is being talked about.

Audio script

a こんにちは。わたしはとしこです。ペットのなまえはプティです。プティはさんさいです。かわいいです。いぬのビスケットをたべます。ペットはなんですか。

b こんにちは。ぼくはまさるです。ペットのなまえはさむらいです。ちょっとこわいです。ねずみをたべます。ペットはなんですか。

c こんにちは。まさこです。私のペットはちいさいです。うるさいです。パンととりのえさをたべます。ペットはなんですか。

d こんにちはしんです。ぼくのペットはおおきいです。くさをたべます。ペットはなんですか。

Vocabulary note

ビスケット	biscuits

- **69/T15 4B** Students listen to the tape and fill in a pet care card for each pet in Japanese. (Students may fill in the katakana names in English.)

Audio script

SPEAKERS: Vet and Persons 1, 2 and 3

a V: もしもし、どうぶつびょういんです。
P1: もしもし、私のペットがびょうきです。
V: そうですか。ちょっとまってください。はい、おなまえは？
P1: やまだきょうこです。
V: はい、でんわばんごうは？
P1: はい、783-0102 です。
V: はい、783-0102 ですね。
P1: はい、そうです。
V: ペットはなんですか。
P1: あひるです。
V: あひるですか。
P1: はい、そうです。
V: ペットのなまえは？
P1: ドナルドです。
V: なんさいですか。
P1: ごさいです。
V: なにをたべますか。
P1: あひるのえさをたべます。
V: はい、じゃ、すぐきてください。
P1: はい、ありがとうございます。

b V: もしもし、どうぶつびょういんです。
P2: もしもし、きむらですが、私のとりが、びょうきです。
V: はい、おなまえはきむらさんですね。
P2: はい、きむらすすむです。
V: はい、でんわばんごうは？
P2: はい、663-1895 です。
V: 663-1895 ですね。
P2: はい、そうです。
V: とりのなまえはなんですか。
P2: やきとりです。
V: おもしろいなまえですね。やきとりはなんさいですか。
P2: いっさいです。
V: やきとりはなにをたべますか。
P2: パンとくだものをたべます。

c V: もしもし、どうぶつびょういんです。
P3: はやく！　ホット・ドッグがへんです。
V: ホット・ドッグですか。
P3: はい、私のペットです。
V: ああ、そうですか。おなまえは？
P3: ホット・ドッグです。
V: いいえ、...
P3: あっ、わたしのなまえですか。
V: はい。
P3: 私はすずきみえです。
V: はい、でんわばんごうは？
P3: でんわばんごうは 383-6971 です。
V: はい、383-6971 ですね。
P3: はい、そうです。
V: ペットのなまえはホット・ドッグですね。
P3: はい、そうです。
V: ホット・ドッグはなんさいですか。
P3: 十一さいです。
V: ホット・ドッグはいぬですね。
P3: いいえ、ねこです。
V: へえ！ねこ！
P3: はい、そうです。
V: じゃ、なにをたべますか。
P3: ホット・ドッグはホット・ドッグをたべます。
V: あっ、なるほど。

Vocabulary notes

どうぶつびょういん	veterinary hospital
びょうき	sick
じゃ、...	Well, then ...
すぐきてください。	Please come immediately.
おもしろい	interesting
くだもの	fruit
へん	strange
あっ、なるほど。	Oh, I see!

- **69/T16** Students read the sentences and tick the *true* (ほんとう) or *false* (うそ) box according to the information given.

べんきょうのベン — ひらがな

83 2A

Character introduced: を

By the end of Unit 6, students will have been introduced to all the hiragana characters, so most of the activities below involve a large amount of revision.

Warm-up

Jumbled word game: the class is divided into two teams

lined up in front of the board. The first player in each team turns away from the board. The teacher writes a jumbled word (or sentence) on the board and the two players turn around and try to be the first to write the word (or sentence) correctly on the board. Points are allocated for correct responses.

Presentation

Play the tape while students look at the Student Book. Stop the tape whenever you hear a 'ding'.

Audio script

SPEAKER: Ben

Hi, Ben here again with the last hiragana. I'll also tell you about how hiragana sounds can be combined to make more sounds, without you needing to learn any new characters. But first, some revision.

I'll choose a character. Point to it as I say it, and then repeat all the characters in that column after me.
か — か、き、く、け、こ
And now another one:
な — な、に、ぬ、ね、の
And finally:
ま — ま、み、む、め、も

Introducing を

When talking about what pets eat, you learnt the expressions なにをたべますか and さかなをたべます. You would have heard the character を after なに and after さかな.

OK, so you're wondering why there are two characters for 'o'? This special を is used after objects words and you'll find more examples of object-を in Unit 8.

Introducing small ょ

Remember the expressions ちょっとまって and べんきょうのベン? You may have noticed that they contain the hiragana character ょ, but it is written slightly smaller than usual.

To work out how to pronounce words which have this small character like べんきょう, take the character before the small ょ, き in this case, and combine the two sounds, き and ょ, to make きょ. Some hiragana combinations with small ょ are written in the purple box on the page. Listen as I say them and repeat after me:

し、しょ
じ、じょ
ち、ちょ
き、きょ
ぎ、ぎょ

Introducing small ゃ and ゅ

These two sounds can also combine with other hiragana, in the same way that small ょ does, although you don't see them as often as small ょ. You might have noticed them in ちゅうがくせい (Junior High School Student) and ガーコちゃん, the name of Kenichi's pet duck.

Practise saying the combination sounds on the page in the purple box. Repeat after me:

し、しゅ
じ、じゃ
ち、ちゅ
き、きゃ
ぎ、ぎゅ

You'll find more hiragana combination sounds on the inside front cover of your Student Book.

Follow-up

- **W 60** かきかた (*How to write*): students practise writing the characters in the boxes using the correct stroke order. Notice the size and position of the small ゃ、ゅ、ょ.
- *Human hiragana/katakana*: the class is divided into small groups. The hiragana combination sounds covered in *Benkyoo no Ben* are written on pieces of paper and put into a hat. Each group selects one combination. The members of the group then lie down and make the character combination with their bodies. The rest of the class try to guess the sound and vote for the best (or most creative) 'character'.
- *Word gaps (variation on jumbled word game)*: the class is divided into teams lined up in front of the board. The teacher writes a word or sentence with more than one character missing. Students turn around and try to write the missing characters. The game can be made a little easier by writing a list of possible characters on the board.
- *Hiragana-ercise*: students come to the front one by one and 'write' a mystery character with their finger. The rest of the class try to identify the character.
- *Hiragana dictation quiz*: the teacher calls out words in hiragana which students must write correctly. For students who have not done much dictation (or whose knowledge of characters is limited), the quiz can be made easier by getting students to fill in the blank spaces in sentences which are already written out, for example こん___は、な__む___す。__うぞ、___し___ [こんにちは、なかむらです。どうぞ、よろしく。*Note*: the last blank space is for the full stop.
- *Hiragana memory game*: the teacher calls out a series of approximately five hiragana. Students try to remember the sequence and write it correctly. Increase the number of characters in each sequence every two or three rounds (or as required). Students could be given bonus points if they write all characters correctly in the right order. The game could be played in pairs to begin with.
- *Hiragana jeopardy*: this game is played like the TV game 'Jeopardy'. Categories of questions are presented to students, with the number of points increasing according to the difficulty of the question. Categories for hiragana questions could include single characters, hiragana words (with no combination sounds), hiragana words (with one or

more combination sounds), jumbled words, dictation, particles, etc.
- Ⓦ **60/T1** With a partner, students practise reading the hiragana aloud. They can take turns or read them together. As a follow-up activity, students can make up some more examples and test their partner.
- Ⓦ **61/T2** Students circle the correct hiragana for the sounds indicated and practise writing them in the boxes provided.
- Ⓦ **61/T3** Using different highlighters or pencils, students colour in the sounds according to whether they are a combination sound, a voiced sound using にごり (*nigori*) or まる (*maru*), a katakana long sound indicator ぼう (*boo*), other hiragana or other katakana.
- Ⓑ **6.1** Hiragana crossword

ごはんとおかず

Ⓢ **84–5**

Warm-up

Pet photo show and tell: using the vocabulary students have learnt so far, they show a picture of their pet and use whatever words (or sentences) they know to describe it. If they can't think of suitable words, other students can make suggestions.

Presentation and follow-up

- *Word scramble*: divide the class into teams. Make word cards for all of the key words including particles. Refer to pages 84–5 of the Student Book for examples. Place all the cards in a box. Students draw out cards and try to make sentences. When it is their turn, each team can throw back a word and draw another card. Points are allocated according to the complexity of the sentence and/or other criteria as appropriate.
- おもしろいあいさつ: students take pets' names and role-play a meeting in the park (or other venue), where they introduce their owners.
- *Magazine cut-outs*: students cut out pictures from magazines and write captions about pets.
- どうぶつあいごのひ (*Pet Care Day*): students could bring photos of their pets (or the real thing) and introduce them to the class.
- *Sentences and questions*: students practise changing statements to questions (and vice versa) by omitting/adding か.
- *Particle の practice*: discuss the use of の with previously learnt vocabulary, for example ともだちのおかあさん、ともだちのおかあさんのなまえ. Extend the clause, for example ともだちのおかあさんのペットのともだちのいぬ, and challenge students to see how long a clause they can understand. Invite students to make up their own long clauses and challenge the other students to explain them in English! You could also introduce the expression うちの ..., for example うちのペット and うちのおかあさん.
- For further grammar explanation refer students to the せつめい section of the Student Book (pages 202–3).

Extension tasks

- Ⓑ **6.2** *More handy uses for の*: this task extends the use of の to ownership of other things and people as in the examples:

ケイトさんのおかあさん	Kate's mother
カーラさんのともだち	Carla's friend
ゆきさんのうち	Yuki's house
わたしのがっこう	My school

- Ⓑ **6.3** *More about names*: this task extends the sentence pattern ペットのなまえはガーコです to talk about the names of family members and friends.
- Ⓑ **6.4** *Three-way information gap*: divide the class into groups of three. Give each person one part of the informational gap and by taking turns in asking, students find out the information they need to complete their sheet.

テーブルマナー

Ⓢ **86–7**

Warm-up

Have you ever ...?: before looking at the photos on page 87, ask students to describe any Japanese houses or buildings they have seen or been into. Ask each person to make a list of adjectives (in English or Japanese) which describe their impression(s) of a Japanese home (even though they might not have seen one).

Presentation and follow-up

- Use the list of words on page 87 as hiragana practice (the students may need help with the three katakana words). Find them on the house plan on page 86 and talk about the features of Japanese houses. The extra information below will give you some points for discussion.
- *Discussion*: draw two columns on the board: 'Similarities' and 'Differences'. Look at the photographs on page 87 and also any other photos which you might have of the interior or exterior of Japanese houses. Ask students to identify features and place them in the appropriate columns. Then see what classifications can be made in terms of different Japanese housing types: traditional and modern housing, apartments, マンション, university dormitories, etc.
- *Customs in the home*: discuss customs followed by Japanese people in their homes, for example removing shoes in the entrance hall, wearing slippers, removing slippers in the *tatami* room, and taking a bath. Ask students to identify customs observed in their own houses, for example on special occasions.
- Ⓑ **6.5** *Natasha's Japanese dream*: students read the diary entry of an exchange student in Japan and fill in the gaps with an appropriate Japanese word

from the list given. Some words are used more than once.

This should also stimulate discussion of experiences as an exchange student to Japan; coping with different customs, feelings and expectations about being an exchange student to Japan; common mistakes made by exchange students, etc.

Extra information

1 げんかん Entrance foyer. All houses, even the smallest apartments, have a げんかん. This is where people remove their shoes and store them in a くつばこ (shoe cupboard). Japanese flower arrangements (いけばな) are often displayed on the cupboard in the げんかん. There is always a step up into the house from the げんかん where スリッパ are placed for guests and family members to put on.

2 スリッパ Slippers. These are scuff-type slippers provided for people to wear inside the house. Each member of the family will have his/her own スリッパ and there will be other スリッパ provided for guests.

3 ろうか Corridor, hallway

4 おうせつま Room for greeting guests. This room is used to entertain guests when they come for a short visit. Japanese tea and sweets are usually served here.

5 いま Living room. This room is often Japanese-style and has *tatami* on the floor, a *kotatsu* and often, these days, a TV.

6 こたつ *Kotatsu*. This is a low table with a heating element under the table top. A square quilt-type cover (こたつぶとん) is placed over the frame and the table top is placed on top. People sit on ざぶとん with their feet under the こたつ. Children often do their homework on the こたつ.

7 だいどころ Kitchen

8 ふろば Bathroom. The ふろば usually consists of two rooms: one to change in, with a washbasin, a cupboard for towels and often a washing machine (see photo 8), and another where the Japanese bath is (photo 9).

9 This room usually has a hand shower attached to the wall. You use this to wash and rinse yourself thoroughly before entering the bath to soak. There is usually a low stool to sit on while you wash yourself. The bath is fairly small but very deep and is filled to the brim with very hot water. The temperature of the water is kept constant by a thermostatically controlled heater. (You can see the controls on the right-hand wall in photo 9.) People usually have baths at night before going to bed, and spend 30–40 minutes just soaking.

10 トイレ This is a Japanese toilet. To use it, stand facing the fixture with one foot on either side of the bowl and squat. Very often plastic slippers are placed outside the toilet door for you to wear into the toilet. Leave your other slippers outside the toilet door and that will indicate that the toilet is occupied. If someone knocks on the toilet door while you are using it, it is customary to knock back to indicate that you are there, rather than call out as we might do.

11 かいだん Stairs

12 とこのま This is the alcove in a Japanese-style room where pieces of art and flower arrangements are displayed. Traditionally, when guests are entertained in the Japanese-style room, they are seated in front of the とこのま. In this way they are considered one of the family's treasures.

13 おしいれ A cupboard with sliding doors in the Japanese-style room to hold ふとん.

14 きゃくま Japanese-style guest room

15 しょうじ Paper screens

16 にわ Garden. Japanese gardens are usually quite small, often with low shrubs and *bonsai* plants. Sometimes a pond, a water fountain or stones are featured.

17 トイレ Toilet. This is a Western-style toilet. Notice the panel at the side. This controls the temperature of the seat and the toilet's other functions, such as bidet, flushing, raising or lowering the seat.

18 こどもべや Children's rooms

19 わしつ Japanese-style room. The furniture in this room is usually quite simple: a low table with ざぶとん and たたみ on the floor. When visitors come to stay, they usually sleep on ふとん in the わしつ. The ふとん which are kept in the おしいれ are laid out on the floor, then aired and packed away after the visitors leave. Slippers must be removed before entering the わしつ.

20 ふとん Japanese-style bedding. This bed consists of a thin, soft mattress layer which is placed directly onto the たたみ. This is covered with a towelling sheet on which the person sleeps. In cold weather a blanket is placed on top, followed by a thick doona, usually with a cotton cover, which is removed and washed after use. The pillow is smaller than Western pillows and is filled with rice husks.

21 ベランダ Veranda. This is a narrow hallway off a わしつ. It is an area where slippers are removed before entering the わしつ. It will sometimes have chairs and a coffee table.

おはし

S 88–9

Warm-up

Introducing がいらいご *(use of 'borrowed' words)*: give students a list of words in Japanese borrowed from

English. Say them aloud and see how many they can identify. Start off with simple ones like foods and sports, and then try some more difficult ones and talk about their origins, for example パソコン、ファミコン、デパート. Then ask students how many Japanese words they have noticed that are used in English, for example *tempura, sushi, sake, karaoke, harakiri, kamikaze geisha, sashimi, bonsai.*

Presentation and follow-up

- *Discussion*: work through the sections in the Student Book on pages 88–9. When discussing がいらいご, give students other examples and see if they can work out the equivalent words in English. Use restaurant menus for examples. Point out to students that some Japanese words have been borrowed from languages other than English, for example パン (French, originally Portuguese?), アルバイト (German).
- *Dictation quiz*: write out a list of words students have learnt or heard, leaving spaces for the combination sounds. Read out the complete words. Students have to write the correct hiragana in the spaces. Some words could be completely blank (if they are familiar to students).
- *Animal noises*: read out other animal onomatopoeia. Students try to guess what animal makes the sound. For example: butterfly ひらひら、horse ひんひん、goat めえめえ、rabbit ぴょんぴょん.
- ... さん／くんはいぬです！A picture of each animal learnt is drawn on a card and placed in a box. A wild card is also placed in the box. Students take a picture (which they do not show to anyone else) and put it back in the box; then another student chooses a picture, and so on. The first student to draw the wild card is 'in'. (The wild card is not put back in the box.) The students then move around the room miming actions made by their animal and making that animal's sound. The student who is 'in' tries to identify someone, saying ... さん／くんは ... です。If the student is identified correctly, s/he joins the 'in' team and tries to identify other students, and the game continues.

おしょうゆ

S 89 Ⓢ 2A

Presentation

Students listen to the tape and repeat the new expressions.

Follow-up

- **W 70/T19** おしょうゆクイズタイム: students circle the correct answer.
- *Exclamations!*: give students simple scenarios and ask them to suggest suitable exclamations. Use words and expressions covered in previous *Oshooyu* sections.
- *Mime*: give students an expression. They have to mime a situation in which it would be appropriate.
- *Punch-line poster*: make a list of expressions (on a poster) which students could use in role-plays and writing for extra 'punch'.

おかし

S 90

Warm-up

Sing the song こぶた、たぬき、きつね、ねこ.

Song

Sing the song on page 90 of the Student Book to the tune of こぶた、たぬき、きつね、ねこ with the actions indicated. It can also be sung in rounds.

Craft activity

Origami rabbit: make an origami rabbit to go with a small box of chocolate eggs for Easter.

Putting it all together

- Have students read the speech bubble in the photograph on page 89 of the Student Book and ask them the following questions in Japanese. Students answer in Japanese. To make the task more challenging, write the questions and ask students to write the answers in Japanese.
  1 えみさんはなんさいですか。
  2 えみさんのいもうとのなまえは？
  3 なおみさんはなんさいですか。
  4 ペットはなんですか。
  5 ペットのなまえはなんですか。
- **W 70/T17** Students use the questions given to survey three students to find out about their pets.
- **W 70/T18** Students bring along a picture or photograph of an imaginary or real pet and tell the class about it in Japanese. They should mention what type of animal it is, its name and age, what it is like and what it eats. This can also be done as a writing task.
  Variation 1: students can bring in their photos or pictures, number them and put them up on a pin-board. Students then give their talks and the rest of the class must guess which pet each person is talking about.
  Variation 2: students bring a photo or picture of their pet. They write three sentences about the pet on a piece of paper, for example what sort of pet it is, what its name is, and what it is like. Put the animal photos and pictures up on a pin-board. Put the sentences in a box and mix them up. One student takes out a sentence and reads it out, while the rest of the class listen and try to find the matching photo.
- *Role-play* わたしのかぞく: take the part of your family's pet. (Choose any animal if you don't have one.)
  – You're out for a walk with your owner and meet your next-door neighbour, who is also with his/her owner.
  – When your owners are distracted you introduce

yourselves and talk about your families. You come from a small family but your friend has a large family.
  – Compare what both of you have to eat and decide who is luckier.
- *Role-play: obedience school for pets*
  – You have decided to open an obedience school for Japanese dogs.
  – You've taught the dogs some basic commands (sit down, stand up, watch, listen, open the door and close the door), which most of the dogs have learnt easily.
  – However, one of the dogs, クロ, keeps getting confused and always does the opposite, unless you give him special attention.
  – Another dog, シロ, shows great potential but doesn't know where she lives or who is in her family.
  – After you've finished training the dogs, give them a final test.
  – They all do well and are given rewards. But, as usual, クロ needs some special attention to get everything right.
- これはかぞくのしゃしんです: students bring some photos of their family and friends to school (or draw a picture if they don't have a photo). They have to tell everyone in their class who the people in the photos are (not forgetting their pets). Here are some phrases they might find useful:
  これはかぞくのしゃしんです。
  これはわたしのいぬです。
  このひとはおかあさんです。
  そして、このひとはおとうさんです。
  このひとはともだちです。

ごちそうさま

S 90

- **W 71** おべんとうクイズ
- *End-of-unit quiz*: students make up questions (which they write on cards) for use in an end-of-unit quiz.
- *Individual progress cards*: write the items listed in *Gochisoosama* onto the photocopiable student progress card on page 138 of the *Moshi Moshi Teacher's Handbook*. You may wish to add other items, for example other language points, cultural understandings, completion of homework or assignment tasks.

Reference to *Yoroshiku National Curriculum Guidelines for Japanese (Moshi Moshi)*

The following is a list of the suggested language exponents presented in *Moshi Moshi* Module 2 かぞくとともだち (*Family and friends*) which have been introduced in Unit 6 of *Obentoo*. In some cases the example has been changed to correspond to the form introduced in *Obentoo*. Appropriate activities from *Moshi Moshi* are suggested below.

Language exponents

- Pets
  ペットは？
  ペットのなまえはなんですか。
  (くろ) です。
  (おおきい) です。
  Note: instead of ペットをかっていますか。
  Obentoo introduces ペットがいますか。
  and (けんいちくん) のペットはなんですか。
- Ownership
  だれのペットですか。
  けんいちくんのペットです。
  だれのですか。
  (...) さん／わたしのです。
- Expressing surprise
  へええ！
  ああそうですか。
  (in addition きゃー！わあ！)
- Exclaiming
  かわいい！

Suggested activities from *Moshi Moshi*

ペットをかっていますか。 Teacher Resources page 15
ペットはどこでしょう。 Teacher Resources page 18

Overview

Unit objectives

Students will be able to:
- ask the date of someone's birthday and respond when asked
- ask the date of some Japanese festivals and holidays and respond when asked
- ask what day of the week it is and respond when asked
- ask what something is and respond when asked
- talk about at least six items which can be used at school or given as presents
- ask someone's Chinese birth sign and respond when asked
- read and write one more katakana and one more katakana sound change
- read and write the kanji for the days of the week
- read and write the kanji for the months of the year and the date
- read and write the kanji for 'holiday'
- read and write short sentences related to the topics covered
- discuss at least one important event which takes place in Japan in each month of the year

Functions and language exponents

1 Asking and talking about the date and the day
(しんごくん)のたんじょう日はいつですか。
(2)月(11)日です。
• (休みは)なん曜日ですか。
• (月曜日)です。

2 Asking and saying what something is
(プレゼントは)なんですか。
(ほん)です。

3 Asking about and saying someone's Chinese birth sign
(トニーくん)はなにどしですか。
(いぬ)どしです。

Key vocabulary and expressions

エマさんのたんじょう日
キャンプ
こどもの日
休み
... はいつですか。
... はなん曜日ですか。

... はなんですか。
ほん
えんぴつ
けしごむ
かみ
とけい
ものさし
ノート

一月～十二月
一日～三十一日

... なにどしですか。
ねずみどし
うしどし
とらどし
うさぎどし
たつどし
へびどし
うまどし
ひつじどし
さるどし
とりどし
いぬどし
いのししどし

日曜日
月曜日
火曜日
水曜日
木曜日
金曜日
土曜日

Script

Students are expected to be able to read and write the key characters and recognise the associated words.

Key characters	*Associated words*
フ／プ	(プレゼント)
日	日曜日
	たんじょう日
	一日
	二日
	十五日
	こどもの日
月	月曜日
	5月
火	火曜日
水	水曜日
木	木曜日
金	金曜日
土	土曜日
休	休み

曜　よう (for recognition only)

Script understandings

- How kanji have one meaning and more than one pronunciation
- The derivation of the kanji for 'month' (月 moon) and 'day' (日 sun)
- The 'celebrations' referred to in naming the days of the week, for example, 日曜日 (Day of the Sun)
- The origin of the kanji 休み (holiday/rest, person taking a rest beside a tree)

Learning how to learn

'Carla's Guide to Avoiding Embarrassment': a feature which looks at 'dos and don'ts' when giving a self-introduction talk in Japanese

Cultural elements

Information about festivals, celebrations and customs observed each month in Japan

Other incidental language introduced

すてき！
きょうは11月17日ですね。
うん
れんしゅうしましょう。
土曜日？
ああ、そうですか。
やめて！
おにいちゃん
... ちゃん

Extension material

- More about asking the date
  なんがつなんにちですか。
- Asking about today's date
  きょうはなんがつなんにちですか。
- Asking about the date of someone's birthday
  たんじょうびはなんがつなんにちですか。
- Use of から and まで when talking about holidays
  休みはいつからですか。
  休みはいつまでですか。
  休みはいつからいつまでですか。

Need some extra words or expressions?
Ask your teacher!

Individual festivals are explained in detail in the *Teeburu manaa* section. Japanese refer to holidays in terms of the seasons

なつ休み	Summer holidays (Japanese refer to holidays in terms of the seasons)	七・五・三	Seven, Five, Three Day
あき休み	Autumn holidays	オーストラリアのひ	Australia Day
ふゆ休み	Winter holidays	クリスマスのひ	Christmas Day
はる休み	Spring holidays	イースター	Easter
おしょうがつ	New Year	スポーツのひ	Sports Day
せつぶん	Bean-throwing festival	うんどうかい	Sports Carnival
ひなまつり	Dolls' Day (Girls' Day Festival)	ぶんかさい	Cultural Festival (School Fête)
はなみ	Blossom Viewing	パーティー	party
こどものひ	Children's Day	ペン	pen
つゆ	the rainy season	おもちゃ	toy
たなばた	Star Festival	にんぎょう	doll
おぼん	Obon Festival	ネクレース	necklace
あきまつり	Autumn Festival	じてんしゃ	bike
たいいくのひ	Sports Day	かばん	bag
ぶんかのひ	Culture Day		

Teaching suggestions

The following suggestions are provided as a guide to lesson planning and should be adapted to suit your teaching style and the learning styles of your students. These tasks are specific to this unit. For more information on general strategies for each section, refer to *Using Obentoo* on pages 3–8.

いただきます

91–3 2B

Warm-up

Guess the concept: write the words in kanji for the days of the week, the dates of the month and the months of the year. Put the words in a hat. Tell students that the words in the hat are from three categories which are all related to the concept of time. On the pin-up board (or felt board) put three cards labelled Concept 1 (e.g. for days of the week), Concept 2 (e.g. for dates of the month), and Concept 3 (e.g. for months of the year). Tell students that you will take out the words one at a time, say what they are and position each under the correct concept label. The students have to listen and try to guess what the concepts are by asking questions to which you can answer 'yes' or 'no'. When students have correctly identified the concepts, leave one word under each concept label and put the rest back in the box. Take them out one at a time again, call out the word and this time the students have to identify under which concept group the word should be placed.

Presentation

- *Using the OHTs*: play the tape while students look at the OHTs and ask them to guess what is happening. As they listen, ask them to write down the number of words they hear which were from one of the concepts they learnt above. Initially, it may be helpful to focus on allowing students just to identify familiar words, before looking at the gist of the story.
- *Frame by frame*: play the story one page at a time and ask students to guess what is happening in each frame. Get students to identify the new words as they emerge. Say each word and have them repeat it after you.

Follow-up

- *Cartoon grab*: copy the cartoon from the Student Book and cut it into frames. Students form teams of 3 or 4 and the pieces of the cartoon are mixed up and put on a desk. The teams compete to see which can rearrange the pieces in the correct order in the shortest period of time.
- Have all students answer the questions on page 93 in their notebooks. Then use them as the questions in a quiz-show game.
- *Mystery presents*: the students each place something of theirs (which they have learnt to say) in a large box. One student then comes out to the front and is blindfolded. The class then asks プレゼントはなんですか。as the student takes out an item from the box, which s/he then tries to identify in Japanese. The class then asks だれのですか。and the owner says わたし／ぼくのです。The owner then comes to the front and the game continues.

どんなあじ？

94–6 2B

1 Asking and talking about the date and the day

Warm-up

- Replay *Itadakimasu* and explore the page as in earlier units.
- Quickly revise the numbers with a game of bingo. Mention the two words for 4, 7 and 9 and

that some pronunciations are used for some purposes and some for others.

Presentation

- Have students cover the text, look at the pictures and listen to the tape first without repeating. Then rewind the tape and have them listen and repeat as usual.
- Listen, look at the sentences and repeat, as in earlier units.
- You may wish to give more examples for listening, looking and repeating. Copy and enlarge the first line of each of the examples and, using the flashcards for the months, dates and days, hold up the cards and have students repeat after you.
- 「一ちょうさん」 *(King Pin No. 1) variation*: students sit in a large circle. One student is いっちょうさん and stands in the middle. A slight gap is made between two students in the circle to indicate each end of the chain: the top and the bottom. いっちょうさん starts by pointing to any one of the students in the circle, who has to say the first date of the month. The next student (towards the 'top') says the next date, and so on. If anyone makes a mistake, he/she stands up and goes to the end of the line. The other students then move up to fill the empty space, and so on. いっちょうさん must also say the date when it is his/her turn in the chain (usually after the person sitting down nearest the 'top'). If いっちょうさん makes a mistake, he/she must also go to the end of the line; the person sitting down nearest the top then becomes いっちょうさん, and so on.

Follow-up

- **W 73/T1 5A** Students listen to the tape and write down the day of the week being mentioned. Then they draw a line to the appropriate event.

Audio script

a **A:** せんせい、テストはなんようびですか。
B: 木曜日です。

b **A:** ねえ、パメラさんのパーティーはなんようびですか。
B: 日曜日です。

c **A:** えんそくは月曜日ですか。
B: いいえ、火曜日ですよ。

d **A:** カレンダーをみて！金曜日は休みですよ。
B: えっ！金曜日？いいね。

e **A:** なんですか。
B: プレゼントです。水曜日はおかあさんのたんじょうびです。

- **W 75/T4** Starting from the *in* arrow, students follow the sequence of numbers from the first of the month to the 31st.
- **W 77/T8** *Part A*: students survey five members of the class to find out their birthdays and write the dates in kanji. *Part B*: students find out the dates of some important school events and write them in kanji.
- **W 78/T9 5A** Students listen to the tape and fill in the different events that occur during the month of May on the calendar.

Audio script

Nakamura: はい、みなさん、五月のスケジュールです。カレンダーをみてください。四月二十九日はみどりの日です。がっこうは休みです。五月三日と五月五日も休みです。

Ben: え！せんせい、もういちど。

Nakamura: 四月二十九日は休みです。五月三日も休みです。それから、五月五日休みです。

Shingo: 四月二十九日と五月三日と五月五日は休みですか。

Nakamura: はい、そうです。だから、四月二十九日、五月三日。それから、五月五日に、休みと書いてください。ゴールデン・ウィークです。

All: うれしい！やったー。

Nakamura: はい。いいですか。きいてください。五月九日はテストです。

All: へえええ！ひぇええ！やだー！

Nakamura: しずかに！しずかに！五月九日、テストとかいてください。

All: はーい。

Nakamura: 五月十八日はえんそくです。

Kate: わーい、えんそくだいすき。

Nakamura: 五月十八日、えんそくとかいてください。

Kate: 五月十八日、え・ん・そ・く・はい。

Nakamura: 十九日、二十日、二十一日はけんどうのキャンプです。みなさんかいてください。けんどうのキャンプは十九日、二十日、二十一日です。できましたか。

Carla: ねえ、二十四日はエマのたんじょうびね。

Yuusuke: そうだよ。パーティーは二十五日です。

Carla: そうね、五月二十五日、パーティー、はい。カレンダーにかいて。

Nakamura: しずかに。みなさん、五月三十一日にまるをしてください。

Harjono: 五月三十一日はなんのひですか、せんせい？

Takako: えんそくですか。
Nakamura: いいえ。
Ben: テストですか。
Nakamura: いいえ。
Yuki: けんどうのキャンプですか。
Nakamura: いいえ。せんせいのたんじょうびです。

Vocabulary notes

スケジュール	schedule
カレンダーをみてください。	Please look at your calendars.
ゴールデン・ウィーク	Golden Week
うれしい	Great!
…とかいてください。	Please write down …
カレンダーにかいて	Write it on the calendar.
まるをしてください。	Please circle it.
なんのひ	What day …

- W 78/T10 Students write sentences about each *Obentoo* student's birthday.
- W 79/T11 Working in pairs, students take turns in asking and answering questions using なんようびですか。
- *Birthday guess I*: students write their names on cards, which are placed in a box. A sheet is passed around the room and students tick the month of their birthday (without showing anyone else). The number of people with their birthday in each month is then written on the board. One at a time, students come to the front, draw out one of the names and, looking at the chart, ask … さん／くんのたんじょうびは …月ですか。 The person then says はい or いいえ. When the month is guessed correctly, that person comes out the front, and so on.
- *Birthday guess II*: play as for *Birthday guess I* but use dates instead of months.

2 Asking and saying what something is

Warm-up

Revise the hiragana or any of the previously learnt vocabulary using cards and the question なんですか。

Presentation

- Listen and repeat and Listen, look at the sentences and repeat as in earlier units.
- *Noun mnemonics*: students make up a mnemonic for each of the new words, for example, とけい the clock goes tick tock.
- *Grab*: students form groups of 6 or 7 and draw pictures for each of the new words so that each group has at least one picture of each new word. The pictures are then placed face up, with the students in each group sitting closely around them. Someone then asks プレゼントはなんですか。 after which the teacher (or another student) says … です。 As the word is called, the students try to be the first in their group to grab the picture. The student in each group with the most pictures wins. Note that for revision, other words could be added from previous units.

Follow-up

- W 79/T12 8 5A Students listen to the tape and answer the questions in English.

Audio script

SPEAKERS: Shingo's Mother and Tony

S.M.: トニーくん。おたんじょうびおめでとう。カナダからプレゼントがきましたよ。あけてください。
T あっ。しんごくんのおかあさん、ありがとう。
S.M.: なんですか。
T: おとうさんからのプレゼントです。
S.M.: おとうさんからのプレゼントはなんですか。
T: ああ、ほんです。
S.M.: きれいね。
T: そうですね。
S.M.: それはなんですか。
T: おかあさんからのプレゼントです。
S.M.: おおきい。トニーくん、あけて。あけて。なんですか。
T: とけいです。
S.M.: チックタック、チックタック、ボーンボーン。おもしろいですね。
T: そうですね。
S.M.: このプレゼントはなんですか。
T: ああ。いもうとからのプレゼントです。
S.M.: へえー。いもうと？プレゼントはなんですか。
T: ちょっとまって。けしごむです。
S.M.: あら、かわいい。これはわたしからのプレゼントです。
T: えっ。ありがとう。なんですか。
S.M.: あけてください。
T: ねこです。かわいい。ありがとう、おかあさん。

Vocabulary notes

おとうさんからのプレゼント
a present from your father
きれい
nice, pretty
おかあさんからのプレゼント
a present from your mother
いもうとからのプレゼント
a present from your younger sister

- **W 80/T13** Students read the captions, match them to the appropriate picture and then write the date of each person's birthday.
- **W 80/T14** Sudents identify each of the items in the suitcase and write them in the spaces provided.
- *Jigsaw puzzle*: students form pairs and draw two items on a single piece of A4-sized cardboard. They then cut up the sheet of cardboard into 25 randomly shaped pieces and put these in an envelope. The envelopes are placed in a hat and each pair of students chooses one envelope. The pairs form groups of 6 or 8 students and compete by taking out pieces of their 'jigsaw', arranging the pieces correctly and identifying the objects in the shortest period of time.
- *Extension*: the structure なんですか。... です。 could be introduced with other classroom vocabulary. Refer to 'Classroom Instructions' on pages 9–10 for further suggestions. Students will generally accept learning a large number of extension words for listening and speaking if the number of items they need to read and write is kept to manageable levels. This encourages them to extend their vocabulary without putting them under pressure to read and write everything immediately.

3 Asking and saying someone's Chinese birth sign

Warm-up

Discuss with class the system of 十二し。 For your information:
The 十二し is the 12 signs of the oriental zodiac. They originated from China and are related to the date, time of day and the compass directions. Each year is represented by an animal. Each animal has certain qualities and it is said that anyone born under a particular animal sign also has those qualities. 十二し changes each year whereas horoscopes change each month. Pictures of these animals and their Chinese character are often featured on New Year's cards (ねんがじょう). The 12- year cycle is illustrated on page 96 of the Student Book.

ねずみどし	子	charming, creative, energetic, generous, quick-witted
うしどし	丑	stubborn, patient, strong, practical, reliable
とらどし	寅	brave, loyal, sociable, active, enthusiastic, self-confident
うさぎどし	卯	witty, happy, artistic, clever, well-respected
たつどし	辰	ambitious, energetic, healthy, honest, stubborn
へびどし	巳	fashionable, quiet, agile, wise, refined
うまどし	午	strong, friendly, competent, fun-loving, independent
ひつじどし	未	caring, creative, helpful, trusting, artistic
さるどし	申	inventive, curious, versatile, clever, quick
とりどし	酉	hardworking, fussy, determined, confident, stylish
いぬどし	戌	loyal, excitable, watchful, outspoken, protective
いのししどし	亥	trusting, reliable, kind, loyal, intelligent

Presentation

Students look at the pictures, listen to the tape and repeat. After listening and repeating, discuss what was said. Next see if the students can repeat the dialogues themselves. In the pairwork task at the foot of page 96 students should pretend to be other people (famous people, members of their family etc.). Teachers may need to provide some information (year of birth) for this so that students can use the chart on page 96 to work out what どし it is.

Follow-up

- **W 81/T16 8 5A** Students listen to the tape and, using the chart on page 96 of the Student Book, work out the ages of each of the family members.

Audio script

a

A: なにどしですか。

B: ぼくはいのししどしです。おとうさんはいぬどしです。おかあさんはねずみどしです。いもうとはへびどしです。そして、おにいさんはさるどしです。

b

A: なにどしですか。

B: わたしはねずみどしです。おとうとはとらどしです。いもうとはたつどしです。おかあさんはいのししどしです。そして、おとうさんはさるどしです。おばあさんはうまどしです。

- **W 82/T17** Students use the chart to find out the birth signs of some famous people.
- **W 83/T18** Students fill in the required details for each family member and work out their Chinese birth signs. As preparation for this task, you should revise the meanings of とし and どし.

> When marking this task with students, you should ask the full question, for example おとうさんのなまえは、なんさいですか、たんじょうびはいつですか、なにどしですか、and require a full answer from students.

- *Teacher survey:* students form pairs. Each pair is

required to find out a particular teacher's Chinese lunar calendar year. The students then research what qualities are said to be found in people born under each lunar calendar sign and assemble these on a large poster. The names of the teachers who were surveyed are taken out of a hat and the class try to guess their lunar calendar sign by asking ... さんは ... どしですか. The pair of students who questioned that teacher answer はい／いいえ.

べんきょうのベン－カタカナ

S 97 2B

Characters introduced: フ／プ

Warm-up

Who has this one?: write the students' names on the board in katakana. Then call out katakana characters at random. Students have to raise their hand if their name contains that character and put their hands on their heads if it does not. The game could be made competitive by giving students a point for each 'hand up/hands on head' they get correct.

Presentation

- Play the tape while students look at the Student Book. Pause the tape whenever you hear a 'ding'.

Audio script

SPEAKER: Ben

みなさん、おめでとう!

Congratulations! You have now learnt all the hiragana - all 46 of them!

There is only one katakana to learn in this unit, and then some kanji on page 99. One of the kanji looks really complicated, but it's actually easy to remember, and people will think you're pretty clever when you can read it!

Katakana

First some revision. The katakana you already know are printed in black in the chart. Point to each one as I say it, and repeat after me:

イ、ニ、ラ、ア、ハ、オ、ケ、ツ、ヘ、エ、ナ、カ、ト

よくできました。

Now look at the character in the yellow box in the chart. Can you work out how it is pronounced?

It's フ. Say it again after me, フ.

Katakana sound change

Remember *maru* - the small circle added to some characters to change the sound?

You already know that by adding maru, ヘ becomes ペ. Similarly, by adding *maru*, フ becomes プ. Look back to *Donna aji?*. See if you can find a word which starts with プ.

...

Follow-up

- W 72 かきかた *(How to write)*: students practise writing the character in the boxes using the correct stroke order.
- S 97 *Find the odd sound*: students select the odd sound in each group of three presented. *Solutions*: 1c, 2c, 3a, 4b, 5b, 6c.
- Have students look at the photos on page 97 and see if they can work out what each of them says. For your information:

木のぬくもりと自然の味
the warmth of wood and the natural taste
クラフトの里
Craft Village
そば打ち
training centre for practical noodle making
木工体験道場
wood craft
シーフードピザ
seafood pizza
エビ・イカ・アサリ・マッシュルーム・ピーマン・オニオン
prawns, squid, clams mushrooms, capsicum, onions
ピザソース
pizza sauce
イタリアンピザソース
Italian pizza sauce

べんきょうのベン－かんじ

S 98–9 2B

Characters introduced: 日、月、火、水、木、金、土、休

Presentation

- Students listen to the tape and answer the questions on Student Book page 98. Teachers may like to have more follow-up discussion about the origins of kanji and provide students with more examples.

Audio script

SPEAKERS: Emma and Ben

Listen to Ben and Emma talking about the new kanji on pages 98 and 99.

E: OK Ben, let me see if I've got this right. The month at the top, 九月、must be the ninth month - that's September, and the other one, 十月 must be the tenth month, October.

B: はい。

E: And the seven words in kanji across the top under 九月 are obviously the days of the week.

B: はい。

E: The first one is 日曜日、that's Sunday; then 月曜日、火曜日、水曜日、木曜日、金曜日 and 土曜日.

B: はい。

E: So why is the first character of Sunday pronounced にち and the last character pronounced び and yet it's the same character? Oh no - don't tell me there are different ways to pronounce the same kanji?!

B: OK, I won't tell you!

E: Oh, great!

B: Before you start complaining, think of 'o-u-g-h' in English. With an 'r' its rough, with a 'c' its cough, and with a 'd' its dough.

E: I guess so. But why use the same character if you are going to say it differently?

B: Well, originally, Sunday was the day to celebrate the sun, and 日曜日 means 'Day of the Sun'. The first character, 日, refers to the sun.

E: So the last character, び, must also have something to do with the sun. I get it - because the days are determined by the sun.

B: Right.

E: Does that character always have something to do with the sun or the day?

B: Always. The meaning of a kanji never changes.

E: But if a kanji always has the same meaning, how can it have different pronunciations?

B: Well, most kanji originally came from China, and they were given Japanese pronunciations so that Japanese people knew what they were. Then when they need more specialised words to do with, say, the sun, they borrowed the Chinese pronunciation and changed it slightly to sound more Japanese.

E: Not a bad idea. So does every kanji have a Japanese and a Chinese pronunciation?

B: Not every one, but most do. And the different ways of pronouncing the kanji are called 'readings'. The Japanese reading is called くんよみ and the Chinese reading is called おんよみ.

E: OK, let me see if I've got it right. The meaning of a kanji never changes, but its reading might. Most kanji have an おんよみ that's the Chinese reading, and a くんよみ which is the Japanese reading.

B: Well done, and you didn't even get them mixed up.

E: Its easy to remember the difference. Japanese boys are called so-and-so くん so the Japanese reading is くんよみ. Back to days of the week. 日曜日 was the day to celebrate the sun, but what about the others?

B: 月曜日 is Day of the Moon, 火曜日 is Day of Fire, 水曜日 is Day of Water, 木曜日 is Day of Trees, or Wood, to be more precise, 金曜日 is Day of Gold, and 土曜日 is Day of the Earth.

E: So if 月曜日, Monday, is the Day of the Moon, then the first character, 月 must refer to the moon.

B: はい。

E: But it's also used for the word 'month', although it's pronounced slightly differently, がつ. September is 九月, October is 十月. What does the moon have to do with the months?

B: Well, ...

E: I know! The months are determined by the cycles of the moon. What about the writing in the circles next to the calendar - 休み? I can see hiragana み and the kanji next to it looks like it's got 'tree' in it. The other part of the kanji looks a bit like a person leaning against the tree having a break ...

B: Or a very short *holiday*, perhaps?

E: That's it, isn't it? I bet that's the kanji for 'holiday'!

B: You're amazing!

E: Hey, this kanji business is pretty clever really.

Students read page 99 of the Student Book and search for patterns in the kanji compounds. Comment on the shapes of the characters and talk about their origins

- Drill students on new kanji, using flashcards.
- Students in groups of 4–5 play *Kanji grab* using kanji flashcards.

Follow-up

- **W 72–3** かきかた *(How to write)*: students practise writing the characters in the boxes, using the correct stroke order.
- **W 73/T2** Students link the kanji with the corresponding hiragana.
- **W 74 /T3** Students follow each day-of-the-month path to find out what activities the *Obentoo* students are doing on that day. Then they write the day in kanji underneath.
- **W 75–6/T5** Students write the appropriate kanji underneath the hiragana.
- **W 76/T6** Students match the hiragana with the appropriate kanji and picture for each month of the year.
- **W 77/T7** Students write the birthday dates in kanji.
- **W 83/T19** Students fill in the crossword with days and dates in kanji.
- *Pass-it-on*:
  – Students are divided into teams (about 5 students in each) and lined up in front of the board.
  – Teacher shows the back people a card with a character on it.
  – They write it with their finger on the back of the person in front of them.
  – The character is passed down the line until the front person writes it on the board.
  – Points are given to the first team to correctly write the character on the board.

- *Kanji relay*:
  - Students are divided into teams.
  - Teacher calls out a kanji or shows a card bearing that kanji.
  - Then the team must write the character on the board in relay, for example, one stroke per student, with the chalk passing on to the next student.
- *Word Gap*: write each student's name (and/or other katakana words introduced) on a separate card, leaving one or more spaces in each word. Students form teams and line up in front of the board. Show a name (or word) card. The first students in each team compete to see who can write the missing characters first. Points are deducted for incorrect stroke order.
- *It's all done with mirrors*: students/teams compete to try to read katakana words on the board without looking at the words directly, but via a mirror!

> You will notice that the kanji 曜 (as in 日曜日) is included on pages Student Book 98-9. It is intended that this kanji be learnt for recognition only and not for writing, but some students particularly interested in kanji may like to practise writing it. The stroke order is as follows:

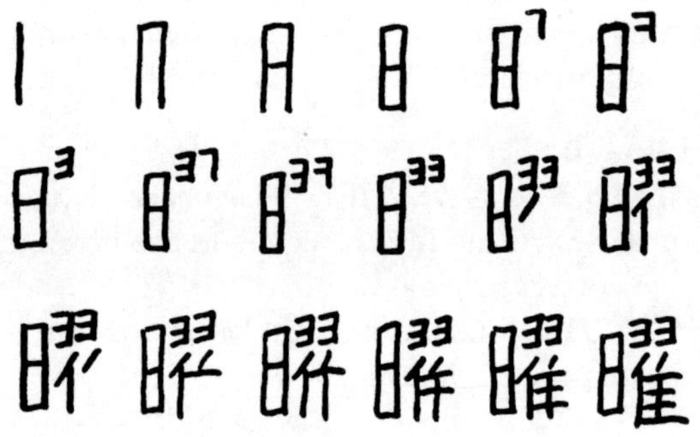

ごはんとおかず

Ⓢ 100–1

Warm-up

Concentration: make small cards (in hiragana/katakana) for each of the words introduced in the unit. Make another set of cards on which one of the characters from each new word is written. All cards are turned face down and students turn over two at a time and try to find matching pairs. If they choose a matching pair, they have another turn. The students compete to see who can collect the most cards.

Presentation

まる／ばつ *(Noughts and crosses)*: word cards are placed in a hat. The class is divided into two teams and one person from each team comes to the front. The representative of Team A starts by taking out two word cards and trying to make a question. If s/he can make a question out of the words, that person puts the question to the representative of Team B. If the person being questioned answers correctly, s/he can make a selection on the まる／ばつ (noughts and crosses) board. If s/he doesn't answer correctly, the questioner can make the selection. After each round, of まる／ばつ, two more players from each team come to the front.

Follow-up

- *Monster bingo*: students draw up a bingo card with three columns headed 月s, 日s and よう日s. They then put five (three or four for a shorter game) words in each column. The teacher (or a designated student) calls out words and students cross them off as they hear them. Minor prizes are given to the first student to complete a whole category. The grand winner is the person who completes the whole card first.
- *Famous people*: collect magazine cut-outs of famous people and find out in which year they were born. Students then write their Chinese lunar calendar year on a caption.
- *My birthday present book*: students write each of their birthdays in kanji on a separate sheet and draw pictures of presents they remember receiving for each birthday. They show the pictures to the class and say as many of the objects as they can in Japanese. (This could be used as an extension activity.)
- Ⓑ **7.1** *More about asking the date*: use this BLM to introduce phrases for asking about dates and から and まで.

テーブルマナー

Ⓢ 102–4

Presentation

- *What's the weather like?*: students look at the photographs and discuss what they observe about the seasons represented. Ask them to suggest how the customs in each picture may have originated.
- *Research and tell*: students form pairs and research one (or more) of the customs or celebrations depicted in each photograph. They then report back to the class by giving a 1–2 minute talk about what they found.

Follow-up

Today/This week in Japan: students contribute information to the weekly/daily school newsletter/bulletin about particular festivals/celebrations which are occurring at that time in Japan.

> Various reference books can be used to obtain further information about festivals and holidays throughout Japan:
>
> - *Illustrated Festivals of Japan* (Japan Travel Bureau, 1987).
> - M. Watanabe and G. Mackereth, *Seasons and Festivals in Japan* (Heinemann, 1992).

おはし

Ⓢ 105

Presentation

- *Silent reading*: students read 'Carla's Guide to Avoiding Embarrassment' in the Student Book and note whether they agree or disagree with the information in each panel.
- *Panels of experts:* students form teams, taking the part of someone (like the *Obentoo* students) who is living in Japan and learning Japanese at a Japanese school. The rest of the class question them about whether they agree or disagree with the points Carla made. The teams take it in turns to answer at the front of the class. To give the task a competitive edge, the class could vote on the best answers.

Follow-up

- じこしょうかい *(Self-introduction)*: students prepare and deliver a short talk about themselves in Japanese and, afterwards, discuss whether they still agree with the points Carla made.
- *Our 'dos and don'ts'*: after giving their talks, students make their own list of 'dos and don'ts' on a poster which is put on the wall.

おしょうゆ

Ⓢ 106 Ⓣ 2B

Presentation

Students listen to the tape and repeat the new expressions.

Follow up

- *How many times?*: students revisit the *Itadakimasu* manga whilst listening to the tape. As they listen, they count how many times each expression is used.
- *Mime*: students form small groups and prepare a simple Japanese dialogue which they mime in front of the class. They should use at least two of the expressions in *Oshooyu*. The rest of the class have to work out what the dialogue is about.
- ... ちゃんです。: students practise introducing the people in their family (from a picture or photo) using the ... ちゃんです。 form.

おかし

Ⓢ 106–7

Song

Sing the song to the tune of *Bibbity Bobbity Boo* (Disney).

Craft activities

- こんぎしのお面 *(Papier mâché masks)*: You will need: a balloon, newspaper, glue, paper masking tape and paint.
  You can make てんぐ (long-nosed goblin) masks or おに (devil) masks. Blow up the balloon, cover half of it with papier mâché, allow it to dry and remove the balloon. The nose of the てんぐ and the horns of the おに are made by twisting additional sheets of newspaper into shape and attaching them with masking tape. Cover the papier mâché with one layer of masking tape to give it a smooth and clean surface to paint it red.
- 達磨 (だるま) *Daruma dolls*
  You will need: a small milk carton or yoghurt container, masking tape, newspaper, paint, and a real だるま to use as a pattern. Cut the top off the container. Fill the container with newspaper and mould it into the だるま shape. Cover it with layers of tape until it is solid. Use extra tape to make the shape of the face. Paint the face and then paint the remainder of the doll red.
- ぼんおどり *(Summer Festival folk dance)*: if you have access to a Japanese person ask her or him to teach you or your students a ぼんおどり. You could dress your female students in ゆかた (summer kimono) and your male students in はっぴ (happi coats) and はちまき (headbands)
- Organise your own 日本語まつり *(Japanese festival)* at your school. A few suggestions:
  - Have a ぼんおどり。
  - Cook and sell Japanese food (やきとり is easy and popular).
  - Prepare and sell *obentoo* lunches to teachers.
  - Have displays of students' work.
  - Local martial arts clubs may be available to do displays.
  - Have an origami-a-thon. (Use them later to decorate classrooms or send origami cranes to Hiroshima for Peace Day on 6 August.)
  - Calligraphy demonstrations and displays.
  - Computer links to other schools teaching Japanese.
  - Decorative vegetable/fruit cutting (this is illustrated in many Japanese cookbooks).

Putting it all together

- **Ⓑ 7.2** カレンダー: enlarge the calendar pages, paste them onto cardboard and cover them with clear Contact. With a whiteboard marker, record the birthdays of the *Obentoo* students, the festivals and public holidays in Japan (see Student Book pages 102–4), and the birthdays of all the students in the class and the teacher. Also record the dates of tests, the athletics carnival, the school fete and other important events. Put it up on your classroom wall and add to it whenever necessary.
- **Ⓑ 7.3** おべんとうゲーム: divide the class into teams of 3–4 people. Have four teams playing at each board, according to the instructions below.
  Preparing the board:
  - Enlarge the game-board to A3 size and colour the squares the colours indicated (use the colours in the Student Book as a guide). Cover the game-board in clear Contact to protect it.

- Use the prepared flashcards or make your own cards and paste them on coloured cardboard according to the type of question (the colours correspond to the coloured bands indicating the sections in the *Obentoo* Student Book: red: いただきます, green: ごはんとおかず, pink: べんきょうのベン, blue: テーブルマナー, purple: おしょうゆ.)
- Place piles of cards on the squares indicated around the *obentoo*.
- Suggestions for questions are given below. If using cards, you should have the answer on the card as well so that students can check each other. (Of course, students will have to be asked the question by a member of another team.) If you don't have time to put the questions onto cards, you can simply have the questions on a sheet under the colour heading and students can ask them from the list.

Some suggestions for game-card questions:

RED
Answer truthfully in Japanese:
こどものひはいつですか。
おたんじょうびはいつですか。
クリスマスのひはいつですか。
ケイトさんのたんじょうびはいつですか。
休みはいつですか。
三月十日はなんようびですか。
二月十一日はなんようびですか。
六月一日はなんようびですか。
九月八日はなんようびですか。
十一月三十日はなんようびですか。
たなばたはいつですか。
ちえこさんのたんじょうびはいつですか。
プレゼントはなんですか。
なにどしですか。
おかあさんはなにどしですか。

GREEN
Translate into English:
十二月十日です。
たなばたは四月七日です。
九月二日は水曜日です。
プレゼントはものさしです。
おねえさんはいぬどしです。

Give the Japanese word for:
6th
14th
31st
5th
9th
Thursday
October
pencil
Year of the Snake
holiday

PINK
Read the following characters:
金曜日
休み
二日
たんじょう日
こどもの日
火曜日
十月四日
三月八日

Write the following in kanji:
すいようび
にがつはつか
にじゅうさんにち
にちようび

BLUE
What is the date of ひなまつり?
When is the rainy season?
What is one thing Japanese people do at New Year?
What is 七・五・三?
When is あきまつり?
When is ぶんかのひ?

PURPLE
What would you say if someone told you some interesting information?
How would you tell someone to stop it!
If something is すてき is it really good, really bad or really scary?
When do you use the word おにいちゃん?
What is the difference between きょうは十一月十七日です。and きょうは十一月十七日ですね。?

Rules of the game:

- The idea of the game is to move from いただきます to ごちそうさま by answering questions from different categories: red: language in context (answering a question appropriately in Japanese), green: structure of language (filling in a missing word/translation into English), pink: script (reading a character/writing a character/reading a sentence aloud), blue: socio-cultural question (answering a question about Japanese people or lifestyle), purple: expressions from *Oshooyu* (giving an appropriate expression in response to a situation/giving and expression in Japanese/English).
- The game can be played by individuals or teams. A maximum of four players (teams) can play at once. Two players start at the top right and finish at the bottom left, and two players start at the top left and finish at the bottom right. Players can only move horizontally or vertically one square at a time. On each square they must answer a question from the pile of cards indicated by the colour. A member of another team asks the question and checks the answer, which is also written on the card.
- If the answer is correct, on their next turn, players can move to the next square. If the answer is

incorrect, they must remain on that square and answer another question from that colour at their next turn. No two players can land on the same square at the same time. The winner is the first player (team) to reach ごちそうさま。

- Ⓦ **81/T15** Pairs of students perform the guided role-play. Students could also make up their own role-plays using the same situation but with different details. These could then be performed in front of the class. You may need to give further explanation of プレゼントをありがとう. You may wish to introduce ほんをありがとう、えんぴつをありがとう、とけいをありがとう、etc. and also ... をありがとうございました.
- かぞくの十二し *(My family's Chinese birth signs)*:
  - Draw your family tree.
  - Under the pictures of your family members, write their names in English, and their birthdays and their Chinese lunar calendar signs in Japanese.
  - Let your partner look at the picture for two minutes.
  - See how many details your partner can then tell you about your family without looking at your picture.
  - Give your partner one point for each correct detail and two points for a correct birthday.
  - When your partner has finished, change over.
- きょうは...: set up a きょうは... segment in your classroom where one student is nominated each lesson to say what the date is in Japanese and write it in kanji in the top right-hand corner of the board. Encourage students to put the date at the top of every page in their notebooks and at the top of each task or test. Marks can be allocated for this.
- なん月ですか。Make a collection of up to 12 photos or pictures of school events or special occasions (an old school magazine can be used). Hold up the pictures one at a time and say the month when the event took place. When students have finished talking about each picture, shuffle the pile and see how quickly they can recall the month for each one.
- *Picture diary*: students draw simple pictures of the school events and these are placed in a file (for safekeeping). A large poster is then drawn for each month (or week) which is placed on the pin-up board. The teacher takes out the event pictures and asks ... はいつですか。The class reply ... 日 or ... 曜日 as appropriate. The pictures are then put on the calendar.
- Ⓢ **107** *Extra reading task*: students look at the photo and read the caption. You may like to make up questions for students to answer, e.g.
  1. When is Sanae's birthday?
  2. What presents does she receive?
  3. How old is she now?
  4. How do you say 'Happy birthday' in Japanese?
- Ⓑ **7.4** *Desk calendar notes*: students use the patterns *(event)* はいつですか。and *(event)* は...がつ...にちです。to find out the dates of the events from their partner to complete the desk calendar notes.

ごちそうさま

Ⓢ **107**

- Ⓦ **84** *Obentoo quiz*. Students can check how well they have learnt the unit by trying the *Obentoo quiz* themselves or teachers can use it as an assessment task.
- *And the question is...*: instead of preparing questions which are used in a class quiz, students prepare answers and the rest of the class have to work out the question.
- *Individual progress cards*: write the items listed in *Gochisoosama* onto the photocopiable student progress card on page 138 of the *Moshi Moshi Teacher's Handbook*. You may wish to add other items, for example other language points, cultural understandings, completion of homework or assignment tasks.

Reference to *Yoroshiku National Curriculum Guidelines for Japanese (Moshi Moshi)*

The following is a list of the suggested language exponents presented in *Moshi Moshi* Module 2 かぞくとともだち *(Family and friends)* which have been introduced in Unit 7 of *Obentoo*. In some cases, the example has been changed to correspond to the form introduced in *Obentoo*. Appropriate activities from *Moshi Moshi* are suggested below.

Language exponents

- Month of birth
  (　) さんのたんじょうびはなん月ですか。
  (三) 月です。
  (わたし) のたんじょうびは (三) 月です。
- Chinese birth sign
  (　) はなにどしですか。
  (... び) どしです。
- Asking about and identifying objects
  なんですか。
  (ほん) です。
- Expressing surprise
  ああ、そうですか。
- Exclaiming
  すてき！

- Congratulating
  (おたんじょうび) おめでとう
  おめでとうございます。

Module 4 Free Time

Asking and giving information about the day:
(きょう) はなんようびですか。
(日よう日) です。

Module 6 The Four Seasons

- Asking and giving information about the date:
  (きょう) はなん日ですか。
  (十一月二十三日) です。
  (こどものひ) はいつですか。
  (五月五日) です。
  (なつやすみ) はいつからいつまでですか。
  (十二月十四日) から (一月三十一日) までです。

Suggested activities from *Moshi Moshi*

十二し Teacher Resources page 14, Student Book page 12
じこしょうかい Teacher Resources page 14, Student Book page 13
たんじょうびカード Teacher Resources pages 14 and 20.

Unit 8

Overview

Unit objectives

Students will be able to:

- ask someone what they eat and drink for breakfast, lunch and dinner, and respond when asked
- talk about at least 20 foods and 6 drinks
- ask about and express likes and dislikes
- ask someone if or how often they eat or drink something and respond when asked
- read and write 10 more katakana
- recognise 9 more katakana sound changes
- read and write short sentences related to the topics covered
- describe at least 10 traditional Japanese dishes
- discuss the art of Japanese calligraphy
- understand the importance of stroke order and balance in Japanese writing

Functions and language exponents

1 Asking and saying what you eat and drink
(エマさん)あさごはんになにをたべますか。
(コーンフレーク)をたべます。
なにをのみますか。
(コーヒー)をのみます。
ひるごはんになにをたべますか。
(チキン)をたべます。

2 Asking about and expressing likes and dislikes
(ケイトさん)、(ピザ)がすきですか。
はい、だいすきです。
はい、すきです。
いいえ、あまり…。
くだものがすきです。

3 Asking and saying if or how often you eat or drink something
(ベンくん)、(ケーキをたべ)ますか。
はい、まいにちたべます。
はい、よくたべます。
はい、ときどきたべます。
いいえ、ぜんぜんたべません。

Key vocabulary and expressions

あさごはんに
ひるごはんに
ばんごはんに
なにをたべますか。
なにをのみますか。
おべんとう
さかな
クーンフレーク
たまご
サンドイッチ
ごはん
ピザ
ハンバーガー
トースト
ミルク
コーヒー
…をたべます。
…をのみます。
スパゲッティ
くだもの
ソーセージ
サラダ
オレンジ・ジュース
チーズ
アイスクリーム

チョコレート
チキン
…がすきですか。
はい、すきです。
はい、だいすきです。
いいえ、あまり…。
カレーライス
にく
ケーキ
おちゃ
こうちゃ
コーラ

…をたべますか。
…をのみますか。

まいにち
よく
ときどき
…たべます。
…のみます。

ぜんぜん
…たべません。
…のみません。

Script

Students are expected to be able to read and write the key characters and recognise the associated words.

Key characters	*Associated words*
キ	ケーキ
コ	コーヒー、コーンフレーク
サ	サンドイッチ
シ、ジ	ジュース
ス	スパゲッティ
ソ	ソーセージ
チ	チーズ
ヒ、ピ	コーヒー、ピザ
ミ	ミルク
レ	カレー

Script understandings

- Learning about more がいらいご, for example those used in menus
- More examples of how ぼう (ー) is used to lengthen sounds in katakana words
- Introducing *nigori* sound changes (katakana)

カ、ガ	ス、ズ
ケ、ゲ	ト、ド
サ、ザ	ハ、バ、パ
シ、ジ	ヒ、ピ
シュ、ジュ	

Learning how to learn

Using examples from the art of calligraphy, attention is given to balance, stroke order, different types of brush strokes and leaving an appropriate amount of space between strokes.

Cultural elements

すきなたべもの。おとうさんとおかあさんがすきなもの。
ぼくがすきなもの。
おじいさんとおばあさんがすきなもの。

A focus on Japanese traditional foods and drinks and the changing tastes of the Japanese.

Extra foods/drinks introduced:

すきやき	みそしる
てんぷら	すし
てりやきチキン	さけ
えびフライ	おこのみやき
ハンバーグ	おかし
とうふ	やきざかな
さしみ	そうめん
つけもの	

Other incidental language introduced

おいしそう！
おいしい！
うーん、おいしいです。
ハジョーノくんのおべんとうをみて！
わたしきらいです。
サラダ？

Extension material

More about あまり
あまりすきじゃありません。
あまりたべません。
あまりのみません。

Need some extra words or expressions? Ask your teacher!

ハムエッグ	ham and egg
なっとう	fermented soybean (sometimes eaten on rice for breakfast)
パン	bread
ラーメン	Chinese noodle soup
ライス	rice served on a Western plate
おにぎり	riceballs
ステーキ	steak
ポーク	pork
やきとり	chicken on skewers
しゃぶしゃぶ	meat and vegetable dish cooked in the middle of the table

(Also see the menu on pages 4–5 of the Student Book.)

Teaching suggestions

The following suggestions are provided as a guide to lesson planning and should be adapted to suit your teaching style and the learning styles of your students. These tasks are specific to this unit. For more information on general strategies for each section, refer to *Using Obentoo* on pages 3–8.

いただきます

108–10 2B

Warm-up

Japanese food–brainstorm: ask students to brainstorm Japanese foods and drinks they know and write these on the board. Tick the ones the students have tried.

Presentation

- *Listen and guess*: without showing students their books (or the OHTs), play the tape of the cartoon story and ask the students to make a note of any foods (or drinks) they recognise. Ask them to guess some of the other food/drink items which they may have remembered but not completely understood. Then ask the students if they picked up any other information from the story, just by listening. Make a note of their suggestions on the board. Finally, repeat the task, showing students the OHTs of the cartoon without the text.
- *Concept attainment*– すき、だいすき、あまり、きらい: draw the pictures below on the board:

  – Show the class a flashcard or picture, for example of スパゲッティ、and ask the question スパゲッティがすきですか。
  – Then point to the first face and answer はい、すきです。

  Repeat using other examples from the cartoon, for example:
  ソーセージがすきですか。いいえ、あまり。
  くだものは？わたしはくだものがだいすきです。
  スパゲッティがすきですか。わたしきらいです。

  The aim is to see if students can identify the concepts by asking questions to which you answer yes or no. When this has been completed, say the words for the students while they listen and repeat. Make this brief, as the words and structures will get plenty of practice later in the unit.
- *Using the OHTs*: play the tape through while students look at the OHTs. As they listen, get them to take notes about which people like (and don't like) which foods and drinks. Ask them to write notes which might explain the other expressions introduced in the story, for example ... をたべますか。... をのみますか。Discuss the gist of the story frame by frame, noting students' guesses on the board.

Follow-up

- **110** Students answer the questions in English.
- *Word recall*: each student cuts out pictures of 10 foods and drinks from magazines and arranges them in a collage. The class is divided into teams. One team starts by showing the other team one of the collages for 15 seconds (or more/less as appropriate). Someone from the opposite team then tries to remember as many of the food/drink words as possible. Points are awarded for correctly identifying each word.

どんなあじ？

111–14 2B

1 Asking and saying what you eat and drink

Warm-up

- Replay *Itadakimasu* and explore the page as in earlier units.
- Present the new vocabulary for foods and drinks

using picture flashcards. The majority of words are 外来語 so have students guess the meaning of each word. Separate the words written in hiragana and drill them. It is recommended that all of the vocabulary for the unit be taught at this point as they can all be used with each *Donna aji*.

- *Food mnemonics*: students make up mnemonics for each of the new food and drink words, for example, たまご = eggs make my tum go funny. (The mnemonic only needs to be loosely connected with the sound of the target word.)
- '*Stand up/sit down*': students play '*Stand up/sit down*' using the food and drink vocabulary introduced above.

Presentation

- Listen and repeat
- Listen, read and repeat.
- Pairwork practice (page 112).

Follow up

- *ESP game*: one student thinks of a sentence, saying what s/he eats or drinks, and other students try to guess the sentence by asking the questions ... をたべますか。 or ... をのみますか。 The student answers いいえ、... をたべません／のみません。 or はい、... をたべます／のみます。
  Variation: all vocabulary items which will fit into a particular sentence pattern are put in a box. The student chooses a word from the box and others guess the word using the sentence pattern.
- Ⓦ **87/T2** Students unjumble the words and rewrite them in Japanese. Then they write the English equivalent.
- Ⓦ **89/T5** Students read and circle the odd word out.
- Ⓦ **90/T6** Ⓒ **5A** Students listen to the conversation between Naoko and her family and write down what everyone decides to eat and drink.

Audio script

SPEAKERS: Naoko, Mother, Father, Takashi

N: おいしそう！
M: なにをたべますか。
N: ハンバーガーをたべます。おかあさんは？
M: うーん。わたしはサラダをたべます。
N: サラダ！うん、おいしそう！あのー、わたしはハンバーガーをたべません。サラダをたべます。
F: なおことおかあさんはサラダをたべますね。
N: はい、そうです。おとうさんはなにをたべますか。
F: カレーライスをたべます。
N: へー、カレーライスもおいしそう!
F: うん。おいしいよ。
N: うん、あのー、わたしはサラダをたべません。カレーライスをたべます。
F: なおこちゃんはカレーライス？
N: はい、そうです。カレーライスをたべます。
F: たかしくん、なにをたべますか。
T: ぼくは、えーと、ぼくはピザをたべます。おいしそう。
F: あっ、ほんとう！わたしもピザをたべます。カレーライスをたべません。なおこちゃん！なにをたべますか。
N: ピザです。ピザをたべます。
F: じゃ、おかあさんはサラダをたべますね。
M: はい。
F: たかしくんはピザをたべますね。
T: はい。
F: おとうさんはカレーライスをたべます。そして、なおこちゃんはピザをたべますね。
N: はい、ピザをたべます。おとうさん、のみものは？
F: みずですよ。みんなみずをのみます。
F&T: みず？まずい！！きらい！！
F: だめ！

Vocabulary notes

おいしそう！	Looks good!
あっ、ほんとう！	Oh, that's true!
みず	water
まずい！！	Yuk!
だめ！	Stop that!

- Ⓦ **90/T7** Students find a partner and ask each other about their eating habits. See the instructions in the Workbook. *Variation*: you may wish to add any other foods you know to the pyramid, including more 外来語 words or some Japanese foods from pages 118–19 of the Student Book. You may also like to compile the individual results for an overall class survey. The results could be summarised in the school newsletter.
- Ⓦ **91/T8** Students carry out the pairwork, reading/speaking/listening task described in the Workbook.
- Ⓦ **92/T9** Students look at the pictures and write a description of what each of the *Obentoo* students like to eat.
- *Meal manager*: to prepare, make sets of the picture cards for the foods and drinks in this unit (three per group). The class is divided into groups of four. The three sets of cards are placed face down and scattered on the table. Students take turns in turning over three cards at a time and trying to

make a sentence saying what they have for a particular meal (indicated by the pictures turned up), for example あさごはんにコーンフレークとくだものをたべます。そして、ミルクをのみます。Only foods/drinks which are considered appropriate for a particular meal can be included in the sentence. (This is determined by the other players.) Any cards included in the sentence are picked up by the player; any not included must be returned face down. The game continues until all of the cards have been picked up. The winner is the player with the most cards at the end of the game. (This task is useful for practising と and そして。)

2 Asking about and expressing likes and dislikes

Warm-up

- *More food and drink mnemonics*: students make up additional mnemonics for each of the new food and drink words.
- *Game—じゃん・けん vocab*: choose seven or eight of the words in this unit which students may be having trouble remembering. Place picture cards face up in a line on the floor between two teams of about 6 students. Starting from each end of the row of cards, the first player in each team jumps over the cards one by one, saying the Japanese word for each. When the two players meet in the middle they do じゃん・けん (refer page 40). The winner keeps going along the line. The loser goes to the end of the team and the next player starts again. When one player gets to the end of the line, s/he must again win a toss (じゃん・けん・ポン) to win the game.

Presentation

- Listen to the tape and repeat. Then listen, read and repeat.
- As a variation on the pairwork task, have students go around the room and ask as many students as they can about the foods and drinks they like or dislike.

Follow-up

- **W 93/T10** Students listen to the tape and list each food and drink mentioned in the appropriate column in English.

Audio script

SPEAKERS: Interviewer (I), Students (P1–4)

a

I: コーヒーがすきですか。
P1: いいえ、あんまり。
I: こうちゃがすきですか。
P1: はい、すきです。
I: おちゃがすきですか。
P1: はい、おちゃがだいすきです。
I: オレンジジュースがすきですか。
P1: はい、すきです。
I: ミルクがすきですか。
P1: いいえ、あんまり。

b

I: スパゲッティがすきですか。
P2: はい、すきです。
I: ハンバーガーがすきですか。
P2: はい、すきです。
I: カレーライスがすきですか。
P2: いいえ、あんまり。
I: ソーセージがすきですか。
P2: はい、すきです。

c

I: チーズがすきですか。
P3: はい、すきです。
I: くだものがすきですか。
P3: はい、だいすきです。
I: サラダがすきですか。
P3: いいえ、あんまり。
I: アイスクリームがすきですか。
P3: はい、だいすきです。
I: ごはんがすきですか。
P3: いいえ、あんまり。

d

I: チョコレートがすきですか。
P4: はい、だいすきです。
I: ケーキがすきですか。
P4: いいえ、あまり。
I: ピザがすきですか。
P4: いいえ、あんまり。
I: サンドイッチがすきですか。
P4: はい、すきです。

- **W 94/T11** Students survey five students in the class to find out their likes and dislikes. They record their responses on the graph.
- **W 96/T13** Students answer the questions in Japanese according to the picture clues.
- *'Stand up/stand up' (a variation of 'stand up/sit down')*: thirteen students are chosen to come to the front to play. Students take the parts of the *Obentoo* students. They write down three foods or drinks from a list on the board: one should be something they like, another something they don't like, and the third something they love. The teacher calls out pairs of sentences, for example, くだものがすきですか。はい、すきです。or コーヒーがすきですか。はい、だいすきです。

or ケーキがすきですか。いいえ、あんまり…。 If the statement is true, they stand up. If it is not true (i.e. it is not one of their chosen words), they sit down. The aim is for the rest of the class to guess which foods (or drinks) each '*Obentoo* student' loves, likes and dislikes. As in 'stand up/sit down', students guessing should not write anything down. To prevent the game lasting too long, it is a good idea to limit the number of vocabulary items for this task.

3 Asking and saying if or how often you eat or drink something

Warm-up

'Stand up/sit down' (a variation) – more foods and drinks: all the students except one (who is the first 'guesser') choose two words from a list of new vocabulary. The teacher reads out the words in random order and the students stand when their first word is called and sit when they hear their second word called out. When the 'guesser' is able to pick someone's two words, s/he calls out ちょっとまって！('just a moment!') and then identifies the words. If correct, that student joins the 'guessers'. 'Guessers' get two points for each word they identify correctly.

Presentation

- Listen to the tape and repeat. Then listen, read and repeat.
- Students find a partner and do the pairwork task at the foot of page 114.

Follow-up

- *Sentence grab*: students collect cut-outs from magazines, for example, advertisements depicting people having a meal or snack, and stick them on A4 sized pieces of cardboard. If single pictures do not convey much information, two or three pictures can be combined to form a collage. (Ideally, each picture will depict at least four or five foods and/or drinks.) The picture cards are placed in a pile face-down on the floor. The teacher (or a student) writes a sentence about each of the foods and drinks in each picture. It is best not to duplicate sentences. The sentences are then cut out and placed face-up on the floor. The class is divided into four teams who sit around the cards. The first person from one team turns over a food/drink picture and the players from each team try to grab the sentences which suit that picture. Teams get a point for each sentence card they grab. The teams take it in turns to turn over the picture cards.
- **W 97/T14** *Part A–listening task*: students listen to the interview and record the information on the chart.

Audio script

SPEAKERS: Interviewer (I), All students (All), Students (P1–10)

I: みなさん、こんにちは。*Kidz Times* magazine のやまだですけど。みなさん、あさごはんをたべますか。えっ、たべません？だめですよ！あさごはんはだいじなものですよ！じゃ、みなさんにきいてみましょう！すみません。

All: はい。

I: *Kidz Times* magazine のやまだですけど。

All: あっ、こんにちは、こんにちは、こんにちは。

I: こんにちは。みなさん、あさごはんをたべますか。

All: はい、はい、たべます。

I: じゃ、あさごはんになにをたべますか。

P1: わたしはまいにちコーンフレークをたべます。そして、コーヒーをのみます。

I: へー、まいにちですか。コーンフレークですか。

P1: はい。

P2: ぼくはトーストをたべます。ときどきたまごもたべます。そして、ミルクをのみます。

I: はい、トースト、ときどきたまご。そして、ミルクですね。

P3: ぼくもまいにちたまごとトーストをたべます。そして、こうちゃをのみます。

I: そうですか。まいにちたまご、トースト、こうちゃですね。

P4: わたしはくだものをたべます。そして、オレンジジュースをのみます。

I: はい、くだものとオレンジジュースですね。はい、あさごはんになにをたべますか。

P5: わたしですか。あっ、あのー、わたしはあさごはんをたべません。

I: あっ、だめですね。あさごはんをたべませんか。

P5: ええ、

I: コーヒーは？

P5: うん、ときどきコーヒーをのみます。

I: ああ、そうですか。ときどきコーヒーですね。みなさん、ありがとうございました。

I: すみません、*Kidz Times* magazine のやまだですけど。

All: へー！*Kidz Times* magazine ですか。

I: みなさん、あさごはんになにをたべますか。

P6: はい、はい、わたしはまいにち、トーストとチーズをたべます。そして、ミルクをのみます。

I: はい、まいにち、トーストとチーズ。そして、ミルクですね。

P7: ぼくはよくたまごとソーセージをたべます。そして、トーストもたべます。ときどきコーンフレークもたべます。まいにち、ジュースをのみます。

I: はい、たまごとソーセージとトーストですね。それから、ときどきコーンフレークまいにちジュースですね。きみは？

P8: わたしはコーンフレークとくだものをたべます。そして、コーヒーをのみます。

I: そうですか。いいですね。コーンフレークとくだものとコーヒーですね。

P9: ぼくはトーストをたべます。そして、こうちゃをのみます。

P10: ぼくもトーストをたべます。こうちゃをのみます。

I: はい、どうもありがとう。みなさん、あさごはんになにをたべますか。じゃまた。さようなら。

Vocabulary notes

Kidz Times magazine のやまだです。
Yamada from the *Kidz Times* magazine

だめですよ。	That's no good.
だいじなもの	important thing

みなさんにきいてみましょう。
Let's ask everyone.

すみません	excuse me
もちろん	of course
わたしですか。	You mean me?
きみ	you (used by boys)
きみは？	How about you?

Part B–speaking task: students conduct their own survey and record the results on the chart.

- **W 97–8/T15 8 5A** Students listen to the tape and fill in the information regarding breakfast, lunch and dinner on the charts.

Audio script

SPEAKERS: Doctor (D), Mr Sato (S)

D: ああ、さとうさん、こんにちは。
S: せんせい、こんにちは。
D: どうぞ、すわってください。
S: どうもありがとう。
D: えーと、さとうさん、まいにちなにをたべますか。
S: うーん、そうですねー。
D: さとうさん、まいにち、あさごはんをたべますか。
S: まいにちですか。うーん、ときどきたべません。
D: ああ、そうですか。じゃ、あさごはんになにをたべますか。
S: うーん。
D: トーストをたべますか。
S: はい、ときどきたべます。
D: コーンフレークをたべますか。
S: いいえ、ぜんぜんたべません。
D: ああ、コーンフレーク... ぜんぜん、たべません。はい。たまごをたべますか。
S: いいえ、ぜんぜんたべません。
D: チーズをたべますか。
S: はい、ときどきたべます。
D: ソーセージをたべますか。
S: はい、ときどき。
D: くだものをたべますか。
S: いいえ、ぜんぜんたべません。
D: くだもの ... ぜんぜんたべません。はい。じゃ、あさごはんになにをのみますか。こうちゃをのみますか。
S: はい、ときどきこうちゃをのみます。
D: コーヒーをのみますか。
S: はい、よくコーヒーをのみます。
D: コーヒーをのもます。はい。ミルクをのみますか。
S: いいえ、ぜんぜんのみません。
D: オレンジジュースをのみますか。
S: いいえ、ぜんぜんのみません。
D: じゃ、そのほかに、なにをたべますか。
S: よくピザをたべます。
D: ピザですか。あさごはんに！
S: はい、ピザをたべます。
D: ああ、そうですか。こんどはひるごはんです。さとうさんはひるごはんをたべますか。
S: はい、まいにちひるごはんをたべます。
D: サンドイッチをたべますか。
S: いいえ、ぜんぜんたべません。
D: おべんとうをたべますか。
S: いいえ、ぜんぜんたべません。
D: ハンバーガーをたべますか。
S: はい、よくたべます。
D: ハンバーガーをたべます。はい。ピザをたべますか。
S: はい、もちろん、ピザがだいすきです。よくピザをたべます。
D: サラダをたべますか。
S: いいえ、ぜんぜんたべません。
D: ああ、サラダぜんぜんたべません。はい。カレーライスをたべますか。
S: はい。ときどきたべます。
D: チーズをたべますか。
S: いいえ、ぜんぜんたべません。
D: ケーキをたべますか。
S: はい、よくたべます。

D: じゃ、なにをのみますか。オレンジジュースをのみますか。

S: いいえ、ぜんぜんのみません。

D: ミルクをのみますか。

S: はい、ときどきチョコレートミルクをのみます。

D: コーラをのみますか。

S: はい、よくのみます。

D: あ、コーラをよくのみます。はい。コーヒーをのみますか。

S: はい、ときどきのみます。

D: そのほかになにをたべますか。

S: ときどきスパゲッティをたべます。

D: ああ、そうですか。じゃ、さとうさん、こんどはばんごはんです。

S: はい。

D: ばんごはんをたべますか。

S: はい、まいにちばんごはんをたべます。

D: ばんごはんになにをたべますか。にくをたべますか。

S: はい。まいにち、にくをたべます。

D: まいにち、にくをたべます。はい。チキンをたべますか。

S: はい、ときどきたべます。

D: サラダをたべますか。

S: いいえ、ぜんぜんたべません。

D: ソーセージをたべますか。

S: はい、ときどきたべます。

D: くだものをたべますか。

S: いいえ、ぜんぜんたべません。

D: あ、くだものをぜんぜんたべません。はい。スパゲッティをたべますか。

S: はい、ときどきたべます。

D: じゃ、のみものは？なにをのみますか。ジュースをのみますか。

S: はい、よくジュースをのみます。

D: コーヒーをのみますか。

S: はい、まいにちコーヒーをのみます。

D: こうちゃをのみますか。

S: いいえ、ぜんぜんのみません。

D: おちゃをのみますか。

S: はい、ときどきのみます。

D: そのほかになにをたべますか。

S: まいにち、チョコレートアイスクリームをたべます。

D: まいにちですか。

S: はい。

D: チョコレートアイスクリームですか。

S: はい。

D: はい、どうもありがとう。

Vocabulary note

そのほかに apart from that

- **W 98–9/T16** Students read the descriptions and match them to the appropriate picture.
- **W 99–100/T17** Students answer questions about themselves in Japanese.

べんきょうのベン―カタカナ

S 115 C 2B

Characters introduced: キ、コ、サ、シ、ス、ソ、チ、ヒ、ミ、レ

Warm-up

The pressure's on!: show flashcards of the katakana characters which have been studied. Each student reads out one card, going around the class. As each card is read correctly, the class score goes up by one. If anyone makes an error, the score goes back by one. A record is kept of the highest score the class is able to reach. This game reinforces the importance of everyone in the class knowing their katakana characters.

Presentation

- Play the tape while students look at the Student Book. Stop the tape whenever you hear a 'ding'.

Audio script

SPEAKER: Ben

Hi, Ben again with some more katakana. One of the best things about knowing katakana is that you can read menus in Japanese. The katakana introduced in this unit are ones you'll find on just about every menu.

But first as usual, some revision. The katakana you already know are printed in black in the chart, point to each one as I say it, and repeat after me.
ア、イ、エ、オ、カ、ケ、ツ、ト、ナ、ニ、ハ、フ、ヘ、ラ

Look at the characters in the yellow boxes in the chart. Can you work out how each one is pronounced?

...

Now look at the group of ten large characters. Point to each one as I say it, and repeat after me.

1 キ
2 コ
3 サ
4 シ
5 ス
6 ソ
7 チ
8 ヒ
9 ミ
10 レ

よくできました。

Katakana sound changes
Now that you know so many katakana, there are lots of sound changes you can make. Some of them are shown in the green box on the page. Look at them now, and repeat after me.

カ　ガ
ケ　ゲ
サ　ゲ
シ　ジ
シュ　ジュ
ス　ズ
ト　ド
ハ　バ
　　パ
ヒ　ビ

There are sound changes in two of the three photos on the page. See if you can find them. Can you find any more in *Itadakimasu*?

…

You'll find more katakana sound changes inside the back cover of your Student Book.

That's it for now. またね！

Follow-up

- *Scratch my back!*: students stand in one line. The student at the back 'writes' a katakana word (or single character) on the back of the student in front, who 'passes' it on to the next student, and so on.
- *Katakana-ercise*: see *Hiragana-ercise* (page 68 of Teacher Notes).
- *Katakana dictation quiz*: see *Hiragana dictation quiz* (page 68 of Teacher Notes).
- Ⓦ **85–6** かきかた *(How to write)*: students practise writing the characters in the boxes using the correct stroke order.
- Ⓢ **115** *Find the odd sound*: students select the odd sound in each group of three presented. *Solutions*: 1c, 2b, 3b, 4a, 5a, 6a.
- Ⓦ **86/T1** Students match each word with the correct picture.
- Ⓦ **88/T3** Students write in the missing katakana.
- Ⓦ **88/T4** Students find the items in the katakana puzzle and write them down.
- Ⓢ **115** Students look at the two pizza advertisements and the photo of a drink bottle and identify the katakana they know. What kind of pizzas are advertised? If they can't work it out, have them use their katakana charts to look up any unknown characters. For your information:
  ミートピザ *meat pizza*
  オニオン・マッシュルーム・トマト・ピーマン・ハム・チキン・イタリアンソーセージ
  onion, mushrooms, tomato, capsicum, ham, chicken, Italian sausage
  チリソースピザ *chilli sauce pizza*
  オニオン・ベーコン・エビ (ダブル)
  onion, bacon, prawn (double)
  コカ・コーラ *Coca-Cola*

ごはんとおかず

Ⓢ **116–17**

Warm-up

- *Sentences, please*: write a string of sentences using as many of the alternatives under each function as possible, but without including punctuation marks such as full stops. Students then see how quickly they can mark where each new sentence begins.
- *Foods only, please*: following on from the above, at the teacher's command, students see how quickly they can highlight (or mark) all the food items. This task can also be used for other categories, such as, drinks, like/dislike, eat/drink.

Presentation

- *Mixed-up Q & A*: two sentences–a question and an answer–are cut into pieces and students see how quickly they can arrange the pieces of each sentence correctly.
- *That's Japanese?*: students choose a question and read it out backwards. The other students have to answer correctly.
- Ⓢ **204–5** *(the* せつめい *section)*: note particularly section C on page 204: exchanging information about what people drink at breakfast time.

Follow-up

- *Class dictation*: each student reads a sentence aloud while the others copy it down.
- *Witch's cauldron*: two large witch's cauldrons are drawn on the board or on large sheets of butcher's paper. Students are asked to write crazy sentences about things they would like their witch to eat (or drink). The class divide into teams and write their sentences on the board (next to their team's cauldron). They then swap sides, each person now selects a sentence and draws a picture of the item in the cauldron. Refer back to vocabulary such as animals, classroom objects and presents.
- まいにち！はやく！Students write down the three daily meals: あさごはん, ひるごはん and ばんごはん. Next to each meal, they write まいにちたべます、よくたべます、ときどきたべます、ぜんぜんたべません、まいにちのみます、よくのみます、ときどきのみます and ぜんぜんのみません. Next to each phrase, they write an appropriate food or drink item, in Japanese. Four students then sit out the front and four more by the board. The teacher calls out a meal and the students by the board have to run to the students sitting down, find out as much as they can about what that person eats and drinks for that meal, and then run back to the board and draw pictures or write words to convey the information to the class. Students get a point for each piece of information they draw/write correctly.

Extension tasks

- Ⓑ **8.1** レストランメニュー Students imagine that they are working at a ファミリーレストラン in Japan, and that the manager has asked them to write up the blackboard menus.
- Ⓑ **8.2** おこのみやきをつくりましょう
- Ⓑ **8.3** *Pairwork*: students practise talking about the foods and drinks they like and dislike.
- Ⓑ **8.4** *Can you find it?*: (Number 1) identify the words in the word maze according to their line and position. Your teacher will give you clues. Find the Japanese word for: cheese, salad, ice-cream, orange juice, chicken, sausage, chocolate, spaghetti, toast, pizza, coffee, cake, milk, cola, hamburger, sandwich, cornflakes, curry and rice, coca cola, McDonalds. (Number 2): identify the words in the word maze according to their line and position. Your teacher will give you clues. Find the Japanese word for: lunch, lunch box, egg, fish, fruit, green tea, rice, western tea, breakfast, every day, sometimes, dinner, eat, often, vegetables, pet food, grass (the expression used before eating), I eat, (the expression used after eating), raw fish, fried seafood and vegetables (tempura), teriyaki, sukiyaki, not at all, I don't drink at all, I don't drink.

テーブルマナー

Ⓢ **118–19**

Warm-up

- Ask students what Japanese food they know, what food they have tried, and what Japanese foods they like and dislike.
- *Getting the gist*: without explaining the information on the page, ask students to identify who they think the people are and what information is being given.

Presentation

Have students try to read the text on pages 118–19 and identify the dishes. You may need to explain any dishes unknown to them. These pages should stimulate discussion about:

- the changing tastes of the Japanese over the three generations.
- the introduction of Western food into the Japanese diet and its effects on their body size and health
- the fast-food industry in Japan: Japanese traditional fast food (そば、うどん、おでん、おこのみやき) v. Western fast food (マクドナルド、ロテリア、ケンタッキー)
- family restaurant chains.

Students may like to compare their own favourite foods with those of their parents.

For your information:

お父さんとおかあさんがすきなもの

– すきやき Beef, vegetables, tofu and broth cooked in a pot in the middle of the table. It is traditionally served with raw egg, in which you dip the hot meat and vegetables just before eating.

– ごはん Steamed rice served in a Japanese rice bowl. If rice is served on a flat plate with a Western dish, it is called ライス.

– みそしる Traditional soup made from a soya bean base and containing fish, vegetables or seaweed and tofu. In some families it is eaten with every meal.

– てんぷら Deep fried seafood and vegetables. It is eaten dipped in a sauce made from soy sauce, さけ and stock.

– てりやきチキン Chicken marinated in a sweet-soy-sauce based sauce and fried or grilled.

– すし Raw fish on mounds of rice (にぎりずし) and seaweed wrapped rolls of rice with fish, vegetables or pickles inside (まきずし)

– さけ Rice wine served hot in winter and cold in summer. It is often drunk before or during a meal with rice crackers or dried fish snacks.

ぼくがすきなもの

– えびフライ Deep-fried crumbed prawn cutlets

– スパゲッティ Spaghetti with meat sauce

– カレーライス Curry with rice

– おこのみやき Savoury pancake filled with a combination of prawns, ham, cabbage, bean sprouts, onion, carrot, etc.. It is cooked on a large barbecue plate and served with a barbecue sauce, mayonnaise and seaweed flakes.

– ハンバーグ A hamburger patty (ハンバーガー is the hamburger in a bun with salad).

おじいさんとおばあさんがすきなもの

– おちゃとおかし Green tea and sweets

– とうふ Tofu (bean curd). Cold tofu with soy sauce, shallots and かつおぶし (as seen in the picture) is called ひややっこ. Tofu is used in soups and one-pot dishes.

– やきざかな Grilled fish.

– さしみ Raw fish.

– そうめん Chilled thin noodles served with a dipping sauce and shallots.

– つけもの Pickled vegetables.

Follow-up

Students refer to pages 4 and 5 of the Student Book and try to read and identify the dishes on the Nakayama Gakuen canteen menu. For your information:

1	うどん	wide noodles in a broth
2	きつねうどん	wide noodles in a broth with fried bean curd skin
3	カレーうどん	wide noodles with curry
4	たぬきそば	thin noodles in a broth with small pieces of tempura batter
5	月見(つきみ)そば	thin noodles in a broth with an egg
6	てんぷらそば	thin noodles in a broth with deep fried prawns and vegetables
7	サンドイッチ	sandwiches
8	カレーライス	curry and rice

9	ラーメン	Chinese noodles in soup
10	おにぎり	rice balls wrapped in seaweed
11	ぎょうざ定食(ていしょく)	meal set of steamed meat dumplings
12	日替(ひがわ)り定食(ていしょく)	daily special set
13	オレンジジュース	orange juice
14	アップルジュース	apple juice
15	サイダ	cider
16	レモネード	lemonade
17	コーラ	cola
18	ファンタ	Fanta
19	ココア	cocoa

いただきまーす！！Let's eat!!
食(た)べた後(あと)は食器洗(しょっきあら)い場(ば)までもどしましょう。
After you eat, return your plate to the washing area.

おはし

S 120–1

Warm-up

Show and tell–Japanese calligraphy: if possible, show students the items mentioned in this section of the Student Book. If it is not possible to find genuine Japanese articles, you may be able to find ink blocks and brushes at an Asian food supermarket.

Presentation

- *Demonstration*: if there are Japanese people in your school community, you could invite someone to demonstrate the points and examples given in the Student Book.
- *Discussion*: ask students to talk about what helps or hinders their ability to write Japanese correctly or smoothly. Encourage students to contribute their suggestions (and talk about their difficulties) and to suggest how they think their writing could be improved.

Follow-up

This is what I think: students put a piece of their writing in a box (without their name). Each student then selects a piece of writing from the box and writes positive comments and suggestions for improvement. (Each suggestion for improvement should be balanced by a positive comment.) The sheets are then put back in the box (or on the floor) and students collect their piece of work.

おしょうゆ

S 122 (tape) 2B

Presentation

- Students listen to the tape and repeat the new expressions.
- *Oshooyu board*: add these expressions to a list on the pin-up board and encourage their use in writing and role-plays.
- *A dialogue a day*: at the beginning of every lesson, a pair of students could perform a very short dialogue incorporating at least one of the *Oshooyu* expressions.
- **W 100/T18** おしょうゆクイズタイム: students circle the correct answer.

おかし

S 123

Songs

- Students sing the song in the Student Book to the tune of *Frère Jacques*. They can then take turns in making up their own verses, keeping the first, second and fourth lines the same.
- Sing the following Japanese song to the tune of さくら:

  さくら、さくら、
  やきとり、てんぷら、
  みそしる、さしみ、
  さくら、さくら、
  やき　にぎり

Craft Activity

- *Make your own Japanese cookbook*: students in groups research a particular Japanese dish. They find the recipe, try cooking some at home for homework, and bring it in for the rest of the class to try. Then they compile the recipes into a class cookbook.

Putting it all together

- **S 108–10** Students go back to *Itadakimasu* and re-read it.
  - They then act out the whole manga.
  - Now ask the students to act out each section, modifying or adding to the story where they can.
  - Write the bulk of the cartoon dialogue in the frames but leave spaces where students can fill in missing characters or words they have learnt to write.
- **W 94–5/T12** Students read the letters and answer the questions in English.
- **S 122** Students look at the photo and try to read the captions. What do they mean?

ごちそうさま

- **S 123** Students make up a caption for each of the photographs on this page.
- いちばんすきなもの *(My favourite things)*: collect pictures of the things you like to eat and drink, things you like a little and things you don't like. Write the following words at the top of a large piece of paper:
  だいすきです。すきです。あまり……。きらいです。and then arrange the pictures under the appropriate word.
  Label the things in Japanese, if you know the words and can write them. Alternatively, make a class list of the words you can't write and and ask your teacher

to write them and make copies. Cut out the words you need and stick them onto your poster.

- メニューをつくりましょう *(Let's make a menu)*: the holidays are approaching and you've got a busy schedule! What you need are some interesting menus to look forward to. What would you like to have for each of these occasions?

えいがのあと	after the movies
ピクニックで	on a picnic
パーティーで	at a party
ビデオをみながら	while watching a video
日本のレストランで	at a Japanese restaurant

Choose one of these headings (or make up your own) and write your menu in Japanese. Display your menus on your classroom wall when you have finished. (This can be done in groups or individually.)

- W **101** *Obentoo quiz*: students can check how well they have learnt the unit by trying the *Obentoo quiz* themselves or teachers can use it as an assessment task.
- *Self-assessment form and discussion*: after students have completed the unit they could assess their own general achievements using the form on page 137 of the *Moshi Moshi Teachers' Handbook*. The form provides space for the students to list what they have achieved, the difficulties they have encountered and strategies they could use for improvement. After students have completed the form, they could discuss the three headings and make suggestions about ways to improve their Japanese.

Reference to *Yoroshiku National Curriculum Guidelines for Japanese (Moshi Moshi)*

The following is a list of the suggested language exponents presented in *Moshi Moshi* Module 3 じぶんのこと (*Things about me*) which have been introduced in Unit 8 of *Obentoo*. In some cases the example has been changed to correspond to the form introduced in *Obentoo*. Appropriate activities from *Moshi Moshi* are suggested below.

Language exponents

- Enquiring about and expressing likes and dislikes
  (スパゲッティ) がすきですか。
  はい、すきです。
  はい、だいすきです。
  いいえ、あまり....。

Module 4: Free time

- Asking and giving information about after-school activities
  なにをたべますか。
  なにをのみますか。
  おべんとうをたべます。
  ミルクをのみます。
- Asking and giving information about frequency
  まいにちたべます。
  よくたべます。
  ときどきたべます。
  ぜんぜんたべません。

Suggested activities from *Moshi Moshi*

- かるた Teacher Resources pages 22 and 25–30
- すきなメニュー Teacher Resources page 22, Student Book pages 18–19
- いちごもすきです。 Teacher Resources pages 22 and 33
- なにをたべますか。 Teacher Resources page 23, Student Book page 17
- さあ、レストランへ！ Teacher Resources page 24, Student Book page 21

Overview

Unit objectives

Students will be able to:

- ask someone what they are going to do on a particular day
- say when and where they are going
- ask about and say with whom they are going
- say what sort of event they are going to or not going to
- read and write five more katakana characters and three more sound changes
- talk about activities which Japanese people do on the weekends
- talk about things they can do to aid their listening comprehension

Functions and language exponents

1 Asking what someone is going to do/Saying where you're going
(なかむらせんせい)は(日曜日に)なにをしますか。
(えいが)にいきます。

2 Saying when and where you're going/Asking and saying with whom you're going
(きょう、レストラン)にいきます。
だれといきますか。
(ちえこさんと)いきます。
一人でいきます。

3 Saying what sort of event you're going to or not going to
(トニーくん)は(土曜日に)なにをしますか。
(テニスのしあい)にいきます。
(しあい)にいきません。(しんごくんのうち)にいきます。

Key vocabulary and expressions

金曜日に
土曜日に
日曜日に
しゅうまつに
きょう
あした
えいが
デパート
がっこう
うみ
パーティー
レストラン
コンサート
ピクニック

... さんと
ともだちと
一人で

サッカーのしあい
テニスのえいが
バレーボールの ...
バスケットボールの ...
ホッケーの ...
オーストラリアのフットボールの ...
からての ...
けんどうの ...
おばあさんのうち
しんごくんのうち

... にいきます。
... にいきません。

Script

Students are expected to be able to read and write the key characters and recognise the associated words.

Key characters	*Associated words*
ク	ピクニック
グ	ラグビー
テ	テニス
デ	デパート
ホ	ホッケー
ボ	バスケットボール
ル	バレーボール
ン	レストラン

Script understandings

- Learning about more がいらいご、for example sports
- Introducing *nigori* sound changes (katakana): グ(ラグビー)、デ(デパート)、ボ(バレーボール)
- More examples of how hiragana, katakana and kanji are used together

Learning how to learn

Through Ben's interview with Carla, further attention is given to the 'art' of good listening, for example, noticing (and 'mimicking') accent, tone of voice and expressions used; extracting important familiar details from unfamiliar (or unnecessary) information; using small amounts of familiar language to maintain the thread or gist of a series of sentences; requesting repetition and/or clarification; and the importance of staying 'switched on' when listening. These expressions are introduced:
すもません。ちょっとわかりません。
すみません、もういちどおねがいします。
「おべんとう」ってなんですか。

Cultural elements

A photo collage shows some places that students might go to each day and during their free time. The photos are supported by captions in Japanese. Other incidental language introduced.
それから
わたしテニスがきらい！
ぼくけんどうがきらい！
まいったなー！
つまらない！
つまらないです。
よかったー！

Extension material

- Asking where someone is going
どこにいきますか。
Where are you going?
あしたどこにいきますか。
Where are you going tomorrow?
- Expressing surprise on receiving information
カーラさんと。ああ、そうですか。
With Carla? Oh, I see!
おばあさんのうち(に)。ああ、そうですか。
To your grandmother's house? Oh, I see!
日曜日に。ああ、そうですか。
On Sunday? Oh, I see!

Need some extra words or expressions? Ask your teacher!

プール	pool
きょうかい	church
かいもの	shopping
やま	mountains
バーベキュー	barbecue

Teaching suggestions

The following suggestions are provided as a guide to lesson planning and should be adapted to suit your teaching style and the learning styles of your students. These tasks are specific to this unit. For more information on general strategies for each section, refer to *Using Obentoo* on pages 3–8.

いただきます

S 124–6 3A

Warm-up

- *Sports and activities, brainstorm*: ask students to brainstorm any sporting or 'free time' words they know in Japanese already and write these on the board. Write katakana words in one section and hiragana words in another. This may stimulate discussion of Japanese martial arts, for example からて、けんどう、あいきどう、じゅうどう、きゅうどう、なぎなた、すもう。
- Then give students some other examples of sports which in Japanese are 外来語 and see if they can recognise them in English, for example バドミントン、バスケットボール、バレーボール、フットボール、ゴルフ、ホッケー、クリケット、ネットボール、ピンポン、ラグビー、ローラーブレード、サーフィン、サッカー、ソフトボール、スケート、スキー、テニス。(Most of these are introduced in Unit 9 or Unit 10.)

Presentation

Listen and guess: without showing students their books (or the OHTs), play the tape of the cartoon story and ask the students to make a note of any sporting or activity words they recognise. Add these to the list(s) on the board above. Show the OHTs and replay the tape, and then ask students if they can 'flesh out' the details of the story (without reading any of the words or looking in their books). The tape could be replayed a third time, frame by frame, with students trying to work out the details of the story. Refer them to their books to answer the questions on page 126. With students looking at pages 124, 125 and 126, replay the tape again, sentence by sentence. Each time students hear a new word, stop the tape and check that they can recognise the word on the page. Also ask them to find other places in the cartoon story where the word is used. See if students can work out the use and meaning of いきません and ... さんの ... (e.g. おばあさんのうち) themselves. Refer to *Benkyoo no Ben* for the new katakana characters.

Follow-up

What a boring weekend!: students work out their own version of the cartoon story, changing the names of the characters, the sports they play and the places they are going to visit. Encourage the students to prepare a story around the most boring weekend activity (or activities) they could imagine. The names of particularly dull movies could be used instead of places.

どんなあじ？

S 127–32 3A

1 Asking what someone is going to do/Saying where you're going

Warm-up

- Replay *Itadakimasu* and explore the page as in earlier units.
- *Place mnemonics*: students make up mnemonics for each of the new place and time words. For example, えいが = Garth is achin' to see the eiga! (*Note:* the mnemonic only needs to be loosely connected with the sound or meaning of the target word.) To provide further help, ask students to think of gestures which suit the sound or meaning of one of the words in the mnemonic, which they can perform each time one of the new words is used in a sentence.

Presentation

- Students look at the pictures on page 127 while listening to the tape. They should try to work out the meaning before they listen and repeat.
- Students listen and repeat; then they listen, read the sentences on page 128 and repeat. Finally they should do the pairwork task on page 128.
- *Head and face mime*: students try to mime the activities and places mentioned in the sentences by restricting movement to their face and head, while other students try to guess (in Japanese) which sentence from pages 127–8 is being mimed. If students show interest in this technique, they could be challenged to perform the mimes by restricting movement to their eyes only!

Follow-up

- **W 105/T5 5A** Students listen to the tape and write down the names of the two speakers in each situation and what one of them is going to do.

Audio script

a **Nakamura:** ゆうすけくん、火曜日になにをしますか。
Yuusuke: あっ、せんせい、こんにちは。火曜日にうみにいきます。

b **Yuki:** はい、まつだゆきです。
Emma: もしもし、ゆきさん、エマです。
Yuki: あっ、エマ、こんにちは。
Emma: こんにちは。ねー、ゆきさん、金曜日になにをしますか。

Yuki: えーと、金曜日ですか、金曜日にえいがにいきます。

c **Harjono:** ケイトさん、日曜日になにをしますか。

Kate: 日曜日、ちょっとまって、金曜日はえいが、土曜日はコンサート、日曜日に、デパートにいきます。

Harjono: へー！！

d **Ben:** けんいちくーん、おはよう。

Kenichi: あっ、ベンくん、おはよう。

Ben: けんいちくん、水曜日になにをしますか。

Kenichi: がっこう。がっこうにいきます。

e **Yuki's Mum:** ケイト、しゅうまつになにをしますか。

Kate: しゅうまつですか。土曜日にピクニックにいきます。そして、日曜日に、パーティーにいきます。

- Students decide where they are going for their holidays and write the places in their diary. Then they ask their friends and record their responses.
- **W 106/T7** Students write sentences in the speech bubbles according to the hints given.
- *Memory test:* from flashcards depicting each of the activities covered in the story (and/or *Donna aji?*), a group of seven students each pick a flashcard, stand in a line and, one at a time, perform a mime to depict the activity on the card they chose. Afterwards, the students change their positions in the line and the rest of the class try to recite the activities in order, using days of the week.

2 Saying when and where you're going/Asking and saying with whom you're going

Warm-up

The longest who's who: one student starts up with, for example ともだちのフットボール. Another student adds to it, e.g. アメリカ人のともだちのフットボール. Another students adds something further, e.g. おかあさんのアメリカ人 のともだちのフットボール, and so on. After each student's addition, the rest of the class repeat the entire statement. The class keep a record of the number of parts in the statement and could try to improve the 'score' later.

Presentation

- Listen and repeat and listen, look at the sentences and repeat as in earlier units.
- *Rubbish!*: students draw flashcards depicting the activities on pages 129–30. Flashcards could also be drawn for additional activities which have been learnt. A template of the days of the week is drawn on the board and one activity card is placed in position for each day of the week. While the rest of the class look to the back of the room, a volunteer picks two days of the week and says which activity s/he is doing on each day; however, for one of the two days, the student deliberately makes a mistake. The student says his/her sentences aloud and then the class look to the front and try to pick which day the person was 'lying' about (by giving the correct sentence(s)). As students become more familiar with the sentences, the volunteers could give three, four or more days at a time, with one or more activities being a 'lie'. The order of the cards should be changed after each volunteer. New cards could be added, depicting other activities.

Follow-up

- **W 107/T8 5A** Students listen to the tape and answer the questions in English.

Audio script

Tony: トニーです。
Sanae: はい。
Tony: さなえさん、こんにちは。
Sanae: Shh. こんにちは。
Carla: カーラです。
Sanae: はい。
Carla: あっ、こんにちは。
Sanae: Shh. こんにちは。
Tony: こんにちは。
Harjono: ハジョーノです。
Sanae: はい。
Harjono: みなさんこんにちは。
All: Shh.
Harjono: ああ、ごめんなさい。こんにちは。
All: こんにちは。
Takako: たかこです。
Sanae: はい、どうぞ。
Takako: ありがとう。こんにちは。
All: Shh.
Takako: あっ、こんにちは。
Yuusuke: ゆうすけです。
All: ゆうすけくん、shh.
Yuusuke: へっ！！！
Sanae: みなさん、こんにちは。これからベンのたんじょうびパーティーのミーティングをします。
Sanae: Shh. ベンのたんじょうびは7月13日です。パーティーは金曜日です。

Harjono: ええ！金曜日？金曜日はだめ。
Sanae: 金曜日になにをしますか。
Harjono: コンサートにいきます。
Yuusuke: ぼくも。
Harjono: へえ、だれといきますか。
Yuusuke: トニーくんといきます。
Harjono: そう？
Tony: はい、そう。
Sanae: じゃ、金曜日はだめ。土曜日は？
Takako: あっ、土曜日はだめ。
Sanae: 土曜日になにをしますか。
Takako: おかあさんとデパートにいきます。
Sanae: ああ、そう。
Carla: わたしはちえこさんとピクニックにいきます。
Sanae: じゃ、日曜日は？みなさん日曜日は？日曜日はいい？トニーくん？
Tony: はい。
Sanae: カーラさん？
Carla: はい。
Sanae: ハージョーノくん？
Harjono: はい。
Sanae: たかこさん？
Takako: はい。
Sanae: ゆうすけくん？
Yuusuke: はい。
Sanae: じゃ、日曜日にパーティーをします。
Sanae: Shh.

Vocabulary notes

だめ	no good
いい	OK, good

- **W 107/T9** For this task students will need a partner and two markers (small buttons or coins). Students place one marker on a picture in the first row and another marker on a picture in the second row. They ask きょう、なにをしますか。 for the first row and だれといきますか。 for the second row. The student's partner must then answer in Japanese. If s/he answers correctly, s/he receives a point. Then students swap over.
- **W 108/T10** Students read the survey alternatives and circle the most appropriate answer.

3 Saying what sort of event you're going to or not going to

Warm-up

'*Stand up/sit down'—more sports*: all the students except one (who is the first 'guesser') choose two words from a list of new vocabulary. The teacher reads out the words in random order and the students stand when their first word is called and sit when they hear their second word called. When the 'guesser' is able to pick someone's two words, s/he calls out ちょっとまって！ ('Just a moment!') and then identifies the words. If the 'guesser' is correct, that student joins the 'guessers'. 'Guessers' get two points for each word they identify correctly.

Presentation

- *Backwards building*: after the class has worked through the tape once, i.e. after listening to the tape, looking at the pictures and repeating, the teacher says the last part of one of the sentences, for example, なにをしますか。 and students try to guess which sentence it is. In the case of this example, the students will not be able to guess, as every question ends with this phrase. The teacher adds one more word to the phrase, building the sentence backwards, for example あした、なにをしますか。 If students cannot guess (or read) which sentence is being referred to, the teacher adds a further word, for example たかこさんはあした、なにをしますか。 Once students have understood the idea, volunteers could take the teacher's part.
- **S 132** Listen, look at the sentences and repeat, as in earlier units.

Follow-up

- **W 109/T11 5A** Students listen to the tape and complete the table.

Audio script

SPEAKERS: Sanae, Nakamura sensei, Yuki, Emma, Kenichi

S: あっ、ゆきさん、けんいちくん、なかむらせんせい、エマさん、きょうはどうもありがとう。アンケートです。しゅうまつになにをしますか。レストランにいきますか。はい、ゆきさん。
Y: はい、いきます。
S: けんいちくん。
K: いいえ、いきません。
S: なかむらせんせい。
N: はい、レストランにいきます。
S: エマさん。
E: はい、わたしもレストランにいきます。
S: コンサートにいきますか。はい、ゆきさん。
Y: はい、いきます。
S: けんいちくん。
K: いいえ、いきません。
S: なかむらせんせい。
N: いいえ、いきません。エマさん。
E: いいえ、コンサートにいきません。

S: ピクニックにいきますか。はい、ゆきさん。
Y: いいえ、いきません。
S: けんいちくん
K: いいえ、いきません。
S: なかむらせんせい
N: はい、いきます。
S: エマさん。
E: はい、ピクニックにいきます。
S: えいがにいきますか。はい、ゆきさん。
Y: はい、いきます。
S: けんいちくん。
K: はい、いきます。
S: なかむらせんせい。
N: いいえ、いきません。
S: エマさん。
E: はい、いきます。
S: デパートにいきますか。はい、ゆきさん。
Y: はい、いきます。
S: けんいちくん。
K: いいえ、いきません。
S: なかむらせんせい。
N: いいえ、いきません。
S: エマさん。
E: はい、いきます。
S: みなさん、そのほかに、しゅうまつになにをしますか。
N: ぼくはテニスのしあいにいきます。
S: ああ、そうですか。はい、せんせいはテニスのしあいですね。
Y: わたしはしゅうまつにうみにいきます。
E: あっ、わたしもうみにいきます。
S: うみですか。ゆきさんとエマさんはうみですね。
K: ぼくはやきゅうのしあいにいきます。
S: ああ、そうですか。
K: はい。そして、サッカーのしあいにいきます。
S: ああ、そう。
K: はい。そして、バスケットボールのしあいにいきます。
S: はい、けんいちくん、やきゅうとサッカーとバスケットボールのしあいにいきますね。どうもありがとうございました。
All: ありがとう。

- **110/T13** Students read the notes and answer the questions in English.
- **111/T14** Students write sentences in Japanese according to the information given.
- **111/T15** *Part A*: students read sentences and find a corresponding picture for each one in the chart.
- **111/T15** *Part B*: students write sentences describing the remaining activities in the chart.

べんきょうのベンーカタカナ

133 3A

Characters introduced: ク、テ、ホ、ル、ン

Warm-up

じゅんばんに *(In the correct order)!*: the class is divided into teams of 5 or 6 students. Flashcards of each of the katakana which have been learnt are placed in a pile. The cards are shuffled and dropped onto the floor. A timer sees how long each team takes to put its cards in the correct alphabetical order. The winning team is the one which can get its cards in alphabetical order the quickest.

Presentation

- Play the tape while students look at the Student Book. Stop the tape whenever you hear a 'ding'.

Audio script

SPEAKER: Ben

Hi, Ben here again with some more katakana.

But first, as usual, some revision. The katakana you already know are printed in black in the chart. Point to the ones I say, and repeat after me.
キ、コ、サ、シ、ス、ソ、チ、ヒ、ミ、レ

Look at the characters in the yellow boxes in the chart. Can you work out how each one is pronounced?

...

Now look at the group of five large characters. Point to each one as I say it, and repeat after me.

1 ク
2 テ
3 ホ
4 ル
5 ン

よくできました。

Katakana sound changes

Three more katakana sound changes are shown in the blue box on the page. Look at them now, and repeat after me.

1 ク、グ
2 テ、デ
3 ホ、ボ

Now look at *Gohan to okazu* on pages 134 and 135. How many words can you find which contain any of the new katakana or their sound changes?

That's it for now. またね！

- Students look at the advertisements on page 133 of the Student Book and identify characters they know.

  For your information:
  東京第一ホテル松山
  Tokyo Dai-ichi Hotel Matsuyama
  お休みの日は外でランチ
  Lunch outside during the holidays
  ピクニックべんとう
  Picnic lunches

Follow-up

- Ⓦ **102** かきかた *(How to write)*: students practise writing the characters in the boxes using the correct stroke order.
- Ⓢ **133** *Find the odd sound*: students select the odd sound in each group of three presented. *Solutions*: 1a, 2c, 3b, 4b, 5c, 6c.
- *Katakana-ercise:* see *Hiragana-ercise* (page 68).
- *Katakana dictation quiz:* see *Hiragana dictation quiz* (page 68).
- Ⓦ **103/T1** Students find as many katakana and kanji as they can in the puzzle and write them in the boxes provided.
- Ⓦ **104/T2** This task focuses on the use of small ッ. Students read the words aloud and match each one with its English equivalent by drawing a line.
- Ⓦ **104/T3** This task focuses on the use of small ィ and ァ. Students read the words aloud and match each one with its English equivalent by drawing a line.
- As a follow-up to these tasks, students could identify names containing small ッ、ィ and ァ in a list of their classmates' names. This can also be done using the names of familiar cities or countries.
- Ⓦ **104/T4** Students write the words in katakana.

ごはんとおかず

Ⓢ **134–5**

Warm-up

Guess!: students make up a story by combining sentences from the second, third and fifth blocks on page 134. They write their sentences in Japanese, if they can, or draw simple pictures to depict the sentences they choose. Other students then try to guess their story by asking questions like えいがにいきますか。The student whose turn it is must answer はい or いいえ. The winning student is the one whose sentences take the longest to guess.

Presentation

- Copy the word flashcards from the Teacher Resource File. Make cards for particles and verbs used on these pages. Give sets to groups of students. Then you call out sentences in English and students must make the sentence correctly in Japanese, using the cards.
- Students make up captions in Japanese for the photos on the double-page spread.
- Ⓢ **135** *Extra reading task*: students read the speech bubbles on the photo and answer these questions:
  1. Why is Yoshiko looking stunned?
  2. What does the caption at the bottom say?
- *Crazy days*: students sit on chairs in a large circle with one student identified as the opening leader. The leader's job is to say one of the days of the week, for example, 水曜日. The next student says 木曜日. The next student can say 金曜日 or あした. If the student says あした, the next student must say 金曜日. The student could instead choose to say きょう, in which case the next student must say 木曜日, and so on. Each time a student makes a mistake, s/he goes to the end of the 'circle' and the other students move one seat closer to the leader's position. Instead of saying 土曜日 a student can say しゅうまつ, but the next student must then say 月曜日. The object is to try to trick the leader into making a mistake and taking his/her position.

Follow-up

- *Class dictation*: each student reads a sentence out aloud while the others copy it down.
- Ⓦ **109/T12** **5A** Students listen to the sentences on the tape and piece together the broken sentences by drawing links. Then put them in the correct order from a to e.
  This task may stimulate discussion of the structure of Japanese sentences: the verb at the end of the sentence, the time word at the beginning, how particles in Japanese are placed *AFTER* the word they refer to, for example, ともだちと 'with a friend', パーティーに 'to a party'. Students may like to draw up a chart of particles they have come across so far, suggesting a meaning or function for each particle; for example, と means 'with', and は is used as a subject marker. (Refer to page 211 of the Student Book.)

Audio script

a 日曜日におかあさんとデパートにいきます。

b 火曜日にともだちとパーティーにいきます。

c 水曜日におにいさんとラグビーのしあいにいきます。

d 土曜日にひとりでともだちのうちにいきます。

e 金曜日にいもうととえいがにいきます。

Extension tasks

- Ⓑ **9.1** どこにいきますか Students read the dialogues and answer the questions in English.

- Ⓑ **9.2** しゅうまつになにをしますか
Students draw as many weekend activities as they can and write a caption under each in Japanese.
- Ⓑ **9.3** *Kate and Ben's diaries*: students practise the pattern ... ようびになにをしますか to complete the missing information from the diaries.

テーブルマナー

Ⓢ 136–7

Warm-up

General discussion: students discuss in English what they know about Japanese teenage lifestyle, the facts and the myths.

Presentation

- Ⓢ **136** しゅうまつになにをしますか。
Students read the speech bubbles and match them to the activities on the opposite page.
- Divide the class into eight groups and have each group research and deliver a short presentation, written or spoken, on one of the activities mentioned on page 137 of the Student Book. Suggestions for research:
  - えいが Movies in Japan, Japanese movies which are available in Australia/New Zealand, Japanese movie stars, Japanese TV.
  - レストラン Types of restaurants in Japan, foods popular with teenagers, coffee shops.
  - がっこう Going to school on Saturday, じゅく、よびこう, school club activities.
  - デパート Japanese shopping habits, types of shops, エレベーターガール、services in Japanese department stores.
  - おばあさんのうち The role of the elderly in Japan, Japanese housing.
  - マクドナルド The Japanese fast-food industry, types of fast food (takeaway), home delivery, convenience meals.
  - じゅうどうのしあい Japanese martial arts, traditional Japanese sports.
  - コンサート The Japanese pop music industry, popular bands/artists, music shows on TV.

Follow-up

On the weekend I…: students make up their own collages of weekly activities, including activities they might do in Japan, and write captions about each one, as in the picture on page 136 of the Student Book.

おはし

Ⓢ 138

Presentation

Discussion: discuss the questions on page 138. Make a list of expressions (for example, asking for repetition) and write these on the board or on a chart.

Follow-up

How to be a bad listener/How to be a good listener: encourage students to contribute their own ideas on how to listen well (and how to listen poorly). Make lists of these and display them on the pin-up board.

おしょうゆ

Ⓢ 139 Ⓣ 3A

- Students listen to the tape and repeat the new expressions.
- *Oshooyu board*: add these expressions to a list on the pin-up board and encourage their use in writing and role-plays.
- いいえ、はい！！！ *Oshooyu* expressions are written on paper raindrops and attached to an umbrella chart. While reciting the rhyme, the raindrops are picked at random. The expression where the rhyme stops must be used in a 2-or 4-line role-play.
いいえ、はい、いいえ、はい
どこに　とまるか　わからない

おかし

Ⓢ 139

Song

Students sing the song in the Student Book to the tune of *Following the leader* from Disney's Peter Pan.

Craft activity

たこ (*Kite*): you will need: four pieces of balsa wood (available from craft shops), a piece of calligraphy paper (半紙), sticky tape and streamers. Trace a Japanese design onto the paper, colour it in, and attach wood at top and bottom with sticky tape, attach two diagonal pieces of wood, and then attach streamers. (Suitable Japanese designs can be found in children's colouring-in books.)

Putting it all together

- Ⓦ **113/T16** Students read the notes from the *Obentoo* students and rewrite the messages in English on the memo pads.
- Ⓦ **114/T17** *Part A*: students follow the あみだくじ puzzle to find out where the *Obentoo* students and teachers are going during the holidays, and with whom. Students write their findings in full Japanese sentences.
- Ⓦ **114/T17** *Part B*: students make up their own あみだくじ, using the names of their classmates. How to make an あみだくじ:
  - Write the 7 days of the week along the first row.
  - Write the names of 7 boys along the second row.
  - Write the names of 7 girls along the third row.
  - Write 7 places or activities along the fourth row.
  - Connect each of the rows with vertical lines.
  - Draw horizontal lines at random connecting the

vertical lines. (You may draw more than one horizontal line between each item.)
  - Follow the puzzle as explained on pages 65-6 of the Workbook.
- どこに *(Where?)*: collect some Japanese pictures of places that students might like to go to during the week. Glue each picture to a piece of cardboard. Divide the class into groups of 5 or 6 people and place a pile of pictures face down in the middle. The first person picks up a picture, shows it to the group and says a sentence about the picture, using the following pattern: 私は … よう日に … にいきます。 I'm going to … (place) on … (day of the week).

  The next person says where the first person is going and on what day, then picks up another picture and says where s/he is going and when.

  The next person says where the first two people are going and when, then picks up another picture and says another sentence. Each group says as many sentences as possible, with each person repeating all previous sentences. The game is not a strict memory test, so students can prompt one another. The cards are placed face down in another pile as they are used.
- しゅうまつになにをしますか。アンケート。 *(Survey–what are you doing on the weekend?)*: you are a town planner and you are trying to find out which facilities in your local area are visited by most people with their families and which are visited by most people with their friends.
  - Make a list of the places in your local area you would like to find out about.
  - Ask five different people in your class if they visit each place. If they do, find out on what day they visit and with whom they go.
  - Also find out the ages of the people who visit each place.
  - Work out any other questions you would like to ask which might help your survey.
  - Ask and answer your survey questions in Japanese and make a brief summary of your results in English, or Japanese if you can.
  - What conclusions can you draw from your survey?
- *Charades*: someone starts by performing three short mimes of places s/he is going to on the weekend. One of the mimes should have a place or activity including の, for example テニスのしあい。 You should also mime with whom you're going. The rest of the class then ask questions until they have guessed the three places the person is going to and with whom s/he is going. The person whose mimes can be guessed correctly in the shortest time is the winner. To make the game more challenging, write lists of activities on pieces of paper and put these into a hat. Each person draws a piece of paper and must mime exactly what is written.

ごちそうさま

- Ⓢ **140** *Extra reading task*: students look at the article at the top of the page and answer these questions:
  - What is being advertised in the red advertisement on the right?
  - When will these events take place?
  - What is the name of the performer in the green advertisement on the left?
  - Where will this event be held?
  - When will it be held?
  - From what time will it be held?

  Advanced or adventurous students may then like to sift through the advertisement and try to read the katakana words which appear. They will be amazed at how much they can find out just from reading the katakana!
- Ⓦ **115** *Obentoo quiz*.
- *Individual progress cards*: from time to time, encourage students to write a brief progress report mentioning (1) what they have achieved, (2) where they have had difficulty, and (3) what they could do to improve their work. You may wish to refer to the student progress card on page 138 of the *Moshi Moshi Teacher's Handbook*
- *Discuss and report back*: students then discuss their progress reports in small groups and a scribe takes note of the groups' common difficulties and suggestions for improvement. These are then reported back to the class.

Reference to *Yoroshiku National Curriculum Guidelines for Japanese (Moshi Moshi)*

The following is a list of the suggested language exponents presented in *Moshi Moshi* Module 2 かぞくとともだち *(Family and friends)* which have been introduced in Unit 9 of *Obentoo*. In some cases the example has been changed to correspond to the form introduced in *Obentoo*.

Language exponents

Asking and giving information about places to go with family and friends:

(かぞく／ともだち)とどこにいきますか。	ええ、いきます。
(レストラン) にいきます。	いいえ、いきません。
(えいが) にいきますか。	

Overview

Unit objectives

Students will be able to:
- ask and talk about hobbies and interests
- respond with at least seven activities
- ask and say what kind of sports someone plays
- respond with at least ten sports
- ask and say if someone can do something
- say they can do something a little or not at all
- read and write six more katakana
- read and understand short passages giving information about hobbies and interests
- talk about interests and hobbies, both modern and traditional, enjoyed by Japanese people
- easily recognise Japanese punctuation, sentence endings and particles in a piece of Japanese writing

Functions and language exponents

1 Asking and talking about hobbies and interests
(トニーくん、)しゅみはなんですか。
(おんがく)です。

2 Asking and saying what kind of sports someone plays
(トニーくん、)どんなスポーツをしますか。
(バスケットボール)をします。

3 Asking and saying if someone can do something
(しんごくん、)(ローラーブレード)ができますか。
はい、できます。
はい、すこしできます。
いいえ、できません。
いいえ、ぜんぜんできません。

Key vocabulary and expressions

しゅみはなんですか。
じょうば
サーフィン
ピアノ
コンピューター
りょうり
おんがく
どくしょ
…です。
どんなスポーツをしますか。

バスケットボールをします。
ラグビーをします。
すいえいをします。
ソフトボールをします。
クリケットをします。
ネットボールをします。
…をします。

ローラーブレード
スケート
インドネシアご
えいご
…ができますか。
はい、できます。
はい、すこしできます。
いいえ、できません。
いいえ、ぜんぜんできません。

Script

Students are expected to be able to read and write the key characters and recognise the associated words.

Key characters	*Associated words*
タ	コンピューター
ネ	ネットボール
ノ	ピアノ
ユ	ジュース
リ	クリケット
ロ	ローラーブレード

Script understandings

- Learning about more がいらいご for example, sports
- Introducing *nigori* sound changes (katakana): ギ(ギター)、ビ(ラグビー)、ピュ(コンピューター)、ポ(スポーツ)

Learning how to learn

- Tricks for brushing up on reading skills
- Spaces between words
- Punctuation
- Sentence endings
- Particles

Cultural elements

A photo collage shows Daisuke's hobbies and those of his mother, father and sister. These pages focus on hobbies which may be familiar to students as well as traditional activities such as さどう、こと、いけばな and ぼんさい。The photos are supported by captions in Japanese.

Other incidental language introduced

ざんねんですね。
きてください。
でも、ちょっと…です。
よいしょ！
どしーん！
ほんとう？
おつかれさま
よいしょ！
すごーい！
しんじられない！

Extension material

Asking what kind of sports, food or music someone likes:
- どんなスポーツがすきですか。
  What sports do you like?
- どんなりょうりがすきですか。
  What food do you like?
- どんなおんがくがすきですか。
  What music do you like?

Need some extra words or expressions? Ask your teacher!

バレエ	ballet	barei
ダンス	dancing	dansu
たいそう	gymnastics	taisoo
スキー	skiing	sukii
スケート	skating	sketo
さいほう	sewing	saihoo
つり	fishing	tsuri
あみもの	knitting	amimono
サイクリング	bike riding	seikuringu
きってしゅうしゅう	stamp collecting	kitte shiyuushiyuu
トランペット	trumpet	toranpeto
ギター	guitar	gita—
うた	singing	uta
チェス	chess	chiesu

Teaching suggestions

The following suggestions are provided as a guide to lesson planning and should be adapted to suit your teaching style and the learning styles of your students. These tasks are specific to this unit. For more information on general strategies for each section, refer to *Using Obentoo* on pages 3–8.

いただきます

141–4 3A

Warm-up

Revise the sports introduced in Unit 9, using the pattern ... がすきですか。

Presentation

Listen and guess:

- Have students listen to the tape while they look at the OHTs.
- Elicit the story from students and make notes in English on the board.
- After the first hearing, have students try to work out the meaning of the expression しゅみはなんですか。(If they can't work it out, you may need to tell them what it is.)
- Students then listen to the tape again and jot down all the sports or hobbies which they can recognise.
- Continue to brainstorm the meaning of the story and pick out familiar words or expressions.
- Finally students look at the manga with text in their Student Books and pick out words or characters they know.
- Play sections of the tape and have students identify the frames.
- Have students answer the questions in English on page 144.

Follow-up

Divide the class into teams of 3 or 4 people. Give each team a photocopy of the manga cut up into individual frames. The teacher plays a section of the tape (3–5 frames) and each team must try to find those frames and place them on the desk in the correct order. The team which identifies the section the quickest receives points/prizes.

どんなあじ？

145–50 3A

1 Asking and talking about hobbies and interests

Warm-up

- Replay *Itadakimasu* and explore the page as in earlier units.
- Students listen to the tape of *Donna aji?*. Look at the pictures on page 147 and see if they can work out the meaning of the dialogues.

Presentation

- Students listen to the tape and repeat the dialogues.
- Then they listen to the tape, read the dialogues on page 146 and repeat.
- Students finally form pairs and practise the structures on page 146.

Follow-up

- Provide students with a copy of the flashcard pages from the Teacher Resource File. In pairs have Student 1 point to a card while asking the question しゅみはなんですか。Student 2 must answer correctly in Japanese. Then swap over. Student 2 asks the question while Student 1 answers. Students must ask and answer as quickly as possible, trying to catch the other one out. Students gain a point for a correct answer and lose a point for an incorrect answer (or if they stumble on the question). The person with the most points at the end of three minutes is the winner.
- W 118/T4 Students listen to the tape and find out the hobbies of each of the people.

Audio script

a

F: フィリップさん、しゅみはなんですか。
M: ぼくのしゅみはコンピューターです。

b

F: わたしはジーンです。わたしのしゅみはおんがくです。

c

M: ミーラさん！
F: はい。
M: しゅみはなんですか。
F: しゅみですか。えーと、どくしょです。しゅみはどくしょです。

d

F: サムさん、しゅみはなんですか。
M: しゅみはサーフィンです。サーフィンがだいすきです。

e

F: しゅみはなんですか、ジョシュアさん。
M: しゅみはスポーツです。ラグビーとクリケットをします。

f

F1: ティファニーさんのしゅみは？
F2: わたしのしゅみはりょうりです。
F1: へー、りょうり？
F2: はい、そうです。

- W 118/T5 Students conduct a survey among five members of their class to find out about their

hobbies.
- **W119/T6** Students answer the question しゅみはなんですか。according to the pictures.

2 Asking and saying what kind of sports someone plays

Warm-up

Write a number of sports in English on the board. (Choose sports which are がいらいご.) Divide the class into two teams and allocate a number to each student in each team. Make sure that two students who have been allocated the same number are sitting approximately the same distance from the board. The teacher calls out a sport in Japanese and a number. The two students who are that number must run to the board and identify the English word for the sport called out. Points are given to the first to identify the sport correctly.

Presentation

- Listen and repeat.
- Listen, read and repeat.
- Pairwork task (page 148).

Follow-up

- **W119/T7** Students conduct a survey among five members of their class to find out what sports they play.
- **W120–1/T8** *Part A*: students read the personal profiles of four Japanese exchange students and answer the questions in English.
- **W120/T8** *Part B*: students make up their own personal profile, using *Part A* as a guide.
- *On the buses* (first revise the sports introduced in the previous unit and sports and hobbies introduced in this unit):
  - Students are divided into teams and sit on chairs in rows.
  - The teacher asks a variety of questions (vocabulary translation questions, しゅみはなんですか、どんなスポーツをしますか。 using flashcards for students to answer, etc.).
  - Only the student in the front row may answer; s/he indicates desire to answer by being the first to stand up.
  - If the answer is correct, the team gains 1 point.
  - If incorrect, the team loses 1 point.
  - Then the front students go to the end of the line and everyone else moves up one seat (keep this moving quickly).

3 Asking and saying if someone can do something

Warm-up

As in previous units.

Presentation

- Listen and repeat.
- Listen, read and repeat.
- Pairwork task (page 150).

Follow-up

- **W122/T9 5B** Students listen to the interviews and complete the table in English.

Audio script

a

Interviewer: みなさん、こんにちは！！、*Kidz Times* magazine のやまだです。きょうはしゅみについてきいてみましょう。

すみません。*Kidz Times* magazine のやまだですけど。

Chieko: へー。ほんとう。

Carla: *Kidz Times* magazine?

Interviewer: はい、そうですよ。おなまえは？

Chieko: ちえこです。

Carla: カーラです。

Interviewer: はい、しゅみはなんですか。

Chieko: しゅみですか。コンピューターゲームです。

Interviewer: そうですか。カーラさんは？

Carla: 日本ごです。

Interviewer: 日本ご？

Carla: はい、日本ごがだいすきです。

Interviewer: そうですか。ありがとうございました。

Chieko & Carla: ありがとうございました。

b

Interviewer: すみません。

Yuki & Takako: はーい。

Interviewer: *Kidz Times* magazine のやまだですけど。

Yuki & Takako: はい。

Interviewer: おなまえは？

Yuki: ゆきです。

Takako: たかこです。

Interviewer: はい、しゅみはなんですか。

Yuki: はい、スポーツです。

Interviewer: ああ、どんなスポーツをしますか。

Yuki: バレーボールをします。

Interviewer: ああ、そうですか。たかこさんは？

Takako: わたしもスポーツです。

Interviewer: どんなスポーツをしますか、たかこさん？

Takako: けんどうをします。

Interviewer: ああ、そうですか。ありがとうございました。

Yuki & Takako: ありがとうございました。

c

Interviewer: すみません、*Kidz Times* magazine のやまだですが。おなまは。

Ben: ベンです。

Shingo: しんごです。

Interviewer: こんにちは。

Ben & Shingo: こんにちは。

Interviewer: しゅみはなんですか。

Ben: しゅみはスポーツです。

Interviewer: どんなスポーツをしますか。

Ben: ラグビーをします。

Interviewer: あっ、ラグビー？

Ben: はい。そして、けんどもします。

Interviewer: へー、けんど ... スポーツがすきですね。

Ben: はい、すきです。

Interviewer: しんごくん、しゅみはなんですか。

Shingo: ぼくもスポーツです。

Interviewer: あっ、はい。どんなスポーツをしますか。

Shingo: ローラーブレードをします。

Interviewer: へー、ローラーブレードができますか。

Shingo: はい。すこしできます。

Ben: しんごくん、ローラーブレードがじょうずですよ！

Shingo: いいえ、へたです。

Ben: じょうずだよ！！

Interviewer: はい、みなさん、ありがとうございました。さようなら。

Vocabulary notes

きょうはしゅみについてきいてみましょう。
Today, let's find out about hobbies.
ローラーブレードがじょうずです。
You're good at rollerblading.
じょうずです。 You're good at it.
へたです。 I'm terrible at it.

- **W122-3/T10** Students read the three profiles and answer the questions in English.
- **W124 /T12** Students ask five classmates about what they can do and fill in the table with their responses.
- **W127/T15** Students answer the questions truthfully in Japanese.

べんきょうのベンーカタカナ

S151 3A

Characters introduced: タ、ネ、ノ、ユ、リ、ロ

Warm-up

- Quickly revise the katakana that students have learnt so far, using katakana flashcards.
- *Hiragana-katakana perfect match*: divide the class into groups of 4 or 6. Give each group small hiragana cards for あ、い、え、お、か、き、く、け、こ、さ、し、す、そ、ち、つ、て、と、な、に、は、ひ、ふ、へ、ほ、み、ら、る、れ、ん (You could revise a smaller number if desired.) The teacher uses the katakana cards for ア、イ、エ、オ、カ、キ、ク、ケ、コ、サ、シ、ス、ソ、チ、ツ、テ、ト、ナ、ニ、ハ、ヒ、フ、ヘ、ホ、ミ、ラ、ル、レ、ン. The teacher holds up one katakana card at a time and, without the teacher saying aloud what the card is, students have to find the corresponding hiragana card. The student in the group with the most cards at the end is the winner.

Presentation

- Play the tape while students look at the Student Book. Stop the tape whenever you hear a 'ding'.

Audio script

SPEAKER: Ben

みんなさん、こんにちは。

It's Ben again with some more katakana.

But first, some revision. The katakana you already know are printed in black in the chart. Point to the ones I say, and repeat after me.

ア、イ、エ、オ、カ、ク、ケ、ツ、テ、ト、ナ、ニ、ハ、フ、ヘ、ホ、ラ、ル、ン

Look at the characters in the yellow boxes in the chart. See if you can work out how each one is pronounced.

...

Now look at the group of 6 large characters. Point to each one as I say it, and repeat after me.

1 タ
2 ネ
3 ノ
4 ユ
5 リ
6 ロ

よくできました。

Katakana sound changes

Look at the katakana sound changes in the blue box on the page. Repeat each one after me.

キ、 ギ
ヒ、 ビ
ヒュ、 ビュ
ホ、 ポ

Now listen to three of the words you have learnt in this unit and see if you can identify the sound changes in each one.

スポーツ、コンピューター、ラグビー

That's it from me. またね！

- Students look at the katakana insets and Yoplait sign in the photograph on page 151 and identify the characters they have learnt so far; then they try to figure out the meanings.
  For your information:
  バリューセット Value set (taken from a menu)
  イタリアンスペシャル・レシピ
  Italian special recipe *(a caption from a cooking magazine)*
  In the Yoplait advertisement:
  フランス生(うま)まれのデザート a dessert from France
  ブチフル beautiful

  Notice the JR (Japan Rail) sign: 渋谷駅(しぶやえき)。This photograph was taken at Shibuya station, a large station in Tokyo.
  These items could stimulate discussion of the use of English words in captions and advertising.

Follow-up

- **W116** かきかた *(How to write)*: students practise writing the characters in the boxes using the correct stroke order.
- **S151** *Find the odd sound*: students select the odd sound in each group of three presented. *Solutions*: 1a, 2a, 3c, 4c, 5b, 6b.
- *Katakana captain ball* (using the characters タ、ネ、ノ、ユ、リ、ロ):
  – Students are divided into teams with 6 a side.
  – Students are lined up as in captain ball, all holding katakana cards.
  One person stands at the front of the line.
  – Each player shows his/her card to the front person (captain) one at a time and then bobs down.
  – The captain reads each of the cards.
  – When the captain has read all the cards, s/he joins the front of the line and the last person comes up to the front and becomes the captain.
  – This continues as a relay until all players have had a turn as captain, with the winners the team to finish first.
- **W117/T1** Students fill in the missing katakana.
- **W117/T2** ことばさがし *(Find-a-word)*: students highlight the words in the puzzle and write them in the spaces provided.
- **W118/T3** Students unjumble the words and write them correctly.

ごはんとおかず

S152–3

Presentation

- Have students look at the sentence structures on page 152. The teacher asks individual students the question しゅみはなんですか。They have to give an answer from the page which no other student has given. If a student gives an answer which has already been given, that student is 'out'. This game should be played quickly so as to catch students out. When all responses have been used up, the student asked should answer わかりません. (Students should not write anything down during the game.) The game can be repeated with the sentence structures on page 153.
- Have students make up captions for the photos on pages 152–3.

Follow-up

- Ask students to answer the questions truthfully. You may need to provide them with more vocabulary to do this. (See *Need some extra words or expressions?* section in Unit 10 Overview.)
- Students look at the photographs on the double-page spread and in a sentence describe each one in Japanese.

Extension tasks

- **B10.1** *More about likes and dislikes*: students practise the questions and responses.
- **B10.2** *Culture match!*: students match each explanation, illustration and description of the various activities by drawing the same coloured line.
- **B10.3** *Personal profiles*: students read the information and fill in the profile sheet at the bottom of the page. Then, using that information answer their partner's questions about the person on their page. Then they swap over.

テーブルマナー

Warm-up

Students discuss the hobbies of their family members and note the similarities/differences between the hobbies of their grandparents, their parents and themselves.

Presentation

- かぞくのしゅみはなんですか。This can be presented as an individual reading task, where students are required to read the captions and make notes in English, or as a group reading task where the class is divided into four groups and each group reads and explains to the rest of the class the captions in a particular section, for example だいすけくん、だいすけくんのおかあさん、だいすけくんのおねえさん、だいすけくんのおとうさん。
- Students may be asked to research the traditional hobbies: さどう、こと、いけばな、ぼんさい、しょどう.

For your information:
さどう Tea ceremony (also called ちゃのゆ or ちゃど). Originally a Buddhist ritual, the tea ceremony is the art of preparing and serving powdered

green tea, observing highly structured rules of sequence and procedure. It may or may not involve the presentation of a whole meal and is practised as a form of meditation. Japanese girls study the art of さどう for many years.

いけばな Flower arrangement (also called かどう)。This developed as an art form in Japan from around the fifteenth century and today has many different schools with many different styles and techniques. There are approximately 3000 いけばな schools in Japan, with 15 to 20 million students.

しょどう Calligraphy. しょどう is the art of writing Japanese (or Chinese) characters with a brush. Many students learn しょどう at school.

ぼんさい This is the art of dwarfing trees or plants by pruning, restricting new growth and wiring the branches to modify shape. Most bonsai range in height from 5 centimetres to approximately 1 metre.

カラオケ Karaoke. Karaoke (the singing of songs backed by recorded musical accompaniment, with the words displayed on video screen) is one of the most popular pastimes in Japanese bars and pubs. It became popular in Japan in the early 1970s.

こと A thirteen-stringed musical instrument played by plucking the strings. It lies flat on the floor and the player sits on the floor in front of it.

おはし

S 156–7

Presentation

Discussion: students read the information on the double-page spread and discuss each section separately. Use the piece of authentic writing on the left of page 156 to demonstrate each of the points made. Have students find the punctuation marks, the sentence endings, the particles and examples of where a word has wrapped around onto the next line. The teacher should read the passages aloud to show the students where to pause (after particles, at commas and at full stops), and how to read the telephone number, inserting の in the spaces (〇三の三一四の二一八四)。

Follow-up

Have students analyse another piece of authentic writing from a book or magazine as they have done above. They need not be able to read or understand it, but they should be able to find the punctuation marks, the sentence endings and the particles.

おしょうゆ

S 158 3A

Presentation

Students listen to the tape and repeat the new expressions.

Follow-up

- **W 127/T16** おしょうゆクイズタイム: students circle the correct answer.
- *Oshooyu board:* add these expressions to a list on the pin-up board and encourage their use in writing and role-plays.
- *Romper room*: a set of flashcards for new expressions is placed on the blackboard ledge or attached to the board with Blu-Tack. Students are then asked to close their eyes while the teacher takes one or two of the cards away. They must identify the missing cards.
- **S 158** *Additional reading task*: students read the speech bubbles and write the names of the five students and their hobbies. As a follow-up, five students in the class can be asked to role-play the picture. (Michiko introduces herself and her friends one by one and each tells her about his/her hobby.)

おかし

S 159

Rap

Students learn and perform the rap to the following beat (the bold syllable takes the beat):

しゅみ**は**
なんですか
スポー**ツ**
おんがく
コンピューター

どく**しょ**
スケー**ト**
ラグビー
からて
ローラーブレー**ド**

Craft activity

かみぞめ *(Paper dyeing)*: you will need calligraphy paper (はんし) or paper towel, vegetable dye, water and elastic bands.

- Fold the paper in halves. Open out and then fold the same two edges into the centre line you have made. Fold these two edges into the centre again. Fold the corner of the strip over to make a triangle. Turn the whole piece over and fold the triangle over straight. Turn the whole paper over again and repeat the folds. Continue this until you are left with a triangle of paper. You may need to fold in any left-over flap.
- Tie elastic bands around corners for a mottled effect.
- Dip the corners in a mixture of vegetable dye and water.
- Leave for about 30 minutes before carefully opening.
- Dry flat.

These can be used for calligraphy, to fold up and make cards, or as wrapping paper.

Putting it all together

- **W123/T11 5B** Students listen to the interviews on tape and fill in the table describing each person's preferences regarding hobbies, sports, food and music.

  Note: as a warm-up to this task, students should practise the pattern:
  どんなおんがくがすきですか。
  どんなりょうりがすきですか。

Audio script:

a

Computer: コン・ピュー・ター・デ・ー・トです。なまえはなんですか。
Kenichi: ふくだけんいちです。
Computer: なまえはふくだけんいちです。なんさいですか。
Kenichi: 12さいです。
Computer: 12さいです。しゅみはなんですか。
Kenichi: ギターです。
Computer: しゅみはギター。どんなスポーツをしますか。
Kenichi: スポーツはぜんぜんできません。でも、バスケットボールがすきです。
Computer: スポーツがぜんぜんできません。でも、バスケットボールがすき。どんなおんがくがすきですか。
Kenichi: ビートルズがすきです。それから、クラシック・ミュージックもすきです。
Computer: ビートルズがすき。クラシック・ミュージックもすき。どんなりょうりがすきですか。
Kenichi: 日本りょうりがすきです。それから、ピザがすきです。
Computer: 日本りょうりがすき。ピザがすきです。あなたのタイプはAです。パートナーはAタイプがぴったりです。

b

Computer: コン・ピュー・ター・デ・ー・トです。なまえはなんですか。
Harjono: ハジョーノ・スダーガーです。
Computer: ハジョーノ・スダーガー、なんさいですか。
Harjono: 12さいです。
Computer: 12さい、しゅみはなんですか。
Harjono: しゅみはスポーツとおんがくです。
Computer: しゅみはスポーツとおんがく。どんなスポーツをしますか。
Harjono: すいえいをします。それから、クリケットとソフトボールがすこしできます。
Computer: スポーツはすいえいとクリケットとソフトボール。
Harjono: あのー、からてとけんどうがぜんぜんできません。
Computer: からてとけんどうがぜんぜんできません。どんなおんがくがすきですか。
Harjono: 日本のポップス・ミュージックがだいすきです。それから、ロック・ミュージックもすきです。クラシック・ミュージックはあんまり。
Computer: 日本のポップス・ミュージックがだいすき。ロック・ミュージックもすき。クラシック・ミュージックはあんまり。どんなりょうりがすきですか。
Harjono: インドネシアりょうりがすきです。それから、おべんとうがだいすきです。
Computer: インドネシアりょうりがすき。おべんとうがだいすき。あなたのタイプはBです。パートナーはBタイプがぴったりです。

c

Computer: コン・ピュー・ター・デ・ー・トです。なまえはなんですか。
Kate: ケイト・ヘンダソンです。
Computer: なまえはケイト・ヘンダソン、なんさいですか。
Kate: 11さいです。
Computer: 11さい、しゅみはなんですか。
Kate: しゅみはスポーツとパーティーです。
Computer: しゅみはスポーツとパーティー、どんなスポーツをしますか。
Kate: じょうばをします。それから、ネットボールとサーフィンとローラーブレードもします。からてとけんどうもすこしできます。
Computer: スポーツはじょうばとネットボールとサーフィンとローラブレード。それから、からてとけんどう。どんなおんがくがすきですか。
Kate: アメリカのロック・ミュージックがだいすきです。
Computer: アメリカのロック・ミュージックがすき。どんなりょうりがすきですか。

Kate: えーと、バーベキューがすきです。ソーセージとチキンとステーキがだいすきです。でも、サラダがきらいです。

Computer: バーベキューがすき。ソーセージとチキンとステーキがすき。サラダがきらい。あなたのタイプはCです。パートナーはCタイプがぴったりです。

d

Computer: コン・ピュー・ター・デ・ー・トです。なまえはなんですか。

Chieko: いしだちえこです。

Computer: なまえはいしだちえこ。なんさいですか。

Chieko: 11さいです。

Computer: 11さいです。しゅみはなんですか。

Chieko: しゅみ？まんがとコンピューターゲームがだいすきです。だから、しゅみはどくしょとコンピューターです。

Computer: しゅみはどくしょとコンピューター。コンピューターですか。スゴイ！！どんなスポーツをしますか。

Chieko: テニスとスキーをします。コンピューターゲームのテニスとスキーですね。

Computer: スポーツはテニスとスキー。コンピューターゲームのテニスとスキー。スゴイ！！！どんなおんがくがすきですか。

Chieko: 日本とアメリカのポップス・ミュージックがすきです。それから、シンセサイザーのおんがくもすきです。

Computer: 日本とアメリカのポップス・ミュージックがすき。それから、シンセサイザーのおんがくもすき。スゴイ！！どんなりょうりがすきですか。

Chieko: えーと、ハンバーガーとコーラがだいすきです。それから、ポテトチップスがだいすきです。アメリカりょうりがすきです。

Computer: ハンバーガーとコーラがすき。ポテトチップスがだいすき。アメリカりょうりがすき。スゴイ！！ぼくもチップスがすき。コンピューター・チップスがだいすき。あなたのタイプはスペシャルタイプです。ぴったりのパートナーはンピューターです。スゴイ！！！ぼくはちえこさんがすきです。

Vocabulary notes

コンピューターデート
Computer Dating Service
ビートルズ
The Beatles
クラシック・ミュージック
classical music
あなたのタイプはAです。
your type is A type
パートナーはAタイプがぴったりです。
As a partner, A type is perfect for you.
ポップス・ミュージック。
pop music
ロック・ミュージック
rock music
シンセサイザー
synthesiser
ポテトチップス
potato chips
コンピューター・チップス
computer chips

- **W 124 /T13** Students read the flyer for the class captain election and answer the questions in Japanese.
- **W 125–6 /T14** Students read the computer dating profiles and jot down notes in English for each. Then they answer the questions at the end.
- スポーツのこうこく *(Sports advertisement)*: you are the owner of a sports clinic and you want to advertise for new members. Make a poster to advertise your favourite sport. Write the name of the sport in large letters. Here are some slogans you could also write:
  みてください。 *Look at this.*
  からだにいいです。 *It's good for you.*
  たのしいです。 *It's fun.*
  せかいでいちばん。 *Number 1 in the world.*
  どうぞ。 *Here it is.*
- うんどうがすきですか。*Do you like exercise?* Perhaps your posters could be part of a school fitness promotion. Talk to your teacher about it.
- スポーツスター・インタビュー *(Sports star interview)*: find a partner and decide who will be the sports star and who will be the interviewer.
  As the interviewer, your task is to find out:
  – the person's name and where s/he is from
  – what sports s/he likes
  – what other sports s/he can do (and can't do)
  – foods and drinks s/he likes
  – what s/he has for meals, because you've heard that it is the secret to his/her success
  – whether s/he will be going to other sporting games while s/he is in town.
  As the star, your task is to:
  – give as much information as you can (you always give more information about yourself than you are asked to give)
  – show your strengths and wide-ranging interests as much as you can (your opponent might be watching the interview on TV and you don't want to show any weakness)

– be very cagey about your eating habits (remember, this is your secret weapon)
– give a good impression while you are in town.

ごちそうさま

- W128 *Obentoo quiz.* Students do the quiz for homework.
- *Individual progress cards*: write the items listed in *Gochisousama* onto the photocopiable student progress card on page 138 of the *Moshi Moshi Teacher's Handbook*. You may wish to add other items, for example other language points, cultural understandings, completion of homework or assignment tasks.
- *Discuss and report back*: students discuss their progress cards in small groups and a scribe takes note of the groups' common difficulties and suggestions for improvement. These are then reported back to the class.

Reference to *Yoroshiku National Curriculum Guidelines for Japanese (Moshi Moshi)*

The following is a list of the suggested language exponents presented in *Moshi Moshi* Module 2 かぞくとともだち *(Family and friends)* which have been introduced in Unit 10 of *Obentoo*. In some cases the example has been changed to correspond to the form introduced in *Obentoo*.

Language exponents

- Asking and giving information about hobbies
  しゅみはなんですか。
  (じょうば)です。
  わたしのしゅみは(サーフィン)です。

The following is a list of the suggested language exponents presented in *Moshi Moshi* Module 3 じぶんのこと *(Things about me)* which have been introduced in Unit 10 of *Obentoo*. In some cases the example has been changed to correspond to the form introduced in *Obentoo*. Appropriate activities from *Moshi Moshi* are suggested below.

Language exponents

- Enquiring about and expressing likes and dislikes
  どんな(スポーツ)がすきですか。
  (テニス)がすきです。
  (すいえい)もすきです。
- Asking and giving information about school subjects and sports
  どんな(スポーツ)をしますか。
  (テニス)をします。

Suggested activities from *Moshi Moshi*

さぶろうさんのかぞく。	Teacher Resources pages 13 and 19
おもしろいともだち、おもしろいかぞく。	Student Book page 11
好きですか。	Teacher Resources pages 22 and 31
Life: Be in it survey	Teacher Resources page 32
せいかくテスト	Teacher Resources page 23 and Student Book page 20

Unit 11

Overview

Unit objectives

Students will be able to:

- ask and talk about free-time activities
- suggest and agree with a course of action
- express and respond to opinions
- read and write five more katakana characters
- recognise seven more katakana sound changes
- talk about Japanese club activities
- prepare a short piece of Japanese writing

Functions and language exponents

1 Asking and talking about free-time activities
(ハジョーノくん)、がっこうのあとでなにをしますか。
(サーフィンのざっしをよみます)。

2 Suggesting and agreeing with a course of action
がっこうのあとでアイスクリームをたべましょう。
はい、(いっしょにたべましょう)。

3 Expressing and responding to opinions
アイスクリームはおいしいですね。
(はい)、(おいしいですね)。

Key vocabulary and expressions

がっこうのあとで
がっこうのまえに
ひまなとき
金曜日のばん
あしたのあさ
あしたのばん
あさ
よる

サーフィンのざっしをよみます。
ほんをよみます。
てがみをかきます。
ラジオをききます。
テレビをみます。
日本のビデオをみます。
けんどうのれんしゅうをします。
しゅくだいをします。
パーティーをします。
ともだちにでんわをします。
ねます。

アイスクリーム
おかし
おちゃ
まんが
からて
ビデオ
カラオケ
シーディー

...をたべましょう。
...をしましょう。
...をみましょう。
...をよみましょう。
...をかきましょう。
...をききましょう。
...をのみましょう。
...にいきましょう。
そうしましょう。
おいしい
まずい
やさしい
むずかしい
おもしろい
つまらない
たのしい

Script

Students are expected to be able to read and write the key characters and recognise the associated words

Key characters	*Associated words*
セ	ソーセージ
マ	マディソン、テーブルマナー
メ	メニュー
ヤ	ジャカルタ、キャンプ
ヨ	チョコレート、ハジョーノ

Script understandings

- Katakana combinations and sound changes: キュ、ジョ、ダ、ディ、ブ、フィ、ベ

Learning how to learn

Emma gives Kate suggestions on how to approach a Japanese writing competition:

- Making of list of things which you can already write about yourself in Japanese
- Underlining as a technique for identifying words which would change when writing about other people
- Why memorising sentences may have limited value
- Taking a long time (to write the sentences out in Japanese) isn't a bad thing
- Adding variety and interest

Cultural elements

Information about Japanese school club activities.

Other incidental language introduced

そして
日本ごで？
いらっしゃい！
ときどき、日本ごでかきます。

Extension material

No extension material is introduced in Unit 11.

Need some extra words or expressions? Ask your teacher!

ひるごはんのまえに	before lunch
しゅくだいのあとで	after homework
ざっし	magazine
しょうせつ	novel
レポート	report (assignment)
テープ	tape

Teaching suggestions

The following suggestions are provided as a guide to lesson planning and should be adapted to suit your teaching style and the learning styles of your students. These tasks are specific to this unit. For more information on general strategies for each section, refer to *Using Obentoo* on pages 3–8.

いただきます

Ⓢ 160–3 Ⓑ 3B

Warm-up

- Students brainstorm a list of club activities which take place in their school and another list with activities which they know (or think) are available in Japanese schools.
- Students research accounts of Japanese school life and add to the list of club activities above.
- Before the students look at the cartoon, the teacher compiles a list of club activities featured in the cartoon and the *Obentoo* students who are involved. Students see if they can guess which student belongs to which club.

Presentation

- Students look at the OHTs of the cartoon and see if they can guess what is happening. The teacher should explain the meaning of サッカーぶ、ぶんげいぶ、えいがぶ、ぶんつうぶ and さどうぶ. Then, with the cartoon divided into segments, the students listen to the tape and work out the dialogue.
- Students answer the questions on page 163.

Follow-up

- Students work through the cartoon, taking a section at a time, and change the names of the students involved, the clubs featured and the activities.
- After students have learnt expressions for the activities featured in the cartoon, the teacher (or a student) reads out one or more activities and students have to guess which club they refer to.
- The teacher takes more examples of club activities (real and fictitious) and, using the sentence pattern ... ぶはなにをしますか、drills the pattern.
  For example: テニスぶはなにをしますか。テニスをします。
  ラグビーぶはなにをしますか。ラグビーをします。
  コンピューターぶはなにをしますか。コンピューターをします。
  アイスクリームぶはなにをしますか。アイスクリームをたべます。
  Teachers may like to do this task after completing *Donna aji?1.*

どんなあじ？

Ⓢ 164–9

1 Asking and talking about free-time activities

Warm up

Replay *Itadakimasu* and explore the page as in earlier units.

Presentation

- Students listen to the tape while looking at the pictures on page 164 and see if they can figure out the meaning of each of the conversations. Then students listen again to the tape and repeat. You may need to pause the tape at the end of each line.
- Students listen, read the sentences on page 165 and repeat.
- In pairs, students practise the new sentence patterns.

Follow-up

- **Ⓦ 131/T5 Ⓑ 5B** Students listen to the interview with Tomoko and write down her schedule for a typical week. Students may write their answers in Japanese or English, depending on their confidence.

Audio script

SPEAKERS: Interviewer and Tomoko

I: ともこさん、まいにち、なにをしますか。
T: まいにち、がっこうにいきます。
I: でも、がっこうのまえになにをしますか。
T: がっこうのまえですか。ええと、あさごはんをたべます。そして、テレビをみます。
I: そうですか。がっこうのあとで、なにをしますか。
T: 月曜日はホッケーです。火曜日はダンスです。水曜日もダンスです。そして、木曜日にテニスのれんしゅうをします。
I: あっ、いそがしいですね。しゅくだいは？
T: よる、しゅくだいをします。そして、ときどき、てがみをかきます。
I: 金曜日のばんは？
T: いいえ、金曜日のばんはしゅくだいをしません。よくビデオをみます。そして、ときどき、ざっしをよみます。

Vocabulary note

いそがしいですね。	You're busy, aren't you.

- **Ⓦ 132/T6 Ⓑ 5B** Students listen to the interview and write in the table what each member of Kyoko's family does in his or her spare time.

Audio script

Kyoko: こんにちは。たなかきょうこです。わたしはひまなときにほんをよみます。テニスをします。そして、おんがくをききます。あっ、おかあさん、しゅくだいですけど、ひまなときになにをしますか。

Mum: ああ、いそがしい！！

Kyoko: おかあさん！

Mum: あとで。

Kyoko: じゃ、おとうさん、ひまなときになにをしますか。

Dad: えっ、ひまなときに？　あっ、しゅくだいですか。

Kyoko: はい、そうです。

Dad: えーと、ひまなときにざっしをよみます。そして、テレビをみます。あっ、ときどきゴルフをします。

Kyoko: はい、ざっしをよ・み・ま・す。テレビをみ・ま・す。ゴルフをし・ま・す。ありがとう、おとうさん。

Dad: うん。

Kyoko: おかあさん、ひまなときになにをしますか。

Mum: あとで、あとで、いそがしい！

Kyoko: はーい。

Grandma: うーん、おいしい。

Kyoko: おばあさん、ひまなときになにをしますか。

Grandma: おちゃをのみます。そして、おかしをたべます。おいしいです。

Kyoko: ああ、そうですか。おちゃをのみます。そして、おかしをたべます。

Grandma: はい、どうぞ、たべなさい、おいしいよ。

Kyoko: ありがとう。おばあさん、ほんをよみますか。

Grandma: いいえ、ぜんぜんよみません。

Kyoko: テレビをみますか。

Grandma: はい、ひるごはんのあとでテレビをみます。

Kyoko: はい、ありがとう、おばあさん。

Mum: ごはんですよー。

Everyone: はーい！

Kyoko: おかあさん、ひまなときになにをしますか。

Mum: ちょっとまって、ごはんのあとでね。

Kyoko: はい。ねー、すすむくん、ひまなときになにをしますか。

Brother: サッカーのれんしゅうをします。

Kyoko: それから、ビデオをみますね。

Brother: はい、そう。

Kyoko: はい、ありがとう。

Brother: うん。

Kyoko: じゃ、おかあさん、ひまなときになにをしますか。おかあさん、おかあさんはひまなときにねます。

Vocabulary notes

いそがしい！！	I'm busy!
たべなさい！	Have some!

- **W 132–3/T7** Students read the questions and then circle the answers which apply to them.
- **W 133/T8** Students survey three friends to find out what they do in their spare time. They should use the questions in Task 7 as a guide. Students then write their answers in Japanese in the table.
- **W 134/T9** Students write sentences in Japanese describing the pictures.
- **W 134/T10** Students complete the sentences by adding a time phrase to the beginning of each.
- Use flashcards to drill new sentence patterns that ask questions using the time phrases presented. For example: 金曜日になにをしますか。がっこうのまえになにをしますか。ひまなときに、なにをしますか。
- おぼえていますか。*–TV game show*:
  - Three contestants are chosen to play.
  - All other students write on a small piece of paper their name and a sentence describing what they do after school.
  - Each student reads out his/her sentence and then hands it in to the compere (the teacher).
  - The compere then puts questions to the contestants based on the audience's sentences. For example:
    ベンくんはがっこうのあとでなにをしますか。
    Contestant answers (for example) サーフィンのざっしをよみます。
    (The contestants must be the first to put their hands up or press a buzzer to answer.)
- *How well do you know your friends?*: the teacher makes a list of students in the class and a list of free-time activities. The teacher (or a student) picks a day of the week and all students write two activities which they would do on that day (in English, or in Japanese if the students are able). The students then select two activities which they think each person would do on the designated day. Students are then asked in Japanese what they do after school and their classmates check their answers.
- Students take the role of celebrities and ask each other what they do after school or in their free time. The dialogues could be performed in front of the class.

2 Suggesting and agreeing with a course of action

Warm-up

- Students look at the thought bubbles within the frames on page 166 and identify in Japanese what the *Obentoo* students are doing. For example:
  1 アイスクリームをたべます。
  2 けんどうをれんしゅうします。
  3 まんがをよみます。
  4 カラオケパーティーにいきます。(From the picture, students will probably identify カラオケをします。)
  5 シーディーをききます。
- Then play the tape and have students look at the pictures on page 166. Discuss the difference in sound and meaning between ... ます and ... ましょう forms.

Presentation

- Students listen to the tape and repeat. (You may need to pause the tape after each sentence to allow time to repeat.)
- Students listen, read the sentences on page 165 and repeat.
- In pairs, students practise the new sentence patterns.
- Students sit in circles and make a different suggestion for each day of the week. If anyone repeats a previous suggestion (or uses a day or date in the wrong order) s/he moves to the end of the circle. Suggestions can only be repeated when they have all been used once.

Follow-up

- **W 135/T11** **5B** Students listen to the conversations on the tape and write down what each pair decides to do. Students may write their answer in English or Japanese, depending on their confidence in writing script.

Audio script

a

A: もしもし、ふくだです。
B: もしもし、けんいちくんですか。
A: はい、そうです。
B: ハジョーノです。こんにちは。
A: ああ、こんにちは。
B: あのう、土曜日、なにをしますか。
A: 土曜日？えーと、ビデオをみます。
B: へえ、なにをみますか。
A: Dracula をみます。
B: へえ、いいね。
A: いっしょにビデオをみましょう。
B: いいね、そうしましょう。

b

A: ひま！！！
B: つまらない。
A: じゃ、シーディーをききましょう。
B: いいえ、つまらないです。
A: ざっしをよみましょう。
B: いいえ、ざっしはつまらないです。
A: えいがにいきましょう。
B: いいえ、えいがはつまらないです。
A: じゃ、パーティーをしましょう。
B: パーティー？いいですね。パーティーをしましょう。
A: そうしましょう。
B: じゃ、ともだちにでんわをしましょう。

c

A: さなえさん、日曜日はカーラのたんじょうびです。
B: そうですか。カーラさんはパーティーをしますか。
A: いいえ、しません。
B: へえ、かわいそう！
A: じゃ、カーラのうちにいきましょう。そして、バーベキューパーティーをしましょう。
B: はい。そして、シーディーをききましょう。そして、バレーボールをしましょう。
A: いいですね。パーティーがだいすきです。

d

A: わたしはしゅくだいがきらいです。
B: うーん。
A: しゅくだいはつまらないです。
B: そうですね。
A: いっしょにレストランにいきましょう。
B: レストラン？
A: はい、ココアをのみましょう。
B: ココア？
A: はい、そして、チョコレート・ケーキをたべましょう。
B: ええ、そうしましょう。

e

A: みきこさん、スポーツがすきですか。
B: はい、すきです。
A: どんなスポーツがすきですか。
B: あきらくんはどんなスポーツがすきですか。
A: ぼくはバスケットボールがすきです。
B: あっ、わたしもバスケットボールがすきです。
A: ぼくはバスケットボールがだいすきです。

B: わたしもだいすきです。

A: ああ、そう。えーと、じゃー、土曜日に、いっしょにバスケットボールのしあいをみましょう。

B: あっ、いいわね。そうしましょう。

A: よかった！！

Vocabulary notes

ひま！	I'm bored!
かわいそう！	the poor thing!

- **135/T12** Students complete the sentences with an appropriate suggestion.
- **136/T14** Students write a suggestion based on each picture.
- *Quickly!*: students draw flashcards depicting (1) after school, (2) days of the weekend, (3) other time words they have learnt. The cards are held up one at a time and the first student who can suggest a suitable course of action puts up his/her hand. Students get a point for each suggestion they make correctly.
- *Word cards*: make three sets of word cards, one set of time phrases, one set of nouns (for example ほんを、サッカーを、ケーキを、テレビを) and one set of verbs in the ましょう form. It is a good idea to make each set on a different coloured cardboard. Students form groups of 2–4 and within a time limit they must make appropriate sentences by putting the cards together. Points are given for each correct sentence; sentences which do not make sense do not gain a point.

3 Expressing and responding to opinions

Warm-up

Students make a list of all the adjectives they have learnt so far. Don't forget the ones introduced in the *Oshooyu* sections like しずか、かわいい、きれい、ひどい、おもしろい (funny), すてき、おいしそう and すごい. Students then match them up with a noun, using the pattern *(Noun)* は *(Adjective)* です。

Presentation

- Students listen to the tape and look at the pictures on page 168. They listen again and repeat. Then they listen, read the sentences on page 169 and repeat.
- *How compatible are you?*: students write a list of activities, foods and drinks, TV programs, etc. In pairs, ask for their partner's opinion about each of the things listed, putting a tick if s/he agrees and a cross if s/he disagrees. Then the partners swap over.

Follow-up

- **135/T13** Using their suggestions from Task 12, students ask other members of the class to do those activities. Students sign in the space provided if they agree with the suggestion, or answer using the pattern if they do not agree.
- **138/T18** Students listen to the conversations and write down in English what each person is talking about and any responses they hear.

Audio script

a **A:** おたんじょうびおめでとう。

B: ありがとう。なんですか。あっ、チョコレート！おいしい！！

b **A:** あしたがっこうにいきません。

B: えっ！なにをしますか。

A: バレーボールのキャンプにいきます。

B: へー！いいね。

c **A:** ローラーブレードができますか。

B: ローラーブレード？いいえ、ぜんぜんできません。ローラーブレードはむずかしいですよ。

d **A:** あしたケイトさんのパーティーにいきますか。

B: いいえ、いきません。

A: えっ、いきません？

B: うん、おばあさんとかぞくのビデオをみます。

A: なんだ、つまらないね。

B: つまらないですよ。

e **A:** なんですか。

B: ペットのほんです。

A: へー！

B: おもしろいですよ。

- **139/T19** *Part A*: students link the nouns on the left to the adjectives on the right.
- **139/T19** *Part B*: students write sentences linking the two words.
- **140/T20** Students write down in Japanese three activities they would like to do. Then they survey people in their class to find out who wants to do the same thing. Students use the pattern いっしょに...をしましょう。If they have the same activity written down, they should answer はい、そうしましょう。おもしろいです。(or some other adjective). If not, they should give a reason for refusing, for example:
  いいえ、...はつまらないです。
  いいえ、...はまずいです。
  いいえ、...はむずかしいです。
  Students should then write the names of the matching people in the second column in Japanese if they can. The winner is the first person

to find a partner for all three activities.
- *Contradict me!:* students form pairs. The first student makes a statement about something, for example アイスクリームはおいしいですね。 The partner has to contradict the statement using an opposite adjective, for example いいえ、まずいです。

べんきょうのベンーカタカナ

S 170 3B

Characters introduced: セ、マ、メ、ヤ、ヨ

Warm-up
- Give students a quick quiz on the katakana they have learnt so far.
- Choose some of the more difficult katakana introduced so far and play the 'Pass-it-on' game:
  - Students are divided into teams (about 5 students in each) and lined up in front of the board.
  - The teacher shows the students in the back row a card with a character on it.
  - They write it with their finger on the back of the person in front of them.
  - The character is passed down the line until the front person writes it on the board.
  - Points are given to the first team to correctly write the character on the board.

Presentation
- Students listen to the tape, repeat the sounds and complete the tasks. Pause the tape whenever you hear a 'ding'.

Audio script

SPEAKER: Ben

みんなさん、こんにちは。

It's Ben again with five more katakana.

But first, some revision. The katakana you already know are printed in black in the chart. Point to the ones I say, and repeat after me.

ク、タ、テ、ネ、ノ、ホ、ユ、リ、ル、ロ、ン

Look at the characters in the yellow boxes in the chart. See if you can work out how each one is pronounced.

...

Now look at the group of five large characters. Point to each one as I say it, and repeat after me.

1 セ
2 マ
3 メ
4 ヤ
5 ヨ

よくできました。

Katakana sound changes

Look at the katakana sound changes and combinations in the green box on the page. Repeat each one after me.

キ、　キュ、
ショ、　ジョ
タ、　ダ
ティ、　ディ
フ、　ブ
フ、　フィ
ヘ、　ベ

Now listen to five of the words you have learnt in this unit and see if you can identify the sound changes or combinations in each one.

サーフィン、バーベキュー・パーティー、クラブ、シーディー、ダンスパーティー

That's it from me. またね。

- Students try to read the signs and advertisements on page 170. For your information:
  メガネスーパー
  glasses supermarket
  これがジャスコの価値あるセール
  This is Jusco's value sale
  マリン
  Marine

Follow-up
- **S 129** かきかた *(How to write)*: students practise writing the characters in the boxes using the correct stroke order. They also identify the 'human characters' at the bottom of the page.
- **S 170** *Find the odd sound*: students select the odd sound in each group of three presented. *Solutions*: 1a, 2b, 3, 4c, 5a, 6b.
- **W 130/T1** Students circle the correct katakana combinations and practise writing them in the boxes.
- **W 130/T2** Students highlight the combination sounds in the words.
- **W 130/T3** Students draw a line between each katakana word and its corresponding word in English.
- **W 131/T4** Students do the crossword puzzle, filling in the words in hiragana.
- *Katakana captain ball:*–The class is divided into teams of five and each student is given a card with one of the new katakana on it.
  - The students line up as in captain ball, all holding katakana cards.
  - One person stands at the front of the line.
  - Each player shows his/her card to the front person (captain) one at a time and then bobs down.
  - When the captain has read all the cards, s/he joins the front of the line and the last person comes up to the front and becomes the captain.
  - This continues as a relay until all players have had a turn as captain, with the winners the team to finish first.

ごはんとおかず

S 171–3

Warm-up

On the buses: (for the procedure, refer to page 106 in these notes): a quiz using all of the verbs learnt so far:
あけます
いきます
います
きます
します
しめます
すわります
たちます
たべます
できます
のみます
みせます
Have students change the ます form to the ません form, English to Japanese, and Japanese to English.

Presentation

- Present the time expressions on page 171 of the Student Book on coloured cards, and discuss with students the meaning and structure. See how many variations of each time clause they can make, for example:
  あしたのばん
  金曜日のばん
  土曜日のばん
  月曜日のばん
  がっこうのあとで
  しゅくだいのあとで
  ばんごはんのあとで
- Do the same with the sentence patterns on the right-hand side of page 171.
- Similar tasks can be done with the language introduced on pages 172 and 173.

Follow-up

- *Sentence perfect match*: write time expressions on one colour card, objects on another colour card and verbs on a third colour card. Divide the class into groups of approximately three students and give a full set to each group. Within a time limit, have them arrange the cards on a desk (or on the board with Blu-Tack) in meaningful sentences. Points are allocated for each correct sentence. The same task can be done using the expressions on pages 172 and 173.
- Nouns (see page 173) are written on cards and placed in one box and adjectives are written on cards and placed in another box. The class is divided into two teams. A representative of each team comes out, draws a card from both boxes and then puts them together to form a sentence, for example アイスクリームはおいしいですね。 If the sentence makes sense (the rest of the class judges), the team gains a point. If it does not make sense, for example アイスクリームはむずかしいですね。 the team loses a point.
- *On the buses* (refer page 106): play the game using the verbs introduced in Unit 11 as well as the verbs previously learnt. Have students change verbs from the ます form to the ましょう form, ます to ません, ません to ましょう, etc.
- Have students read the extra reading passage on page 171 and make a list of Izumi's friends and what they do after school. Why do we feel sorry for Izumi?
- Have students read the speech bubble on page 173. What does it say?
- Have students make up captions for the photos on pages 171, 172 and 173 for example しんごくんはがっこうのあとでしゅくだいをします。
- *Extra reading tasks*: have students recognise as many katakana as they can in the photos on page 172.
  For your information:
  Movie posters for *Broken Arrow* and *Babe*
  CD by ZARD, a Japanese pop group, with Izumi Sakai on vocals
  Ice-cream stand:

アイスクリーム	*ice-cream*
￥１００	*100 yen*
バニラ	*vanilla*
チョコレート	*chocolate*
抹茶（まっちゃ）	*green tea*
ラムレーズン	*rum 'n' raisin*
チョコミント	*choc mint*
ソフトクリーム	*soft serve*

- **B 11.1** *A-mazed*: in the maze there are 20 words and expressions. Students try to find them and put them into the sentences below.
- *Pictionary*: divide the class into teams of 3–4. Have them play Pictionary against other teams, using the sentences on the *Gohan to okazu* pages. (A member of one team draws a picture to illustrate a sentence and the other members of his/her team must guess the sentence in a time limit. Points are given for correct answers within the time limit.)

テーブルマナー

S 174–5

- Use these pages as a springboard for discussion about Japanese club activities. For your information:
  Club activities are offered by the school and are held before or after school. Each school has a wide range of activities for students to try, from sports clubs to music clubs and traditional cultural activities. The clubs are organised by teachers and/or senior students. They are usually held in the school grounds and are open only to students attending that school. The school club may, however, compete against other school clubs in regional competitions on weekends. Students take their involvement in club activities just as seriously

as they take their study. They tend to stay in one or two clubs throughout their school life and move from a こうはい to a せんぱい in the one club. The system of seniority within clubs is also taken very seriously. The こうはい are expected to show respect for the せんぱい by bowing whenever they meet, both within the club activity time and at any time during the day. In turn, the せんぱい are expected to look after the こうはい within the school.

- **Ⓑ 11.2** *Find someone who…*: photocopy the cards on the left onto one colour card and the cards on the right onto another colour card. Give one card to each student, making sure that both cards in each pair have been given out. The student with the question must find the student who has the description of the club activity.
  Alternative: white out the 2nd, 4th, 6th ... card on the left and 1st, 3rd, 5th ... card on the right. Make copies and hand them out to Person A in each pair of students. Then white out the opposite cards, copy them and hand them out to Person B in each pair of students. Have them ask each other questions and fill out the missing information.
  Alternative: make sets of cards and divide the class into groups of 4 students. Put the cards face down on the desk. Students take turns at turning over two cards in an effort to match the question with the correct answer.

おはし

Ⓢ 176

Presentation

Have two students act out the conversation between Emma and Kate. Discuss the questions at the bottom of the page.

Follow-up

- The Japan Foundation runs a Japanese speech contest and a Japanese essay competition each year. Encourage students to enter these competitions.
- Have students prepare a short self-introduction composition or a composition about their best friend.
- *Focus on dictionary skills*: show students how to look words up in a Japanese–English dictionary. Have students look up some words they already know in a Japanese–English dictionary and an English–Japanese dictionary.

おしょうゆ

Ⓢ 177 Ⓣ 3B

Presentation

- Students listen to the tape and repeat the new expressions.
- 日本ごで *and* ときどき、日本ごでかきます: have students replace 日本ご with other languages.
- *How many times?:* students listen to the tape of the cartoon story again and count how many times each expression is used.

おかし

Ⓢ 177

Song

Sing the song to the tune of Sukiyaki.

Craft activity

こいのぼり *(carp streamer)*: refer to page 147 of *Japanese Culture – Resources and Activities* by Karan Chandler (Nelson ITP, 1996).

Putting it all together

- **Ⓦ 136/T15** Students write a letter to a friend.
- **Ⓦ 137/T16** Students read Toshio's letter to David and answer the questions in English.
- **Ⓦ 138/T17** Students write a reply to Toshio's letter.
- **Ⓦ 140-1/T21** *Part A*: students read the invitations and write as much information about them as they can in English.
- **Ⓦ 141/T21** *Part B*: students design a notice for their school fête or for a party.
- **Ⓦ 141/T22** Students answer the questions in Japanese.
- いらっしゃい！ *Step right up!*: you and a partner are making a TV commercial for your favourite school club. In the commercial, you should say the name of the club and what you do. In the short time that remains, you've decided to
  – EITHER say the day and something you might be doing, followed by your partner, who talks about another day, and so on
  – OR give the information about your club as an interview between yourself, as the club member, and your partner, as the 'passer by in the street' who's interested in joining.
  – Don't forget to mention all the parties you have. Make your opinions about the club and its activities very obvious–remember, you want lots of people to join.
- お休みのスケジュール*(Holiday schedule)*: the holidays are approaching and this time you're going to plan ahead! Pick a date and a day and write it at the top of the page. Draw pictures of the activities you plan to do. Don't forget to include meals and snacks you might want to have. When you've finished, go around the class and ask the other students what they plan to do. Mark on your schedule when you find someone who has planned the same activity as you. Don't forget to give your opinions about what other people have planned too!

- ゲームショーレポーター *(Game show reporter)*: you are interviewing people to go on a TV game show. You have a group of four people and you ask them questions about what they do in their spare time in order to find the most interesting person to appear on the show. Each person you interview tries to sound more interesting than the previous person. They are also quick to give their opinions about what other people like doing–of course, what *they* do is always more interesting than what anyone else does!
- **B 11.3** しゅうまつに！: students make arrangements for the weekend and record them on the right-hand side of the sheet. The information on the left indicates whether they like the idea or not. They should use the patterns:
  ...（に）...を ... ましょう。
  はい、そうしましょう。... は ...です。
  or いいえ、... は... です。
  For example:
  A: 金曜日のばん、ざっしをよみましょう。
  B: はい、そうしましょう。ざっしはおもしろいです。
  B: 土曜日にシーディーをききましょう。
  A: いいえ、シーディーはつまらないです。

Students take turns in asking and answering. More than one activity should be suggested for each time slot.

ごちそうさま

- **W 142** *Obentoo quiz*: Students complete the self-study quiz and swap books with another student for marking.
- *Individual progress cards*: write the items listed in *Gochisoosama* onto the photocopiable student progress card on page 138 of the *Moshi Moshi Teachers' Handbook*. You may wish to add other items, for example other language points, cultural understandings, completion of homework or assignment tasks.

Reference to *Yoroshiku National Curriculum Guidelines for Japanese (Moshi Moshi)*

The following is a list of the suggested language exponents presented in *Moshi Moshi* Module 4 フリータイム (*Free-time*) which have been introduced in Unit 11 of *Obentoo*. In some cases the example has been changed to correspond to the form introduced in *Obentoo*. Appropriate activities from *Moshi Moshi* are suggested below.

Language exponents

- Asking for and giving information about after-school activities
  がっこうのあとでなにを(し)ますか。
  (ともだち)の(うち)にいきます。
  そのあとでなにを(し)ますか。
- Making and responding to suggestions
  (日曜日)になにを(し)ましょうか。
  (えいが)をみましょう。
  ええ、(み)ましょう。
  いいえ、(ビデオをみ)ましょう。
- Stating opinions
  (クリケット)は(おもしろい)です。
  (これ)は(まずい)です。
- Disagreeing
  いいえ、(おいしい)です。
- Emphasising opinions
  (おいしい)ですよ。
  そうですよ。

Suggested activities from *Moshi Moshi*

いつかいものにいきますか。
Teacher Resources pages 36 and 39
メッセージ
Teacher Resources page 36, Student Book page 26
いつ行きましょう。
Teacher Resources page 36, Student Book page 27
じゅんばんに！
Teacher Resources pages 37 and 42
ちょうさ：ひまなじかん
Teacher Resources pages 38 and 44
どうですか。
Teacher Resources page 38, Student Book page 30
まんが
Teacher Resources Pages 38 and 43

Overview

Unit objectives

Students will be able to:

- ask what someone did and respond when asked
- ask what something was like and respond when asked
- ask what means of transport someone uses and respond when asked
- read and write all of the katakana characters
- recognise one more katakana sound change
- talk about events in the Japanese school year
- talk about strategies they have used to learn Japanese

Functions and language exponents

1 Asking what someone did/Saying what you did
(しんごくん)、きのうなにをしましたか。
(くつをかいました。そして、カセットをききました)。

2 Asking and saying what something was like
(カーラさん、)(パーティーは)どうでしたか。
(たのしかったです。)

3 Asking what transport someone uses/Saying what transport you use
(しんごくん)なんでいきましたか。
(ローラーブレード)でいきました。

Key vocabulary and expressions

...曜日
... 月 ... 日
きのう
...曜日のばん
休みに
なにをしましたか。

... さんのかぞくにあいました。
えんそくにいきました。
ローラーコースターにのりました。
ダンスをしました。
日本のえいがをみました。
てがみをかきました。
カセットをききました。
コーラをのみました。
ケーキをたべました。
くつをかいました。
ほんをよみました。

すいえいたいかい
えんそく
なつ休み
キャンプ
うんどうかい
しけん
ぶんかさい
クリスマス・パーティー
... はどうでしたか。

おもしろかったです。
つまらなかったです。
やさしかったです。
むずかしかったです。
おいしかったです。
まずかったです。
たのしかったです。

なんでいきましたか。
ローラーブレードで
バスで
じてんしゃで
でんしゃで
タクシーで
しんかんせんで
...さんのくるまで
あるいて

Script

Students are expected to be able to read and write the key characters and recognise the associated words.

Key characters	*Associated words*
ウ	ウィークエンド
ヌ	ヌガー、ヌードル
ム	アイスクリーム
モ	モー・モー
ワ	ワン・ワン
ヲ	

Script understanding

- Katakana sound change ウィ

Learning how to learn

Students reflect on their study of Japanese:

- The first few lessons
- Listen and guess
- Speaking Japanese
- Reading and writing Japanese
- Japan and the Japanese people
- Learning another language

Cultural elements

Events in the Japanese school year:

- にゅうがくしき
- キャンプ
- しけん
- なつ休み
- しゅうがくりょこう
- うんどうかい
- ぶんかさい
- そつぎょうしき

Other incidental language introduced

日本ごができませんでした。
びっくりしました。
とても
日本のかしゅ
せんせいのチームがかちました。
はじめてふぐをたべました。
からだにきをつけて。
ダンスをしませんでした。
わすれないで。
しあわせ！
すこしつまらなかったです。
かわいそうに！
アメリカからレポーターがきました。

Extension material

- Past negative of verbs ... ませんでした。
- ... ましたか。
- ... にいきましたか。
  いいえ、いきませんでした。
- Use of particle に in おかあさんにてがみをかきました。
- はじめて for the first time

Need some extra words or expressions? Ask your teacher!

なつ休みに	during the summer holidays
ふゆ休みに	during the winter holidays
はる休みに	during the spring holidays
あき休みに	during the autumn holidays
クリスマス休み	during the Christmas holidays
じてんしゃにのりました。	I rode a bike.
スケートボードにのりました。	I rode a skateboard.
ジーパンをかいました。	I bought some jeans.
スカートをかいました。	I bought a skirt.
シャッツをかいました。	I bought a shirt.
ズボンをかいました。	I bought some trousers.

Teaching suggestions

The following suggestions are provided as a guide to lesson planning and should be adapted to suit your teaching style and the learning styles of your students. These tasks are specific to this unit. For more information on general strategies for each section, refer to *Using Obentoo* on pages 3–8.

いただきます

Ⓢ179–80 Ⓣ 3B

Presentation

- Divide the class into groups of 3–4 students. Give them each a section of the text to read and prepare. Have the students present their section to the class by reading it aloud and translating it, by reading it aloud and acting it out, or simply by explaining it in English. The teacher should elicit from the students some of the sentence patterns contained in the text (ました、バスで、...かったです)。Students should try to explain the meaning and the usage.
- Then play the tape section by section. In their groups, the students discuss the meaning and structure. They should first focus on words or expressions which they have learnt before and list them on the board or on large sheets of butcher's paper. Then they listen to the tape again, focusing on new words and expressions. Students list them on the board or on large sheets of butcher's paper.
- Students then complete the questions on page 183.
- Alternatively, pages 179–80 can be introduced by listening to the tape first and then dividing the class into groups for the reading task.

Follow-up

Have students list the events in the school year mentioned in the *Itadakimasu* section and, using the school calendar, write the dates of each of those events in their own school. The rest of this task can be completed in the Putting It All Together section *(Memories of this year).*

Ⓢ181–3 Ⓣ 3B

Presentation

Pages 181–3 can be introduced directly after the previous pages or can be left until after the *Donna aji?* section has been completed. If they are done immediately, they can be treated in a similar way to the previous section (listening to the tape, reading in groups, etc.). If they are done after *Donna Aji?* they can be presented in the following way:

- Discuss the title 一年間の思い出一年二組み
- Present the pictures without the text, either as OHTs or as flashcards (copy and enlarge the pictures). Have students try to make up at least one sentence for each picture. Then have them listen to the tape and match the text to the correct picture. Finally have students read and understand each caption.

どんなあじ?

Ⓢ184–9 Ⓣ 3B

1 Asking what someone did/Saying what you did

Warm-up

- Replay *Itadakimasu* and explore the page as in earlier units.
- Use flashcards to revise the verbs learnt so far in their ます forms.

Presentation

- Students look at the pictures on page 184 and listen to the tape. Discuss the meanings of each.
- Students listen to the tape, look at the pictures and repeat the Japanese.
- Students listen to the tape, read the text on page 185 and repeat the Japanese.
- Students form pairs and practise the structures at the bottom of page 185.

Follow-up

- Students go back to the pictures on page 184 and expand the dialogues so that the second speaker asks the first speaker what s/he did. Students can be asked to act out their expanded dialogues.
- **Ⓦ146/T4** Students answer the questions truthfully in Japanese.
- **Ⓦ146–7/T5** Students read the sentences and in the space next to each person in the picture on page 146 they write the number of the relevant sentence. They also write T if the sentence is true or F if it is false.
- **Ⓦ147/T6** First the students write down three things that they did on the weekend. Then in pairs they try to find out what their partner did by asking questions which must be answered with はい、...ました。or いいえ、...ませんでした。(see the examples on page 147 of the Workbook). After each sentence has been guessed, they count up the number of questions needed to guess it and write the number in the box provided. After both students have had a turn to ask questions, they add up the points and the person with the smallest number of points is the winner. You may like to have a tournament where winners do the task again with other winners until a champion is left.

2 Asking and saying what something was like

Warm-up

Hold up a series of pictures cut from magazines and ask students どうですか。*(What is it like?)*. Revise the adjectives already learnt, as well as any from this unit that students can remember from the *Itadakimasu* pages.

Presentation

- Students look at the pictures on page 186 and listen to the tape. Discuss the meanings of each.
- Students listen to the tape, look at the pictures and repeat the Japanese.
- Students listen to the tape, read the text on page 187 and repeat the Japanese.
- Students form pairs and practise the structures at the bottom of page 187.

Follow-up

- Using photos from the previous year's year book/ school magazine ask students ... はどうでしたか。 If students have been on an excursion during the year, the questions can be based on it.
- **W149/T9** Students write captions for the holiday pictures.
- **W149/T10 5B** Students listen to the tape and write how the speaker feels about the items mentioned. Students may write in English or in Japanese, depending on their confidence.

Audio script

A: なつ休みはどうでしたか。
B: たのしかったです。

A: しけんはどうでしたか。
B: むずかしかったです。

A: すしはどうでしたか。
B: まずかったです。

A: クリスマス・パーティーはどうでしたか。
B: つまらなかったです。

A: ぶんかさいはどうでしたか。
B: おもしろかったです。

A: 日本ごはどうでしたか。
B: やさしかったです。

- **W150/T11** Students listen to the Japanese exchange students talking about how they spent their holidays. They fill in the table in English or Japanese.

Audio script

SPEAKERS: Everyone, Teacher, Students (P1-4)

E: せんせい、おはようございます。
T: ああ、みなさん、おはよう。おやすみはどうでしたか。
E: よかった、おもしろかった、よかった。
T: なにをしましたか。
P1: わたしはゴールドコーストにいきました。まいにちおよぎました。
E: へえ、まいにち？
P1: ええ、とてもたのしかったです。
P2: ぼくはニュージーランドにいきました。
E: へー、ニュージーランド？
P2: はい。そしてね、バンジージャンプをしました。
E: へー、こわい！
P2: こわかったですよ。でも、すごくよかったです。
P3: ぼくはまいにちえいがをみました。
E: うそ！
P2: ほんとうですよ。まいにちみました。Greater Union Cinema でアルバイトをしました。
E: へー、どうでしたか。
P2: たのしかったです。まいにちポップコーンをたべました。
P4: ねえ、ねえ、ねえ、わたしはトム・クルーズにあいました。
Girls: わー、すごーい、どうして？わたしはトム・クルーズにラジオのコンテストのてがみをかきました。
E: へえー、しんじられない！
P4: そしてね、トム・クルーズさんといっしょにレストランにいきました。
E: わーー、うそ！
P4: わたしはチキンをたべました。トムさんもチキンをたべました。
E: わー、どうでしたか。
P4: おいしかったです。！！
E: ちがーう。！！トムさんはどうでしたか。
P4: ああ、トムさんはとてもやさしかったです。

Vocabulary notes

ゴールドコースト	Gold Coast
およぎました。	I swam.
バンジージャンプ	bungee jumping
ポップコーン	popcorn
ラジオのコンテスト	radio contest
いっしょに	together
とても	very

- **W150/T12 5B** Students listen to the tape and fill in the table in English or Japanese.

Audio script

SPEAKERS: Teacher and Emiko

T: えみこさん、月曜日に、がっこうのあとでほんをよみましたか。

E: いいえ、よみませんでした。しゅくだいをしました。

T: はい。じゃ、火曜日に、ほんをよみましたか。

E: はい、よみました。おかあさんとコンサートにいきました。でも、コンサートはつまらなかったです。だから、ほんをよみました。

T: ああ、そうですか。水曜日に、ほんをよみましたか。

E: はい、よみました。おにいさんとスケートにいきました。でも、スケートはむずかしかったです。ぜんぜんできませんでした。だから、ほんをよみました。

T: はい。じゃ、木曜日に、ほんをよみましたか。

E: はい、よみました。日本ごのテストをしました。でも、テストはやさしかったです。だから、テストのあとで、ほんをよみました。

T: はい。じゃ、金曜日に、ほんをよみましたか。

E: はい、よみました。かぞくとスパゲッティのレストランにいきました。でも、スパゲッティはまずかったです。スパゲッティをたべませんでした。だから、ほんをよみました。

T: ああ、そうですか。土曜日に、ほんをよみましたか。

E: はい、よみました。おねえさんとパーティーにいきました。でも、パーティーはつまらなかったです。だから、ほんをよみました。

T: はい。じゃ、日曜日に、ほんをよみましたか。

E: いいえ、よみませんでした。ともだちのうちにいきました。わたしたちはビデオをみました。でも、ともだちはこわいえいががきらいです。だから、ともだちはほんをよみました。

ああ！！ともだちのうち！！

- **W151/T13** In pairs, students use the picture clues to find out what their partner did and what it was like.

3 Asking what transport someone uses/Saying what transport you use

Warm-up

Transport banzai: make bingo cards with pictures of nine means of transport. The teacher calls out the words and students cross them out as they hear them. The first person to cross out a row wins, then the first person to cross out the whole card wins.

Presentation

- Students look at the pictures on page 188 and listen to the tape. Discuss the meanings of each.
- Students listen to the tape, look at the pictures and repeat the Japanese.
- Students listen to the tape, read the text on page 189 and repeat the Japanese.
- Students form pairs and practise the structures at the bottom of page 189.

Follow-up

- **W155/T19 5B** Students listen to the tape and write down where the people went and what means of transport they used.

Audio script

a

Harjono: なんでがっこうにいきましたか。
Yuusuke: じてんしゃでいきました。

b

Kate: なんできょうとにいきましたか。
Tony: しんかんせんでいきました。

c

Kate: なんでキャンプにいきましたか。
Emma: でんしゃでいきました。

d

Yuusuke: なんでえいがにいきましたか。
Kate: バスでいきました。

e

Harjono: なんでともだちのうちにいきましたか。
Tony: ローラーブレードでいきました。

- **W155/T20** Students follow the あみだくじ puzzle to find out who went where, with whom and by what means of transport. They write the information out in full sentences.
- **W156/T21** Students answer the questions in Japanese.

べんきょうのベンーカタカナ

S190 3B

Characters introduced: ウ、ヌ、ム、モ、ワ、ヲ

Warm-up

- Replay *Itadakimasu* and explore the page as in earlier units.
- Choose about 20 previously learnt katakana and write them randomly on the board. Divide the

class into two teams. Give each student a number (in Japanese), ensuring that the students with the same number are equidistant from the board. The teacher then calls out a number and a katakana. The two students with that number run to the board and find the character called out. Points are allocated for the fastest correct answer.

Presentation

- Students listen to the tape and complete the tasks.

Audio script

SPEAKER: Ben

みんなさん、こんにちは。

Ben here again with some more katakana.

But first, some revision. The katakana you already know are printed in black in the chart. Point to the ones I say, and repeat after me.

ク、セ、タ、テ、ネ、ノ、ホ、マ、メ、ヤ、ユ、ヨ、リ、ル、ロ、ン、

Look at the characters in the yellow boxes in the chart. See if you can work out how each one is pronounced.

...

Now look at the group of six large characters. Point to each one as I say it, and repeat after me.

1 ウ
2 ヌ
3 ム
4 モ
5 ワ
6 ヲ

よくできました。

Katakana sound changes

And finally - one more sound change. Look at the characters in the green box on the page and repeat after me.

ウ、ウィ

Look at *Now try this* on page 190 and use the new sounds you've learnt to work out what the words say.

...

That's it from me. またね。

- Students read the advertisement at the top of the page. For your information:
  マック・モーニング *Mac Morning* (from an advertisement from McDonald's morning menu)

Follow-up

- **W 143** かきかた *(How to write)*: students practise writing the characters in the boxes using the correct stroke order.
- **S 190** *Find the odd sound*: students select the odd sound in each group of three presented. *Solutions*: 1b, 2a, 3c, 4a, 5b, 6b.
- **W 144 /T1** Students fill in the blanks in the katakana chart.
- **W 144/T2** Students find the appropriate character in the balloon to fill in the blank spaces.
- **W 145/T3** Students find the words in the puzzle and circle them. Then they write each one next to the correct picture below.
- Have students make up a puzzle similar to that in Task 3 above. The puzzles can be passed around the class for other students to do.
- Now that students have learnt all of the katakana, give them a list of names of students in the class and have a competition to see who can read them the quickest. (This is best done as a team game.)
- Game: *First to five hundred* (see instructions in the *Okashi* section).

ごはんとおかず

S 191–2

Warm-up

Have students go back to Unit 11 and make a list of time expressions which take particle に and a list of those which don't.

Presentation

- Discuss with students the structures presented in Unit 12. Have them notice the use of different particles in different situations, and formulate rules for the use of を、に、で、 etc. Refer to the *Setsumei* section (pages 208–9) and also to the particle chart on page 211.
- Focus discussion on verb forms introduced in *Obentoo* and refer to the verb chart on page 210.
- Focus on adjective forms introduced in *Obentoo* and refer to the chart on page 209.

Follow-up

- **W 148/T7** Students change the sentences from the present tense to the past tense.
- **W 148/T8** Students complete the reference table with the present positive form, the past positive form and the suggestion form.
- **W 151/T14** Students change the sentences from the present tense to the past tense.
- **B 12.1** はじめて: students listen to the conversations about activities people have done for the first time and then complete the descriptions.

Audio script

a **A:** はじめておちゃをのみましたか。
B: はい、はじめてです。
A: どうでしたか。
B: おいしかったです。
A: へー、すきですか。
B: はい、だいすきです。

b **A:** はじめてローラーブレードをしましたか。
B: はい、はじめてしました。

A: どうでしたか。
B: うん、すこしできました。でも、むずかしかったです。

c A: はじめて日本のえいがをみましたか。
B: はい、はじめてみました。
A: どうでしたか。
B: おもしろかったです。でも、日本ごがわかりませんでした。

d A: はじめてカンガルーをたべましたか。
B: はい、はじめてたべました。
A: どうでしたか。
B: うーん、まずかったです。

e A: はじめてかんじをかきましたか。
B: はい、はじめてかきました。
A: どうでしたか。
B: やさしかったです。

f A: はじめて日本人にあいましたか。
B: はい、はじめてあいました。
A: どうでしたか。
B: たのしかったです。

Vocabulary notes

わかりませんでした。	I didn't understand.
カンガルー	kangaroo

- Students make up a caption for each of the photos on pages 191–2.
- Copy the sentence patterns onto cards and cut into sections. When the teacher calls out a sentence in Japanese or in English, the students must construct the sentence on the desk as quickly as possible.
  Alternative: The teacher calls out a question and students make up an appropriate answer, using the cards.
- *Pass it on*:
  - Students are directed to write a time phrase on a piece of paper (the teacher directs discussion as to whether or not it needs a particle).
  - They fold it over so that it can't be seen and pass it on to the next person.
  - The next student writes the name of a person in the class followed by は.
  - They fold it over so that it can't be seen and pass it on to the next person
  - The next student writes the name of another person in the class, followed by と.
  - They fold it over so that it can't be seen and pass it on to the next person.
  - The next person writes a means of transport, followed by で.
  - They fold it over so that it can't be seen and pass it on to the next person.
  - The next person writes a place, followed by に.
  - They fold it over so that it can't be seen and pass it on to the next person.
  - The next person writes いきました.
  - They fold it over so that it can't be seen and pass it on to the next person.
  - The last person reads the sentence aloud to the class.

Extension tasks:
- Ⓑ**12.2** にっきをよみましょう: students read the diary entry and answer the questions in English.
- Ⓑ**12.3** *More about verbs*: students practise the various verb tenses.

テーブルマナー

Ⓢ **193–4**

Warm-up
- Students identify the main events in their school calendar, for example the swimming carnival, athletics carnival, school camp, school fête and exams. If possible, the teacher should give a Japanese translation for each event.
- Students list similarities and differences between Japanese and Australian school life.

Presentation
Divide the class into groups and have each group read the information on one of the events. The group can then further research their event and present more information to the rest of the class in the form of an oral presentation or a project. If there is a Japanese exchange student in the school, s/he can be invited to the class and asked questions about each of the events. If not, students may write to penfriends or E-mail students in Japan to ask about school life, or obtain information via the Internet.
For your information:
- The school year begins around 5 April. There are three terms. Term 1 is from April to July. The summer holidays are from July until September. Term 2 starts in September and goes until the winter holidays from 23 December until mid-January. Term 3 is from January to March.
- にゅうがくしき、the school entrance ceremony. All students and teachers gather in the school hall to welcome the new First Year students. There are many speeches by students, teachers and community members to welcome the new students. A representative of the First Years reads an oath promising to work hard and live up to the expectations of the school. Many messages of good luck from local junior high schools or primary schools and other organisations are read.
- キャンプ、Some schools run a school camp for the students in a particular year. It is often held

towards the end of Term 1.

- しけん、exams. Mid-term and final exams are held each term. Not all subjects are examined in the mid-term exams, but all are examined in the end-of-term exams.
- なつやすみ、the summer holidays. During the summer holidays, most students are expected to do some homework and assignments.
- しゅうがくりょこう、the annual school trip. This is a big excursion attended by all students and all teachers of a particular year. (Sometimes the principal goes along too.) It lasts about five days and students usually travel to famous destinations in Japan. They are expected to complete an assignment during that time, but are usually given quite a bit of freedom while on the excursion.
- うんどうかい、the school athletics carnival. This involves the whole school and is a competition between the school years. Along with the ぶんかさい、 it is probably the highlight of the school year. Students train vigorously for months before the うんどうかい. There are a range of events, from serious athletic events to novelty events like the three-legged race. This ensures that all students are involved. The events on the score card (page 194 of the Student Book) are as follows:

  １００メートルきょうそう 100 m race.
  ２００メートルきょうそう 200 m race.
  ３００メートルきょうそう 300 m race.
  パンくいきょうそう (lit. 'bread-eating race')–students run up to a row of pieces of bread hung on strings, with their hands held behind their backs; the winner is the first to eat the bread without using hands.
  かいものきょうそう (lit. 'shopping race')
  にんげんピラミッド human pyramid.
  つなひき tug o' war.
  ににんさんきゃく three-legged race.
  たまいれ ball throw–teams of students throw balls into a basket on top of a pole; the team with the most balls in the basket within a time limit is the winner.
  ダンス dance.
  おうえん cheering–group displays using placards, flags or streamers are judged; cheering is usually done to the beat of the たいこ (big drum).
  リレー relay (usually the last race of the day).
- ぶんかさい、the school cultural festival (like a school fête). This is held around November every year. It is a festival open to the public where school clubs set up exhibitions, there are performances by school drama groups and music groups, and there are performances and presentations put on by each class. Some ぶんかさい、especially university ぶんかさい、go on for several days.
- そつぎょうしき、graduation ceremony. Like the にゅうがくしき, the そつぎょうしき is a formal occasion where graduating students are presented to the principal and receive their graduation certificates in front of staff, parents and the student body.

  Photos on page 193:
  (Anticlockwise from top left)
- Lining up for assembly in the playground
- しゅうがくりょこう–a school visit to Miyajima
- The famous Tori gate at Miyajima
- しんかんせん、the Bullet Train (students often travel on the Bullet Train during their しゅうがくりょこう.)
- They often stay in a りょかん、Japanese-style inn, while on the しゅうがくりょこう.
- Images of school holidays with friends
- Students chatting in a classroom at lunchtime
- Exams at school

Photos on page 194:

- ダンス、dance at the うんどうかい
- リレー、relay
- にんげんピラミッド、human pyramid
- たいこ、the big drum–students practising for the おうえん (cheering)
- Presentation of a play as part of the ぶんかさい
- たまいれ、ball throw at the うんどうかい
- The ぶんかさい is a chance for each of the school clubs to advertise their activities; foreign exchange students are often involved in the ESS (English Speaking Society)
- At the end of the year, students always write a message in each other's autograph books
- Ⓑ**12.4** 中山学園の一年: you will need: the game board enlarged to A3 size, buttons or counters to indicate players position, list of questions.

  Instructions:

  Follow the path around the board answering questions about Japanese school life. Students must begin at the にゅうがくしき (school entrance ceremony). Students take turn in throwing the die and moving the required number of spaces. The student must answer the question corresponding to the number on which they land. If the question is answered correctly, s/he may stay on that space. If it is answered incorrectly, s/he must go back to his/her previous space and throw again at his/her next turn. The winner is the first to reach their そつぎょうしき (graduation ceremony).

  Questions:

  一 What is にゅうがくしき？
  二 What month does the Japanese school year begin? (April)
  三 What does mean いちがっき mean? (1st term)
  四 Approximately what time does school begin? (8.30 am)
  五 What do students do before they go to their classrooms? (change their shoes)
  六 Where do students go when the morning bell rings? (to their homeroom)
  七 How many terms are there in the Japanese school year? (3)

八 How many sets of exams do junior high school students have each year? (6-half-yearly's and yearly's in each term)

九 What is the Japanese word for exam? (しけん)

十 What must students do at the end of the school day? (clean the classrooms おそうじ)

十一 How long are the summer holidays? (5 weeks)

十二 In what months do the summer holidays fall? (July-August)

十三 What is しゅうがくりょこう? (school trip)

十四 In what kind of accommodation do students usually stay during their school trip? (りょかん Japanese style inn)

十五 How do students usually go on their school trip? (by bullet train しんかんせん)

十六 What always happens on the school trip? (have a class photo taken)

十七 What is the 'sports carnival' in Japanese? (うんどうかい)

十八 What month is the sports carnival held? (October)

十九 Who do students compete against in the うんどうかい? (students from other grades)

二十 What is だまいれ? (a competition to throw as many balls as possible into a basket in a specified time)

二十一 What is ににんさんきゃく? (three-legged race)

二十二 What is つなひき? (tug o' war)

二十三 What month is the ぶんかさい? (November)

二十四 Name three things you would find at a ぶんかさい. (food stalls, games, entertainment, club stalls)

二十五 Name three clubs which students can join. (sports, tea ceremony, music, calligraphy, science, debating). (see Student Book page 174-5)

二十六 What is おばけやしき? (ghost house)

二十七 What colour are most boys' school uniforms? (black)

二十八 When are the winter holidays (ふゆやすみ)? (December-January)

二十九 What month is the end of the school year? (March)

三十 What do students receive at the そつぎょうしき? (そつぎょうしょ graduation certificate)

おはし

Presentation

- Discuss with students the skills they have acquired in learning Japanese. Discuss with them what part of the language was the most difficult, the most easy, the most enjoyable, etc.
- Have students answer the questions on page 195, either as a whole class or in small groups.
- Have students make a poster advertising the study of Japanese in their school.

Images of Japan:
– こうよう the famous autumn leaves of the Japanese maple (もみじ)
– ふじさん、 Mt Fuji
– まいこさん in Kyoto
– Tokyo at night

おしょうゆ

Presentation

S 196 3B

- Students listen to the tape and repeat the new expressions. You may need to discuss the structure of some of the items in *Oshooyu*, for example アメリカからレポーターがきました。すこしつまらなかったです。はじめて、ふぐをたべました。 Provide extra examples of each of these structures.
- *How many times?*: students listen to the tape of the cartoon story again and count how many times each expression is used.
- **W 156/T23** おしょうゆクイズタイム: students circle the correct answers.

おかし

S 197

Song

Students sing the song to the tune of *Old MacDonald*.

Game

First to five hundred: (a game to practise reading katakana, although it can be adapted to use for testing hiragana or structures and vocabulary): to make the game board, you will need a large piece of cardboard, clear Contact, thick clear plastic (available from hardware stores), invisible sticky tape, cardboard in five different colours, and a thick black marker.

- Write the heading 'First to Five Hundred' at the top of the piece of cardboard and five headings underneath from left to right:
  - Katakana singles
  - Names
  - Foods
  - Patterns
  - Sound changes
- Cover the board in clear Contact.
- Cut 10 cm x 8 cm rectangles of clear plastic.
- Attach them to the cardboard in five rows of five under the five headings, with sticky tape on three sides to make a pocket.
- Using the coloured cardboard, make five cards of 8

cm x 7 cm cards of each colour.
- On the first colour cards, write single katakana (one on each card), increasing in difficulty.
- On the second colour cards, write names in katakana (one on each card), increasing in difficulty.
- On the third colour cards, write katakana foods (one on each card), increasing in difficulty.
- On the fourth colour cards, write katakana patterns (e.g. ア、カ、サ、タ or ア、キ、ス、テ or タ、ト、ナ、ノ)–students should say the next two kana in the pattern.
- On the fifth colour cards, write combination sounds or sound changes (one on each card), increasing in difficulty.
- Write 20 on the back of the cards with the easiest questions, 40 on the next, 60 on the next, 80 on the next and 100 on the most difficult questions.
- Put the cards in the pockets with the question face down (the number of points showing).

To play:
- Divide the class into teams.
- Students choose a category and a point value, for example 'Names for 20'.
- The teacher shows the team the card and they must read it. (In the 'Patterns' category, players must give the next two kana in the pattern.)
- If the players answer the question correctly, they receive the points allocated to that question.
- The first team to reach 500 points is the winner.

Teachers may like to make a number of cards for each point value to play a variety of games.

Craft activity

Origami pocket: use old photocopy paper from the recycling bin at school; students can dye the paper first if they like–see the instructions on page 109).

Now that students can read all of the hiragana and katakana, they may like to make their own cards. This origami pocket will be useful to keep them in.
- Fold the paper in half lengthwise.
- Fold in half sideways just to make a centre line.
- Open out and fold the two sides into the centre.
- Squash fold the two sides into triangles.
- Fold the corners to the back.
- Fold down the two top flaps.

Putting it all together

- **Ⓦ152/T15** Students read the diary entry and write a brief summary of it in English.
- **Ⓦ152/T16** Students write an account of their own first date in Japanese, using the diary entry in Task 15 as a guide.
- **Ⓦ153/T17** Students read the account of the camping trip and answer the questions in English.
- **Ⓦ154/T18** Students read Sally's account of her excursion and answer the questions in English. They also write an account in Japanese of an excursion of their own.
- **Ⓦ156/T22** Students write a letter in Japanese to their penfriend in Japan, describing their last holiday.
- ことしのおもいで *(Memories of this year)*:
  - Students collect a series of photos (or draw pictures) of memorable things which have happened during the year.
  - They arrange the photos in a sequence and write the date and day next to each one.
  - They also write a short caption for each photo or picture, which could include saying where they went, by what means they went there, what they did, whom they met there, with whom they went and what it was like.
  - The picture sequences can be made into a booklet or a poster and displayed in the classroom.
  - Students can be asked to select one of the pictures and tell the class about it in Japanese. They could begin with わたしのいちばんいいおもいでです。 ('This is my best memory')
- こんしゅうのベストえいが (*This week's Best Movies)*: students write the names of five classmates down the side of the page. They interview the five students and ask them if they watched any movies last week. The interviewers write the names of the movies they watched at the top and then ask them what the movie was like, giving rating points to each of the movies according to the responses. Then they find out which movies got the best and worst ratings in the class. Here are some questions students could use and the points to give for each answer.
  せんしゅう、えいがをみましたか。
  はい、みました。
  いいえ、みませんでした。
  なにをみましたか。
  「....と....」をみました。
  「....」はどうでしたか。
  すごくつまらなかったです。*(0 points)*
  つまらなかったです。*(1 point)*
  まあまあでした。*(2 points)*
  おもしろかったです。*(4 points)*
  すごくおもしろかったです。*(5 points)*
  (This task can also be done with TV shows.)
- 20のしつもん *Twenty questions*: on a piece of paper, students write down five things: a place they went to, with whom they went, what they did, what it was like and by what means of transport they went there. The rest of the class ask questions like デパートにいきましたか。and ...さんといきましたか。to which students must truthfully answer はい or いいえ. The person who has to have the most questions asked is the winner.
- **Ⓑ12.5** *Emiko's and Daisuke's holiday:* students read the postcard on their own sheet and use it to answer their partner's questions. Students then ask their partner where Daisuke/Emiko went during their holidays. They find out what Daisuke/Emiko did on the dates mentioned and fill in the table. Teachers should first elicit from students the questions they will need to find out the

information. For example:
だいすけくん／えみこさんはなつ休みに
どこにいきましたか。
だいすけくん／えみこさんはなつ休みに
なにをしましたか。
8月10日になにをしましたか。
8月17日になにをしましたか。
8月12日になにをしましたか。
8月15日になにをしましたか。
depending on students' confidence with script they may fill in the table in English or Japanese.

ごちそうさま

197

- Students work with a partner and go through the list of outcomes in the *Gochisoosama* section, asking each other at least one question on each.
- **157** *Obentoo quiz.*
- *Self-assessment form and discussion*: after students have completed the unit they could assess their own general achievements using the form on page 137 of the *Moshi Moshi Teachers' Handbook*. The form provides space for the students to list what they have achieved, the difficulties they have encountered and strategies they could use for improvement. After students have completed the form, they could discuss the three headings and make suggestions about ways to improve their Japanese.

Reference to *Yoroshiku National Curriculum Guidelines for Japanese (Moshi Moshi)*

The following is a list of the suggested language exponents presented in *Moshi Moshi* Module 4 フリータイム (*Free-time*) which have been introduced in Unit 12 of *Obentoo*. In some cases the example has been changed to correspond to the form introduced in *Obentoo*. Appropriate activities from *Moshi Moshi* are suggested below.

Language exponents

- Asking and giving information about after school activities
  (きのう) がっこうのあとでなにを (し) ましたか。
  (ともだち) の (うち) にいきました。
- Asking and giving information about transport
  なんで (がっこう) にいきましたか。
  (じてんしゃ) でいきました。
- Stating opinions
  (キャンプ) は (たのしかった) です。
- Disagreeing
  いいえ、(つまらなかった) です。
- Emphasising opinions
  (たのしかった) ですよ。

Suggested activities from *Moshi Moshi*

アンケート：ウィークエンド Teacher Resources pages 36 and 40
どうでしたか。Teacher Resources pages 36 and 41
何をしているでしょう。Teacher Resources page 37, Student Book page 28
けんじくんからのてがみ Teacher Resources page 37, Student Book page 29

Obentoo song

chorus

にほんごは　たのしい
おべんとうは　おいしい
1, 2, 3, 4, 5
さあ、おべんとうよ

にほんに　いきましょう
ともだちに　あいましょう
1, 2, 3, 4, 5
さあ、おべんとうよ

verse 1

あ　か　さ　た　な　は　ま
ひらがな、かたかな
い　き　し　ち　に　ひ　み

あ　か　さ　た　な　は　ま
ひらがな、かたかな
い　き　し　ち　に　ひ　み
にほんごは　すごい

chorus

verse 2

う　く　す　つ　ぬ　ふ　む
ひらがな　できる
え　け　せ　て　ね　へ　め

う　く　す　つ　ぬ　ふ　む
ひらがな　できる
え　け　せ　て　ね　へ　め
ちょっとまって、あのうね

chorus

verse 3

お　こ　そ　と　の　ほ　も
みんな、おべんとうよ
にほんごは　やさしい

お　こ　そ　と　の　ほ　も
みんな、おべんとうよ
にほんごは　やさしい
みなさん、いっしょに！

chorus

Donna aji? rap

ペコペコはらペコ
たかこの　おべんとう
あまい、あつい、おいしい
へえ！！どんなあじ？

Workbook solutions

Unit 1

3 **a** ゆ, **b** き, **c** こ, **d** ハ, **e** た, **f** エ
4 **b** Takako, Yuusuke: saying goodbye
c Emma, Mr Nakamura: saying goodbye
d Harjono, Emma: it's morning
Yuki, Takako: it's morning
e Yuusuke: saying goodbye
5 **a** 5, **b**, 1 **c**, 4 **d**, 6 **e**, 3, **f** 2
6 **a** 3, **b**, 6 **c**, 1, **d** 2, **e** 7, **f** 4, **g** 5
7 **a** おやすみなさい。おやすみなさい。
b おはようございます。おはようございます。
c さようなら。さようなら。
d ぼくは ... です。
e おなまえは。
f はい, ... です。
8 **c** ✓, **d** ✓, **e** ✓, **f** ✓, **g** ✕, **h** ✕, **i** ✕, **j** ✓
9 **a** Takako, **b** Yuusuke, **c** Yuki, **d** Kate, **e** Harjono, **f** Emma, **g** Nakamura
11 **a** お, **b** こ, **c** た, **d** ま, **e** ハ, **f** な, **g** さ, **h** ゆ, **i** ケ, **j** き, **k** エ
12 **a** なかむらせんせい
b こんにちは。
c ゆき
d ゆうすけ
e おはようございます。
f たかこさんですか。
g いいえ, さなえです。
h さようなら。
i またあした。
j おなまえは？

おべんとうクイズ

1 **a** in the morning, **b** Goodbye., **c** こんにちは。
2 **a** Good morning, **b** Hello, **c** Goodbye, **d** See you tomorrow, **e** Takako, **f** Yuki, **g** Mr Nakamura, **h** Yuusuke, **i** Emma, **j** Harjono, **k** Kate
3 (Own name) です。
4 **a** 3, **b** hiragana, **c** katakana, **d** 46, 46
5 **a** ゆ, **b** た, **c** さ

Unit 2

1 ち, き, て, ま, さ, す, け, た, ゆ, ハ, エ ア, ケ, オ, イ, ニ, カ, ト, 日, 本
2 **a** 3, **b** 4, **c** 5, **d** 1, **e** 2
3 **a** た, **b** エ, **c** ケ, **d** ハ, **e** ゆ, **f** ゆ
4 **a** け, **b** し, **c** て, **d** イ, **e** オ, **f** ナ, **g** ニ, **h** へ
5 **a** Kate, **b** Emma, **c** Yuki, **d** Tony, **e** Harjono, **f** Shingo, **g** Takako, **h** Yuusuke
6 **a** ちえこさん
b しんごくん
c けんいちくん
d みなさん
e せんせい
f すわってください。
g あけてください。
7 **a** ベンくん
b カナダ
c カーラ
d インドネシア
e オーストラリア
f トニーくん
g ニュージーランド
h エマ
i ケイト
j ハジョーノ
8 **a** 3, **b** 1, **c** 5, **d** 2, **e** 7, **f** 4, **g** 6
9 Teacher to correct
11 **a** Emma, Australia
b Harjono, Indonesia
c Kate, New Zealand
d Tony, Canada
e Carla, America
f Ben, Australia
g Yuusuke, Japan
12 **a** 7 わたしはたかこです。日本からきました。
b 6 わたしはエマです。オーストラリアからきました。
c 3 わたしはケイトです。ニュージーランドからきました。
d 1 ぼくはハジョーノです。インドネシアからきました。
e 2 わたしはカーラです。アメリカからきました。
f 5 ぼくはトニーです。カナダからきました。
g 4 ぼくはベンです。オーストラリアからきました。
13 **a** みなさん、こんにちは。ぼくは Michael Jackson です。アメリカからきました。
b こんにちは。ぼくのなまえは Kieren Perkins です。オーストラリアからきました。
c こんにちは。わたしは Kiri Te Kanawa です。ニュージーランドからきました。
d ぼくは Jim Carrey です。カナダからきました。どうぞよろしく。
15 **a** オーストラリアからきました。
b 日本からきました。
c アメリカからきました。
d インドネシアからきました。
e カナダからきました。
f ニュージーランドからきました。
16 **a** Hurry up.
b えーと...
c wish someone luck
d すみません。
e you're happy because you won
f あのうー
g That's right.
17 **a** ちょっとまってください。
b みなさん
c どこからきましたか。
d きいてください。
e みせてください。
f 日本からきました。
g すわってください。
h けんいち
i ちえこ
j しんご
18 **a** ニュージーランド
b エマ
c インドネシア
d オーストラリア
e ハジョーノ
f ベン
g カナダ
h トニー
i カーラ
j アメリカ
k ケイト

おべんとうクイズ

1 **a** where they're from
b stand up
c ドアをしめてください。
d look at something
e be quiet
f open the door
2 **a** こ, **b** み, **c** てください。**d** さん, **e** ま, **f** し, **g** な
3 **a** 日本
b オーストラリア
c 日本
d カナダ
e 日本
f アメリカ
g 日本

Unit 3

1 b, e, f, j, l, o, q, t
2 **a** いしかわ
b せき
c たかはし
d いでいし
e さかい
f たなか
g あかい
h おき
3 **a** ちえこ
b ベン
c さなえ
d カーラ
e たかこ
f なかむらせんせい
4 **a** たけし
b きみこ
c みちこ
d あきこ
e まさお
f まちこ
g ますみ
h さちこ
i あけみ
j ゆみこ
k たか
l ちゆみ
5 一 4, 二 6, 三 3, 四 5, 五 4, 六 2, 七 1, 八 2, 九 1, 十 1
6 Teacher to correct
7 **a** 八, **b** 十三, **c** 十三, **d** 七, **e** 十四, **f** 二十, **g** 六, **h** 八 **i** 十二, **j** 五, **k** 十七, **l** 六
8 **a** 九, 十一, 十三
b 十一, 十四, 十七
c 九, 十一, 十二
d 五, 四, 六
e 七, 六, 五, 四, 三, 二
9 **a** Indonesia, 12 years old
b New Zealand, 11 years old
c Australia, 12 years old
d America, 13 years old
11 **a** 2, **b** 4, **c** 5, **d** 1, **e** 3
12 **a** 十四, **b** 三十, **c** 六, **d** 十一, **e** 十九, **f** 七, **g** 十六, **h** 三十一, **i** 十五, **j** 二十八
13 **a** あけみは八さいです。
b たかは七さいです。
c なおこは十二さいです。
d たけしは十五さいです。
e ちせかは十四さいです。
14 **a** 7, **b** 5, **c** 6, **d** 4, **e** 1
15 **a** 764 3987
b 487 6363
c 194 8220
d 255 9071
16 Teacher to correct
17 **a** なんさいですか。
b わたしは十七さいです。
c ケイトさんは十一さいです。
d カーラさんは十三さいです。
e でんわばんごうは?
f 九七六四三八一九です。
18 Teacher to correct

おべんとうクイズ

1 **a** someone's age
b Happy Birthday
c 十三さいです。
d けんいちくん
2 **a** 三, 四, 五, 六, 七, 八
b 十, 十一, 十二, 十三, 十四
c 九, 十一, 十三, 十五, 十七
d 二, 八, 九, 十, 十二, 十六
3 (telephone number)です。
4 **a** Your name
b Your age
c Where you are from
d Your telephone number
7 **a** なんさいですか。
b でんわばんごうは？
c おはようございます。
d わたし。
e ぼく

Unit 4

1 う, え, く, ど, ひ, び, ね, に, め, ら, よ, む, ん, す, じ, ま, イ, と, カ, オ
2 **a** Sanae, Japanese
b Tony, Canadian
c Emma, Australian
d Harjono, Indonesian
e Kate, New Zealand
f Carla, American
3 **a** Harjono, Jakarta
b Tony, Vancouver
c Kate, Auckland
d Sanae, Kobe
e Emma, Sydney
f Carla, Madison
4 **a** 4, **b** 1, **c** 2, **d** 6, **e** 5, **f** 3
5 **a** Albert Einstein, America
b Elvis Presley, Gracelands
c Ned Kelly, Australia
d Marilyn Monroe, Hollywood
6 **a** 7, **b** 4, **c** 5, **d** 2, **e** 1, **f** 3, **g** 6
7 **a** 日本人は日本からきました。
b カナダ人はカナダからきました。
c インドネシア人はインドネシアからきました。
d ニュージーランド人はニュージーランドからきました。
e オーストラリア人はオーストラリアからきました。
8 **a** Hiroshima, **b** Matsuyama, **c** Sapporo, **d** Tokyo, **e** Kyoto, **f** Nara, **g** Kumamoto, **h** Aomori
9 **David:** みなさん、こんにちは。ぼくは David です。ぼくは十五さいです。Melbourne からきました。どうぞよろしく。
Amy: みなさん、こんにちは。わたしはオーストラリア人です。うちはシドニーです。わたしのなまえは Amy Gibson です。わたしは十四さいです。どうぞよろしく。

10 Carrie: わたしは Carrie Baker です。アメリカ人です。アメリカからきました。うちは Nebraska です。でんわばんごうは九八七·九六二二です。わたしは十三さいです。

Hasan: わたしは Hasan Karini です。インドネシア人です。インドネシアからきました。うちは Jakarta です。でんわばんごうは七四二·六八五六です。わたしは十二さいです。

Mutsuko: わたしはみやざきむつこです。日本人です。日本からきました。うちはとうきょうです。でんわばんごうは七八八·八五三一です。わたしは十六さいです。

Tracey: わたしは Tracey Shawです。わたしはオーストラリア人です。オーストラリアからきました。うちは Victoria です。でんわばんごうは九五二三·六八七四です。わたしは十七さいです。

Takuya: ぼくはすずきたくやです。日本人です。日本からきました。うちはおおさかです。でんわばんごうは五七六·八八二五です。わたしは十四さいです。

11 a Tomoko, Junior High School Year 1
b Peter, Year 9
c Sophie, Year 11
d David, Year 8
e Tracey, Year 8

12 a I am Nina. I am a friend. I am American. My home is in New York. I am 15 years old. I am in Year 9.
b I am Ken. My home is in Wellington. I am a New Zealander. I am 16 years old. I am in Year 10.
c I am Masumi. I am a Japanese friend. My home is in Nagasaki. I am 14 years old. I am in second year at Junior High School.

13

とし	**日本のがくねん**	**オーストラリアのがくねん**
七さい	しょうがく一ねんせい	一ねんせい
八さい	しょうがく二ねんせい	二ねんせい
九さい	しょうがく三ねんせい	三ねんせい
十さい	しょうがく四ねんせい	四ねんせい
十一さい	しょうがく五ねんせい	五ねんせい
十二さい	しょうがく六ねんせい	六ねんせい
十三さい	ちゅうがく一ねんせい	七ねんせい
十四さい	ちゅうがく二ねんせい	八ねんせい
十五さい	ちゅうがく三ねんせい	九ねんせい
十六さい	こうこう一ねんせい	十ねんせい
十七さい	こうこう二ねんせい	十一ねんせい
十八さい	こうこう三ねんせい	十二ねんせい

14 a みほさんは十四さいです。
ちゅうがく三ねんせいです。
b トニーさんは十二さいです。
七ねんせいです。
c ニーナさんは十さいです。
五ねんせいです。
d よしたかさんは十五さいです。
こうこう一ねんせいです。
e えみさんは十三さいです。
ちゅうがく二ねんせいです。

15 なんさいですか。
なんねんせいですか。
うちはどこですか。
おなまえは？
でんわばんごうは？
All end in か or は？

16 Teacher to correct

17 a エマ, 十二, 七, オーストラリア, シドニー
b トニー, 十二, 七, カナダ, ヴァンクーバー
c ケイト, 十一, 六, ニュージーランド, オークランド

18 a はじめ。
b なんさいですか。
c ぼくも。／わたしも。
d でんわばんごう
e うちはどこですか。
f なんねんせいですか。
g 八ねんせい
h しょうがく
i ちゅうがく
j こうこう
k 日本人
l おわり。

19 a ラーニさんはオーストラリア人です。
b ニーナさんはアメリカ人です。
c ケーさんはカナダ人です。
d みかさんは八ねんせいです。
e たかしくんは十三さいです。八ねんせいです。
f ひできくんはなんねんせいですか。

20 a you want someone to repeat what s/he has said
b you give something to someone
c saying goodbye to a friend you often see
d as well as that
e on your friend's birthday
f before eating

おべんとうクイズ

1 a where you live
b I'm a New Zealander
c I'm American
d I'm Japanese

2 a Tokyo, **b** Kobe, **c** Kyoto, **d** Hiroshima, **e** Sapporo, **f** Nara, **g** Matsuyama, **h** Sendai

3 a パースです。
b 八ねんせいです。
c 九三三一·四一二三です。
d 十三さいです。
(or students' own answers)

4 a S, **b** J, **c** P, **d** P, **e** S, **f** S, **g** J, **h** P

5 a T, **b** F, **c** T, **d** F, **e** T, **f** F

6 a karate, **b** judo, **c** teriyaki, **d** sushi, **e** Honda, **f** Toyota **g** karaoke, **h** Suzuki

Unit 5

1

一	いち
二	に
三	さん
四	よん／し
五	ご
六	ろく
七	なな／しち
八	はち
九	く／きゅう
十	じゅう
一人	ひとり
二人	ふたり
四人	よにん

2 See inside front cover of Workbook or Student Book for complete hiragana chart.

3 a 十一人です。
b 十人です。
c 三人です。
d 十一人です。
e 六人です。
f 十人です。
g 九人です。
h 十九人です。

4 a 3, **b** 4, **c** 1, **d** 2

5 a Me, Kyoko, 13
b Dad, Osamu, 42

c Mum, Keiko, 41
d Younger brother, Susumu, 10
Kyoko's younger brother is in Primary School Year 5

6 **a** 8, **b** 7, **c** 5, **d** 6, **e** 3, **f** 1, **g** 4, **h** 2

7 **a** おとうさん
b おかあさん
c いもうと
d おねえさん
e おばあさん
f おじいさん
g おにいさん
h おとうと

8 **a** おにいさん, おとうさん, おとうと, おかあさん, さなえ
b おかあさん, おとうさん, いもうと, トニー
c おかあさん, おとうさん, いもうと, おじいさん, おばあさん, たかこ

10 **Nakamura sensei:** bird, rabbit
Sanae: rabbit
Yuki: goldfish
Yuusuke: dog, bird
Tony: dog, cat

11 Teacher to correct

12 **a** うま
b うさぎ
c いぬ
d ねこ
e とり
f きんぎょ

14 **a** おとうと
b おとうさん
c きんぎょ
d おねえさん
e ごさい
f うるさい
g せんせい

16 **a** いいえ、いません。
はい、います。
b 五人です。
はい、います。
いいえ、いません。
c 六人です。
いいえ、いません。
はい、います。
いいえ、いません。
はい、います。

18 Teacher to correct

19 **a** うさぎ
b とり
c おとうと
d うま
e いもうと
f せんせい
g おたんじょうび
h しょうがく二ねんせい
i おはようございます。
j ねこ
k うち
l なんさいですか。
m おねえさん
n はい
o いぬ

おべんとうクイズ

1 **a** おかあさん
b おとうさん
c おねえさん
d おばあさん
e おにいさん
f おじいさん
g いもうと
h おとうと

2 **a** I am Tony. I come from Canada. I am 12 years old. There are four people in my family: Mum, Dad, my younger sister and me. I have a dog and a cat.
b I am Sanae. I am Japanese. I am 12 years old. There are five people in my family: Mum, Dad, my older brother, my younger brother and me. I have a pet rabbit.

3 **a** T, **b** T, **c** T, **d** F, **e** T, **f** T

4 **a** 3, **b** 7, **c** 5, **d** 6, **e** 1, **f** 4, **g** 2

Unit 6

2 **a** きゃ, **b** しょ, **c** ひゃ, **d** にゅ, **e** ちゅ

3 Teacher to correct

4 **a** Kenichi, duck, Gako, 2
b Masao, dog, Puti, 1
c Kimiko, snake, Hari, 3
d Shin, goldfish, Fin, 3
e Sanae, rabbit, Mimi, 2

5 **a** うま
b あひる
c ねこ
d へび
e うさぎ
f とり
g いぬ
h きんぎょ

6 **a** きんぎょ
b へび
c いぬ
d とり
e あひる
f うま
g うさぎ

7 **a** dog, **b** duck, **c** horse, **d** snake, **e** rabbit

8 **a** Nick, dog, small
b Sue, bird, noisy
c Honda, cat, big
d Sally, rabbit, cute
e David, dog, scary

9 **a** 7, **b** 2, **c** 5, **d** 6, **e** 12, **f** 11

10 **a** me, dog, Hana, small
b friend, goldfish, Kin, big
c younger brother, duck, Honey, noisy
d older sister, snake, Nina, scary

11 **a** けんいち, あひる, ガーコ
b ケイト, へび, サム
c エマ, きんぎょ, すし
d カーラ, うま, せいこう
e ちえこ, いません

12 **a** カーラ, うま
b けんいち, あひる
c エマ, きんぎょ
d ケイト, へび

13 **a** エマさんのペットは きんぎょです。
なまえはすしです。ちいさいです。
b ケイトさんのペットはへびです。
なまえはサムです。こわいです。
c カーラさんのペットはうまです。
なまえはせいこうです。おおきいです。
d さなえさんのペットはうさぎです。
なまえはミミです。ミミはかわいいです。
e ベンくんのペットはいぬです。
なまえはポチです。ポチはうるさいです。

14 **a** dog, **b** snake, **c** bird, **d** horse

15 a Yamada Kyoko, 783 0102, duck, Donald, 5 years old, pet food
b Kimura Susumu, 663 1895, bird, Yakitori, 1 year old, bread, fruit
c Suzuki Mie, 383 6971, cat, Hotdog, 11 years old, Hotdog
16 a うそ, **b** うそ, **c** ほんとう, **d** ほんとう, **e** うそ
17 Teacher to correct
19 a Congratulations, **b** you're disappointed, **c** you disagree, **d** you agree, **e** You're kidding!, **f** That's disgusting!

おべんとうクイズ

1 a あひる
b エマ
c へび
d カーラ
e うさぎ
2 a Bags, **b** Sam, **c** Fin, **d** Carrington, **e** Chirp, **f** Don
3 a だれのいぬですか。
b ねこのなまえはなんですか。
c ゆきさんのペットはなんですか。
d へびはなにをたべますか。
4 a vegetables, **b** meat, **c** bread and vegetables, **d** grass
5 a はい、いぬがいます。
b しろです。
c にくをたべます。
d ねこです。
(or students' own answers)

Unit 7

1 a Thursday, test
b Sunday, Pamela's party
c Tuesday, excursion
d Friday, holiday
e Wednesday, Mum's birthday
2 にちようび, 日よう日
げつようび, 月よう日
かようび, 火よう日
すいようび, 水よう日
もくようび, 木よう日
きんようび, 金よう日
どようび, 土よう日
3 a 火, **b** 水, **c** 日, **d** 土, **e** 木, **f** 月, **g** 金
4 Refer to Student Book page 223 for the list of dates.
5 （さんじゅうにち）三十日（むいか）六日（にじゅうろくにち）二十六日（みっか）三日（さんじゅういちにち）三十一日（じゅういちにち）十一日（にじゅういちにち）二十一日（はつか）二十日（ついたち）一日（ようか）八日（ここのか）九日（とおか）十日（じゅうににち）十二日（じゅうよっか）十四日（じゅうごにち）十五日（にじゅうさんにち）二十三日（よっか）四日（じゅうろくにち）十六日（じゅうくにち）十九日（にじゅうににち）二十二日（にじゅうごにち）二十五日（ふつか）二日（にじゅうしちにち）二十七日（いつか）五日（にじゅうよっか）二十四日（にじゅうはちにち）二十八日（じゅうはちにち）十八日（じゅうしちにち）十七日（なのか）七日（じゅうさんにち）十三日（にじゅうくにち）二十九日
6 a 3, **b** 5, **c** 2, **d** 9, **e** 11, **f** 12, **g** 1, **h** 7, **i** 8, **j** 6, **k** 4, **l** 10
7 a 五月二十四日
b 七月十三日
c 五月五日
d 二月二十日
e 十一月二十一日
f 三月十五日
8 Teacher to correct
9 May 3: holiday
5: holiday (Golden Week)
9: test
18: excursion
19–21: kendo camp
24: Emma's birthday
25: Emma's party
31: Teacher's birthday
10 b けんいちくんのたんじょうびは十月十日です。
c たかこさんのたんじょうびは十二月二十三日です。
d しんごくんのたんじょうびは十一月二日です。
e さなえさんのたんじょうびは八月三十日です。
11 Teacher to correct
12 a book, **b** clock, **c** eraser, **d** cat
13 a 3, 3/6 **b** 4, 25/8 **c** 5, 1/4 **d** 1, 16/2 **e** 2, 30/10
14 a コンピューターゲーム
b プレゼント
c ものさし
d とけい
e ノート
f えんぴつ
g けしごむ
h かみ

16

	Family member	Chinese birth sign
a	Yasushi	wild pig
	Dad	dog
	Mum	rat
	younger sister	snake
	older brother	monkey
b	Hiroko	rat
	younger brother	tiger
	younger sister	dragon
	Mum	wild pig
	Dad	monkey
	Grandma	horse

Teacher to correct answers for age

17 a いぬどし
b ひつじどし
c とらどし
d ねずみどし
e たつどし
f とりどし
g さるどし
h うしどし
i へびどし
j いのししどし
18 Teacher to correct
19

Across		Down	
1	六月	2	月よう日
5	金よう日	3	火よう日
6	木よう日	4	一日
9	日よう日	7	日よう日
11	十二月	8	十一月
14	五月十日	10	九月
16	三月七日	12	二十日
17	土よう日	13	四月八日
18	九日	14	五日
19	水よう日	15	十四日

おべんとうクイズ

1 a birthday
b 六月十二日
c 八月五日
d にがつよっか
e 木よう日
f the day of earth
g your Chinese birth sign
h write with it

i 五月五日
j Wednesday, 11 September

2 a 十月二十三日
b 一月六日
c 四月二日
d 七月十日
e 五月二十日
f 三月三十一日
g 九月十八日
h 十二月一日

3 a 十一月十日です。
b とりどしです。
c 土よう日です。
d 十二月二十五日です。
e 十月十八日です。
(or students' own answers)

4 a Bean throwing festival, **b** Dolls' day festival, **c** Children's day festival, **d** Cherry blossom viewing, **e** Star festival

Unit 8

1 a 12, **b** 16, **c** 20, **d** 8, **e** 5, **f** 1, **g** 15, **h** 2, **i** 4, **j** 22, **k** 25, **l** 7, **m** 13, **n** 23, **o** 6, **p** 3, **q** 9, **r** 21, **s** 17, **t** 10, **u** 14, **v** 11, **w** 24, **x** 18, **y** 19

2 a ひるごはん lunch
b にく meat
c くだもの fruit
d あさごはん breakfast
e おべんとう lunch box
f さかな fish
g たまご egg
h ごはん rice
i ばんごはん dinner
j おちゃ green tea
k こうちゃ tea

3 a スパゲッティ
b チキン
c コーラ
d サンドイッチ
e アイスクリーム
f トースト
g コーンフレーク
h ピザ
i ハンバーガー
j ミルク
k カレーライス
l コーヒー

4 a コーンフレーク, トースト
b ソーセージ, スパゲッティ, サンドイッチ, カレーライス, ハンバーガー, ピザ, チキン, ミート, サラダ
c ミルク, コーヒー, オレンジ·ジュース, コーラ
d ケーキ, アイスクリーム
e サンドイッチ
f チョコレート
g カレーライス
h ミルク
カナダ
オーストラリア

5 a すみません
b サラダ
c ケーキ
d スパゲッティ
e おちゃ

6 a curry and rice, water
b salad, water
c pizza, water
d pizza, water

9 a カーラさんはひるごはんにサラダサンドイッチとケーキをたべます。オレンジ·ジュースをのみます。
b ケイトさんはばんごはんにチキンとサラダとアイスクリームをたべます。ミルクをのみます。
c なかむらせんせいはあさごはんにコーンフレークとトーストとたまごをたべます。こうちゃをのみます。
d ハジョーノくんはばんごはんにピザとサラダとくだものをたべます。オレンジ·ジュースをのみます。
e すずきせんせいはあさごはんにくだものとコーンフレークをたべます。オレンジ·ジュースとおちゃをのみます。
f ゆうすけくんはひるごはんにスパゲッティとチーズとくだものをたべます。

10 a	green tea	tea, orange juice	coffee, milk
b	—	spaghetti, hamburger, sausage	curry and rice
c	fruit, ice-cream	cheese	salad, rice
d	chocolate	sandwich	cake, pizza

12 a Nina, **b** Yumiko, **c** Masaki, **d** Masaki, **e** Nina, **f** Yumiko, **g** Nina, **h** Yumiko, **i** Nina, **j** Masaki

13 a たまごとトーストをたべます。
b こうちゃをのみます。
c おべんとうとくだものをたべます。
d コーラをのみます。
e さかなとごはんをたべます。
f おちゃをのみます。
g はい、だいすきです。
h はい、すきです。
i いいえ、あんまり...。
j はい、だいすきです。

14 Part A
a 3, **b** 6, **c** 1, **d** 3, **e** 1, **f** 2, **g** 3, **h** 3, **i** 2, **j** 2, **k** —, **l** 1

15 Breakfast
often: coffee, pizza
sometimes: toast, cheese, sausage, tea
never: cornflakes, eggs, fruit, milk, orange juice
Lunch
often: hamburger, pizza, cake, cola
sometimes: curry and rice, milk, coffee, spaghetti
never: sandwiches, *obentoo*, salad, cheese, orange juice
Dinner
every day: meat, coffee, chocolate ice-cream
often: juice
sometimes: chicken, sausage, spaghetti, green tea
never: salad, fruit, tea

16 a 2, **b** 3, **c** 4, **d** 1

17 a トーストとコーンフレークをたべます。
b はい、ときどきたべます。
c オレンジ·ジュースをのみます。
d はい、まいにちのみます。
e はい、おべんとうをたべます。
f いいえ、ぜんぜんたべません。
g はい、たべます。
h コーラをのみます。
(or students' own answers)

18 a something is wonderful
b stop doing something
c Oh, I see!
d delicious
e you hate something

おべんとうクイズ

1 a あさごはんになにをたべますか。
b コーヒー

c いただきます。
d ごちそうさま。
e every day
f never
g だいすきです。

2 a ば, b ひ, c あ, d ひ／ば, e あ, f あ, g ば, h ひ／ば, i あ, j ば

3 a トーストをたべます。
b サンドイッチをたべます。
c にくとやさいをたべます。
d はい、すきです。
e はい、すきです。
f いいえ、あんまり...。
(or students' own answers)

4 a beef hotpot, b skewered chicken, c raw fish on rice, d deep-fried seafood, e meat and vegetables, f rice balls

Unit 9

1 ツ, イ, ラ, サ, ヒ, ア, オ, キ, コ, ソ, レ, カ, ナ, ニ, ス, ト, フ, エ, ケ, ハ, チ, ヘ, シ, 日, 火, 月, 休, 水, 木, 金, 土, 三

2 a cricket, b basketball, c soccer, d pet, e hockey, f football, g picnic, h Olympics, i cassettes,

3 a party, b spaghetti, c Fiona, d Phillip, e family, f Vancouver, g Madison, h surfing, i Fanta, j CD

4 a フットボール, b テニス, c バレーボール
d サッカー, e ホッケー, f バスケットボール
g レストラン, h デパート, i コンサート
j ピクニック, k パーティー

5 a Yuusuke, Teacher: go to the beach on Tuesday
b Yuki, Emma: go to the movies on Friday
c Kate: go to the department store on Sunday
d Kenichi, Ben: go to school on Wednesday
e Kate: go to a picnic on Saturday, party on Sunday

6 Teacher to correct

7 a パーティーにいきます。
b デパートにいきます。
c ピクニックにいきます。
d うみにいきます。
e コンサートにいきます。
f レストランにいきます。
g がっこうにいきます。
h えいがにいきます。

8 a Ben's birthday party
b Some are going to a concert
c Someone is going to the department store with his/her Mum, someone is going on a picnic with Chieko
d Sunday

10 a 友だちといきます。
b おじいさんといきます。
c ひとりでいきます。
d かぞくといきます。
e ひとりでいきます。
(or students' own answers)

11

	Yuki	Kenichi	Mr Nakamura	Emma
restaurant	yes	no	yes	yes
concert	yes	no	no	no
picnic	no	no	yes	yes
movie	yes	yes	no	yes
dept. store	yes	no	no	yes
other?	beach	baseball, soccer and basketball match	tennis match	beach

12 b 火曜日にともだちとパーティーにいきます。
c 水曜日におにいさんとラグビーのしあいにいきます。
d 土曜日にひとりでともだちのうちにいきます。
e 金曜日にいもうととえいがにいきます。

13 a Junji enquires about a baseball match on Saturday.
b He is going to his grandfather's house.
c Masao is going with his father.
d She is going to the movies with Kenji on Sunday and then out to a pizza restaurant. She will also go to Masami's party.

14 b さなえさんはたかこさんのうちにいきます。
c たかこさんはベンくんのうちにいきます。
d カーラさんはしんごくんのうちにいきます。
e ベンくんはさなえさんのうちにいきます。

15 **Part A**
a 14, b 3, c 10, d 13, e 7
Part B
2 火よう日にともだちとうみにいきます。
4 木よう日にともだちとバスケットボールのしあいにいきません。
5 金よう日にともだちとレストランにいきます。
6 月よう日におかあさんとおばあさんのうちにいきます。
8 水よう日におかあさんとデパートにいきます。
9 木よう日におかあさんとえいがにいきません。
12 火よう日にひとりでえいがにいきます。
15 金よう日にひとりでデパートにいきません。

16 a 9/10
Mum
Takako
I won't go to Grandma's house on Saturday. I will go to the movies with Chieko and her Mum. I will have popcorn and cola.
b 28/11
Mrs Fukui
Emma
Tuesday is Carla's birthday. I will go to the party with Kate, Yuki and Sanae. I will have dinner and also cake. I won't go to tennis practice.
c 10/9
Shingo
Tony
Today we are going to a Japanese restaurant with the teacher. I will eat sushi and drink green tea. I love sushi. I won't go on the picnic.
d 23/11
Dad
Kenichi
I will go to the concert tomorrow with John. John is an American friend from school. Today I will go to the department store and not the beach. I won't eat dinner.

17 b 月よう日にケイトさんはしんごくんとえいがにいきます。
c 火よう日にすずきせんせいはなかむらせんせいとレストランにいきます。
d 水よう日にカーラさんはゆうすけくんとコンサートにいきます。
e 木よう日にちえこさんはトニーくんとうみにいきます。
f 金よう日にさなえさんはけんいちくんとたかこさんのうちにいきます。
g 土よう日にゆきさんはベンくんとバスケットボールのしあいにいきます。

おべんとうクイズ

1 a the weekend
b えいがにいきます。
c whom you are going with
d あしたコンサートにいきます。

e いきません
f ちえこさんのうちにいきます。
g いいえ、テニスのしあいにいきません。
h ひとりでいきます。

2 a うみ
b ひとりで
c テ
d ル
e ン

3 a パーティーにいきます。
b いいえ、いきません。
c ともだちといきます。
d はい、いきます。
e いいえ、いきません。
(or students' own answers)

Unit 10

1 a コンピューター
b バスケットボール
c クリケット
d ローラーブレード
e ソフトボール
f ネットボール
g ピアノ
h サーフィン
i インドネシアご
j ラグビー

2 a チーズ
b ミルク
c ピアノ
d チキン
e テニス
f キャンプ
g サッカー
h スケート
i ラグビー
j スポーツ
k レストラン
l パーティー
m クリケット
n ピクニック
o コンサート
p サーフィン
q ソフトボール
r コンピューター
s ローラーブレード

3 a ピアノ
b レストラン
c ピクニック
d ラグビー
e スケート
f デパート
g コンピューター
h バスケットボール
i ローラーブレード
j ネットボール
k クリケット
l ソフトボール

4 a computing, **b** music, **c** reading, **d** surfing, **e** rugby, cricket, **f** cooking

5 Teacher to correct

6 a どくしょです。
b からてです。
c ピアノです。
d コンピューターです。
e すいえいです。
f おんがくです。

7 Teacher to correct

8 a Jun Itoi | computing, rock music
13 years
6 May | soccer, karate,kendo
Junior High School Year 2
Kobe

b Eri Katayama | reading, music
14 years
23 October | volleyball, swimming
Junior High School Year 3
Nagasaki

c Mayumi Ishino | cooking, piano
15 years
16 September | skating, softball
Senior High School Year 1
Tokyo

d Toru Goto | piano, rollerblading
13 years
22 April | surfing
Junior High School Year 2
Osaka

9 Ben: rugby, kendo
Chieko: computer games
Yuki: volleyball
Carla: Japanese
Shingo: rollerblading
Takako: kendo

10 a Matsuyama, Yamamoto
b Ishida, Yamamoto
c Matsuyama
d Ishida, Matsuyama
e Matsuyama

11

a	guitar	basketball	Beatles classical	Japanese food pizza
b	sport music	swimming cricket softball	Japanese pop rock	Indonesian lunch box
c	sport party	karate, kendo horseriding netball surfing rollerblading	American rock	barbecue sausage chicken steak
d	reading computer games	tennis skiing	Japanese and American pop synthesizer	American hamburger cola potato chips

12 Teacher to correct

13 Part A
a 十四さいです。
b アデレードです。
c スポーツです。
d はい、できます。
e ポップスミュージックがすきです。

Part B
Teacher to correct.

14 b From Sapporo. Is 17 years old. Hobby is sport. Loves skating. Plays rugby and tennis. Can swim a little.Goes to the movies on weekends. Likes scary movies. Has a pet rabbit and dog.

c Is 16 years old. Hobby is music. Loves rock and pop music. Likes guitar. Practises on weekends. Canユt play any sport. Can speak French. Sometimes goes to French restaurants. Loves hamburgers, pizza, spaghetti, cake and chocolate. Hates salad.

d Is 17 years old. From Kyoto. Hobbies are computing and reading. Hates sport. Has a pet goldfish. On weekends, goes on picnics. Likes fruit,

hates meat.
e Is 15 years old. From Sendai. Hobby is sport. Tennis and swimming. Likes rugby but no good at it. Likes rock music. Hates computing and cats. Likes dogs. Goes to sports matches on weekends.
a, d
b, e
c, e

15 a スポーツです。
b ネットボールがすきです。
c いいえ、できません。
d ポップスがすきです。
e はい、できます。
f スパゲッティがすきです。
g いいえ、できません。
(or students' own answers)

16 a つまらない！
b よかった！
c going somewhere else
d きてください。
e Thanks for your hard work.
f すごーい！

おべんとうクイズ

1 a your hobbies
b すいえいをします。
c if you can skate
d いいえ、ぜんぜんできません。
e singing to a music video
f a musical instrument

2 a コンピューター
b ネットボール
c できます
ぜんぜん
d できます
e スポーツ

3 a どくしょです。
b すしがすきです。
c いいえ、できません。
d じょうばです。
e すいえいをします。
f ポップスがすきです。

Unit 11

1 **a** キュ, **b** チャ, **c** ニョ, **d** ピュ, **e** キョ, **f** ジャ
2 **a** ピュ, **b** キュ, **c** チョ, **d** ジュ
3 **a** emu, **b** barbecue, **c** chocolate, **d** party, **e** camp, **f** Jakarta, **g** weekend, **h** Madison, **i** juice
4

Across		Down	
1	いつ	2	つまらない
3	おいしい	3	おもしろい
6	ちいさい	4	いち
9	いらっしゃい	5	あさ
10	すし	7	いっしょに
11	はい	8	いますか
12	いきましょうか	10	すし
16	にん	11	はたち
17	ちゅうがく	13	きてください
20	だれの	14	うん
21	うち	15	もういちど
22	さどうぶ	18	ものさし
23	まど	19	しんぶん
		21	うま

5 まいにち
がっこうにいきます。
がっこうのまえ
あさごはんをたべます。テレビをみます。
がっこうのあと
月曜日
ホッケーとしゅくだいをします。
がっこうのあと
火曜日
ダンスとしゅくだいをします。
がっこうのあと
水曜日
ダンスとしゅくだいをします。
がっこうのあと
木曜日
テニスのれんしゅうとしゅくだいをします。
よる
金曜日
ビデオをみます。ざっしをよみます。
しゅくだいをしません。

6 Kyoko: reads books, plays tennis, listens to music
Mother: sleeps
Father: reads magazines, watches TV, plays golf
Grandmother: drinks green tea, eats sweets, watches TV
Susumu: soccer practice, watches videos

7 a あさごはんをたべます。
b しゅくだいをします。
c うみにいきます。
d ビデオをみます。
e デパートにいきます。
f ざっしをよみます。
(or students' own answers)

8 Teacher to correct

9 b ひまなときにえいがをみます。
c ひまなときにほんをよみます。
d ひまなときにおんがくをききます。
e ひまなときにケーキをたべます。
f ひまなときにパーティーをします。
g ひまなときにこうちゃをのみます。
h ひまなときにてがみをかきます。

10 b まいにち
c がっこうのあとで
d 金よう日のばん
e あした
f しゅうまつ
g 土よう日のばん
h 土よう日のあさ
i きょう
(or students' own answers)

11 a Watch a video. (Dracula)
b Have a party (will telephone their friends),
c Go to Carla's house and have a barbecue party. Listen to CDs and play volleyball.
d Go to a restaurant. Drink cocoa and have some chocolate cake.
e Go to a basketball match on Saturday.

12 b レストランにいきましょう。
c テニスをしましょう。
d コーヒーをのみましょう。
e しゅくだいをしましょう。
f ビデオをみましょう。
g サーフィンをしましょう。
h アイスクリームをたべましょう。
i コーラをのみましょう。
j カラオケをしましょう。
(or students' own answers)

14 b ざっしをよみましょう。
c カラオケをしましょう。
d シーディーをききましょう。
e えいがをみましょう。
f でんわをしましょう。

15 こんにちは、
金よう日にがっこうのあとで日本のレストランにいきましょう。すしをたべましょうか。

でんわをしてください。
ヘレンより
(or students' own answers)

16 a 14 years old
b Junior High School Year 2
c 4 people
d Sachiko
e Primary School Year 6
f soccer
g everyday after school
h Saturday
i play soccer
j what are his hobbies
does he play sport
what does he do after school

17 Teacher to correct

18 a birthday present (chocolate): delicious
b volleyball camp: good
c rollerblading: difficult
d watching family videos: boring
e pet book: interesting

19 **Part A**
たのしい: a, c, d, f, g, i, j, k, m, n, o, q, r, t
おもしろい: c, d, f, g, i, k, n, o, q, r
つまらない: a, c, d, f, g, i, j, k, m, n, o, q, r
おいしい/まずい: b, e, h, l, p, s
やさしい/むずかしい: a, d, f, i, j, k, m, n, t
(or students' own answers)

Part B
a チョコレートはおいしいです。
b 日本ごはやさしいです。
c パーティーはたのしいです。
d ほんはおもしろいです。
e コーヒーはまずいです。
f ピザはおいしいです。
g すいえいはむずかしいです。
(or students' own answers)

21 **Part A**
a Friday 31 May
Teacher's birthday
Come to the pool after school, play games, listen to music
ring Kate: 555 3724

b Saturday: Soccer Club Party. After the soccer match, have a barbecue. Come to school, drink cola, dance. 1:00pm at school.

c 20 June: Video Party. Come to Ben's house. Watch Australian videos, eat popcorn. At 6:00pm.

Part B Teacher to correct

22 a しゅくだいをします。
b あさごはんをたべます。
c ほんをよみます。
d えいがをみます。
e ネットボールをします。
f テレビをみます。
(or students' own answers)

おべんとうクイズ

1 a after school
b Friday morning
c CDをききましょう。
d はい、そうしましょう。

2 a アイスクリームをたべましょう。
b ざっしをよみましょう。
c にっきをかきましょう。
d カラオケパーティーにいきましょう。

3 a おいしい
b むずかしい
c やさしい
d おもしろい
e たのしい
(or students' own answers)

4 **a** ク, **b** セ, **c** ヤ, ヨ, **d** ア, ウ, オ

5 school excursion

6 bullet train

7 Tokyo

8 **a** つまらない, **b** おいしい, **c** むずかしい

Unit 12

1 See inside back cover of Workbook or Student Book for complete katakana chart.

2 a ウール
b ヌードル
c ゲーム
d メモ
e モーニングティー
f ワンピース
g アイスクリーム

3 a サラダ
b ケーキ
c テレビ
d ジュース
e アイスクリーム
f スケジュール
g バンジー
h ミック・ジャガー
i メニュー
j ペット
k チョコレート
l オリンピック
m ピラミッド
n プレゼント
o オーストラリア
p バーベキュー

4 a いいえ、ほんをかいました。
b はい、アイスクリームをたべました。
c はい、うみにいきました。
d いいえ、コンピューターゲームをしました。
e はい、トーストをたべました。
f いいえ、バスにのりました。
(or students' own answers)

5 **a** 7 T, **b** 2 T, **c** 5 T, **d** 1 T, **e** 13 T, **f** 4 T, **g** 14 T, **h** 11 T, **i** 9 T, **j** 3 T, **k** 10 T, **l** 6 T, **m** 8 T, **n** 12 F

6 Teacher to correct

7 a えんそくにいきました。
b コーラをのみました。
c ほんをかいました。
d チョコレートケーキをたべました。
e カセットをききました。
f ともだちにあいました。
g でんしゃにのりました。
h なにをしましたか。
i じてんしゃでいきました。
j ゆきさんにてがみをかきました。

8

a	かきます	かきました	かきましょう
b	よみます	よみました	よみましょう
c	みます	みました	みましょう
d	たべます	たべました	たべましょう
e	いきます	いきました	いきましょう
f	かいます	かいました	かいましょう
g	のみます	のみました	のみましょう
h	ききます	ききました	ききましょう
i	します	しました	しましょう
j	のります	のりました	のりましょう
k	あいます	あいました	あいましょう

9 b えんそくにいきました。ローラーコースター

にのりました。たのしかったです。
- **c** がっこうにいきました。バレーボールをしました。おもしろかったです。
- **d** デパートにいきました。くつをかいました。やすかったです。
- **e** えいがにいきました。ポップコーンをたべました。おいしかったです。
- **f** キャンプにいきました。バーベキューをしました。たのしかったです。

10 a たのしかったです。
- **b** むずかしかったです。
- **c** まずかったです。
- **d** つまらなかったです。
- **e** おもしろかったです。
- **f** やさしかったです。

11

a	Gold Coast	swimming	very enjoyable
b	New Zealand	bungee jumping	scary, great
c	Greater Union Cinema	watched movies ate popcorn	enjoyable
d	restaurant	met Tom Cruise ate chicken	very kind delicious

12 月 Did homework.
- 火 Went with Mum to a concert. Read a book.
- 水 Went skating with her older brother. Read a book.
- 木 Had a Japanese test. Read a book.
- 金 Went to a spaghetti restaurant with her family. Read a book.
- 土 Went to a party with her older sister. Read a book.
- 日 Went to a friend's house and watched videos. Her friend read a book.

14 a ごはんはおいしかったです。
- **b** えいがはつまらなかったです。
- **c** うんどうかいはたのしかったです。
- **d** 日本ごはやさしかったです。
- **e** ほんはおもしろかったです。
- **f** コーヒーはまずかったです。
- **g** テストはむずかしかったです。

15 ★ Telephoned Samantha on Wednesday night.
- ★ Went skating on Saturday night with Samantha. Went by train, it was fun.
- ★ After skating, ate hamburgers and drank cola. It was delicious.
- ★ After that, went to Samantha's house and watched a scary movie with Samantha and her Mum. Samantha likes scary movies. It was really scary.
- ★ Ate ice-cream together.

16 Teacher to correct

17 a They went by bus.
- **b** They had a treasure hunt.
- **c** They ate spaghetti and fruit.
- **d** It was horrible.
- **e** They had kendo practice and played Japanese games.
- **f** They ate yakitori, salad and rice and drank orange juice.
- **g** As Harjono doesn't like yakitori.
- **h** They danced.
- **i** Naoko

18 Part A
- **a** 4 November
- **b** They went to a restaurant.
- **c** She went with her Japanese class
- **d** She ate tempura and rice.
- **e** It was delicious.
- **f** She drank green tea.
- **g** It was awful.
- **h** They went to a Japanese supermarket.
- **i** They bought alot of Japanese sweets.

Part B

Teacher to correct

19 a school, bicycle
- **b** Kyoto, bullet train
- **c** camp, train
- **d** movie, bus
- **e** friend's house, rollerblades

20 a エマさんはトニーくんとでんしゃでバスケットボールのしあいにいきました。
- **b** ケイトさんはベンくんとくるまでともだちのうちにいきました。
- **c** ちえこさんはハジョーノくんとあるいてうみにいきました。
- **d** ゆきさんはけんいちくんとバスでがっこうにいきました。

21 デパートにいきました。
おかあさんといきました。
くるまでいきました。
おもしろかったです。
(or students' own answers)

22 Teacher to correct

23 a いらっしゃい!
- **b** in Japanese
- **c** don't want you to forget them
- **d** surprised
- **e** a little boring
- **f** and

おべんとうクイズ

1 a what you did in the holidays
- **b** how was it?
- **c** how you got there?

2 a あいました
- **b** のりました
- **c** みました
- **d** かきました
- **e** かいました
- **f** ききました

1 e, **2** b, **3** f, **4** a, **5** c, **6** d

3 a おもしろい
- **b** たのしい
- **c** やさしい
- **d** まずい
- **e** つまらない
- **f** むずかしい

4 a ビデオをみました。
- **b** ともだちとみました。
- **c** おもしろかったです。

(or students' own answers)

5 九月三日（水）がっこうにいきませんでした。テニスのしあいにいきました。バスでいきました。そして、テニスをみました。アイスクリームをたべました。たのしかったです。

6 a ローラーブレード
- **b** タクシー
- **c** ダンス
- **d** カセット
- **e** コーラ
- **f** アイスクリーム